LOURDES COLLEGE LIBRARY

3 0379 1005 0570 2

361.32
Sc 4

Spirituality and Religion in Social Work Practice

Decision Cases With Teaching Notes

WITHDRAWN

DUNS SCOTUS LIBRARY
LOURDES COLLEGE
SYLVANIA, OHIO

Edited by T. Laine Scales
Terry A. Wolfer
David A. Sherwood
Diana R. Garland
Beryl Hugen
Sharon Weaver Pittman

D1501363

Council on Social Work Education
Alexandria, Virginia

02-317

Development of the decision cases in this book was supported in part by grants from the Lilly Endowment, Inc., and a Millennium Project Grant from the Council on Social Work Education.

Situations and events depicted herein may be based on actual events. In many cases the names of persons and agencies and certain facts related to the cases have been changed to protect anonymity. Other uses of names are by permission of the persons involved. The authors and editors wish to thank the many case reporters, whose names have been withheld, for their cooperation in making these accounts available for the benefit of social work students and practitioners.

The cases and teaching notes have been prepared solely to provide material for class discussion and not to suggest either effective or ineffective handling of the situations depicted.

Please read the Using and Distributing Cases section on p. v for more information on distributing contents of this book.

Copyright © 2002 by the Council on Social Work Education, Inc.
All rights reserved. No part of this book may be reproduced or transmitted in any manner whatsoever without the prior written permission of the publisher.

Council on Social Work Education
1725 Duke Street, Suite 500
Alexandria, VA 22314-3457
www.cswe.org

Library of Congress Cataloging-in-Publication Data

Spirituality and religion in social work practice: decision cases with teaching notes / edited by T. Laine Scales ... [et al.].
        p. cm. — (Teaching social work)
Includes bibliographical references and index.
  ISBN 0-87293-092-0
  1. Social service—Religious aspects—Case studies. 2. Social workers—Religious life—United States. I. Scales, T. Laine. II. Series.
  HV530 .S667 2002
  361.3—dc21
                        2002005772

Printed in the United States of America

Contents

Using and Distributing the Cases v

Preface vii

Case Details ix

Introduction: Spirituality and Religion, Decision Cases, and Competent Social Work Practice 1
David A. Sherwood, Terry A. Wolfer, and T. Laine Scales

Essay: Case Method Teaching in the Social Work Classroom 11
T. Laine Scales

01 This Work Is My Religion 21
David A. Sherwood

02 Good Medicine 29
Diana R. Garland and Karen Grubb Gilbert

03 Loss and Faith 37
Ann Fleck-Henderson and Michael P. Melendez

04 Dying to Talk About Death 43
Terry A. Wolfer

05 To Tell the Truth 50
Leola Furman and Roger Aker

06 Ya Me Voy! (I'm Going Right Now!) 57
Linda B. Morales and T. Laine Scales

07 Some Day… 63
Nancy K. Brown and Terry A. Wolfer

08 What's a Supervisor to Do? 73
Sharon Weaver Pittman and Luis A. Perez

09 To Leave or Not to Leave: That Is the Question 81
    Erlene Grise-Owens

10 Do We Have to Go Now? Challenges in Foster Care and Adoption 91
    Elisabeth Kenny

11 Helping the Homeless: Our Way or the Highway 100
    Beryl Hugen and Pam Doty-Nation

12 I Will Not Be God's Entertainment 106
    Michael E. Sherr and Terry A. Wolfer

13 Why Can't They Make This Place More Jewish? 117
    Evelyn Hoffman and Dennis R. Myers

14 These Things Happen: Confronting Dual Responsibilities 127
    Helen Wilson Harris, David A. Sherwood, and Elizabeth H. Timmons

15 Reason to Believe 137
    T. Laine Scales, Linda B. Morales, and Elisabeth Kenny

16 A Tale of Too Many Relationships: Bonds, Boundaries, and Borders 146
    Raymond Lisauckis, Carol A. Sherwood, and David Davis

17 A Cursed Child? 153
    Ann Fleck-Henderson and Michael P. Melendez

18 Grace 159
    Claudette Lee and Terry A. Wolfer

19 Not in My House! 165
    T. Laine Scales

20 Sugarland's Dilemmas 173
    Harvey Stalwick and Doreen L. Holding Eagle

21 Seeking, But Not Finding 181
    Miriam McNown Johnson

22 Developing Community in Truman Village 191
    Wendy Sellers Campbell and Terry A. Wolfer

About the Editors and Contributors 203

Using and Distributing the Cases

This text was written for educators, with each case followed by a Teaching Note that includes a case synopsis, suggested learning outcomes, discussion questions, and other materials for instructor use. As explained below, electronic versions of the cases, without teaching notes, are available from the Council on Social Work Education's (CSWE) website, along with other features to support teaching.

The cases are obviously intended for use in courses, seminars, or other educational settings. However, copyright restrictions apply on all materials in the text, and we ask that individuals, schools, and organizations obtain proper copyright permissions to copy or distribute materials from the book.

Following the "fair use" exception to current copyright law (Title 17, Section 107, U.S. Code), individuals are able to distribute, reproduce, or display any materials in this category for *one-time* or *spontaneous noncommercial purposes*, including distribution in an educational setting, provided CSWE's copyright is indicated or otherwise preserved from the original format and the material is not altered in design or content.

Multiple or regular uses of these materials—including planned use in courses, field seminars, or other educational venues—should receive prior written permission from CSWE. Readers are encouraged to visit the Council's website to arrange copyright permissions or to send students to the website to purchase cases.

Spirituality and Religion in Social Work Practice on the Web

CSWE has set up a special section on its website—www.cswe.org/spirituality—as a resource for educators using the cases in this text. Among the features of the section is a discussion forum on using the case method of teaching and on integrating spiritual and religious content into social work education.

Educators who have purchased the book can register to download electronic versions of the cases, and they can arrange copyright permission to distribute the cases in class. Payment of fees by credit card will provide instant copyright permissions for educators, schools, libraries, or copy centers. If offline payment is preferred, users can submit a request for permission that will be followed up in writing.

Finally, educators can also direct students to purchase electronic versions of the cases from the website.

We hope you will make use of the resources available online and contribute your own ideas to the discussion forum.

Preface

When the editors first assembled in 1999 to begin creating this text, we all agreed on three important goals. First, we wanted to create a resource that would be useful for social work programs in state and other nonsectarian institutions, as well as those that are faith-based. This resource will assist instructors as they respond to the expectation that all accredited programs teach about religion and spirituality as a significant dimension of human diversity. In addition, we wanted to design a text that would be useful across the entire social work curriculum, including human behavior and the social environment, professional values and ethics, social policy, research, and practice methods with individuals, families, groups, organizations, and communities. Finally, we wanted the cases to be widely available at a reasonable cost to students.

We have received reports of success in the first two areas from the many instructors who pilot-tested the cases in their different institutional settings across the country. The instructors noted exciting classroom discussions and indicated that these cases are useful in a variety of classes. In the third area, we are thrilled that new media are being used to help instructors and students access cases and use them in their classrooms. As the "Using and Distributing the Cases" section indicates, the Council has published "student versions" of the cases—without the teaching notes or discussion questions included in this book—for online purchase and download. An online forum is also available for instructors to share successes and obstacles to using the cases in their courses. We hope readers will visit www.cswe.org/spirituality to share their experiences with the book and to find out more about case method teaching and integrating content on spirituality and religion into their curricula.

Many social work educators use cases or vignettes in their teaching, and this text is intended to strengthen their skills in this areas. Chapter 2, in particular, details an experiential, inductive approach to learning that facilitates active engagement on the part of students. As educators, we have found these cases extremely useful in our own classrooms for engaging students as they consider the many dimensions of religion and spirituality they will encounter in social work practice. The cases were prepared solely to provide material for class discussion. Because these are topics that commonly generate strong emotions and value dilemmas in both students and faculty, we created cases that would challenge students to consider the complex values and decisions related to these subjects. One reason this collection is so powerful is that the cases are not imaginary stories used to illustrate a point. Instead, they are actual cases reported by real practitioners, with identifying details disguised for purposes of confidentiality. The teaching notes provided after each case are intended to be a starting point for class preparation and not to present effective or ineffective methods of handling the situation depicted.

We owe a great debt to our case reporters who shared their very personal stories and helped us to refine our renditions of their experiences. We cannot thank them each by name, as their identities must be kept anonymous to protect them, their agencies, and their clients.

The editors and authors received financial support for our case-writing workshop from the Baylor School of Social Work, from the Lilly Endowment, Inc., and from a Millennium Grant awarded by the Council on Social Work Education.

We also received valuable training from the Pace University Center for Case Studies in Education. Two of the editors attended the Center's yearly conference in Vancouver, BC, "Enlivening Teaching: Using Discipline-Based Cases and Classroom Research to Improve Learning and Teaching," and found useful information as well as helpful mentors among the conference leaders, particularly Dr. Rita Silverman and Dr. John Boeher.

Finally, we would like to thank the three anonymous reviewers recruited by the Council on Social Work Education. They all provided insightful comments that improved the book manuscript.

As explained in Chapter 1, we chose the decision case method for this resource because we think it is ideal for addressing content on spirituality and religion. We hope that you will find these cases useful as you bring discussions of these important topics into all of your social work courses.

Case Details

This table is intended to assist instructors in selecting cases for classroom use. It is not intended as an exhaustive list of key issues addressed in the cases. The teaching notes following each case provide a more thorough indication of possible teaching objectives and uses for individual cases.

Case No.	Gender, Ethnicity	Central Spiritual/Religious Traditions	Primary Practice Level	Field of Practice	Practice Setting	Spiritual/ Religious Issues	Other Practice Issues
01–This Work Is My Religion	Client(s): F & M, Serbian; Worker(s): Ethnic Albanian, Euro-American	Islam, Orthodox	Macro, mezzo	International social work	Refugee resettlement policies	Freedom of expression in the workplace; agency conflict; Client groups in religious conflict; Justice in conditions of religious and ethnic diversity	Faith-based organizations; staff relationships/conflict; ethical fund-raising; Bridging divisions rooted in ethnic, religious, political, and class differences
02–Good Medicine	Client(s): unspecified, Native American; Worker(s): F, Native American	Native American, indigenous spirituality	Micro, macro	Homelessness, mental health	Private agency	Spirituality and ritual as resources; Spiritual and professional development of the worker	Community organizing; Community politics
03–Loss and Faith	Client(s): F, Jewish; Worker(s): M, Latino	Judaism	Micro, mezzo	Mental health	Private practice	Religious group boundaries: belonging and exclusion; Religious authority; Tensions with religion of one's family of origin	AIDS; Gay and lesbian issues
04–Dying to Talk About Death	Client(s): F, unspecified; Worker(s): F, unspecified	Spirituality	Micro, macro	End-of-life care	Hospital	Spiritual issues in end-of-life care; Use of religious or spiritual resources; Influence of personal experience	Practitioner/client boundaries; Interdisciplinary relations; Advocacy; Palliative care; Transference and countertransference

(continues next page)

Case No.	Gender, Ethnicity	Central Spiritual/Religious Traditions	Primary Practice Level	Field of Practice	Practice Setting	Spiritual/ Religious Issues	Other Practice Issues
05–To Tell the Truth	*Clients:* F, unspecified *Workers:* F, unspecified	Christianity	Micro, macro	Housing	Faith-based agency	Managing volunteers from faith-based organizations Interaction between spiritual and religious values and professional social work values	Who is the client? Clarity of agency policies Values and ethics
06–Ya Me Voy!	*Client(s):* M, Latino *Worker(s):* M, Latino	Curanderismo	Micro, mezzo, macro	Medical social work	Hospital	Religious and spiritual traditions and rituals as methods of healing Spiritual and professional development of the worker	International social work Worker as interpreter of culture for other professionals Cross-cultural issues
07–Some Day...	*Client(s):* F, unspecified *Worker(s):* M, Arabic, F, Euro-American	Islam	Micro	Mental health	Private agency	Religious tradition as basis of human behavior Inter-faith marriage Inconsistent religious practice	Therapeutic alliances (individual/couple) Being stuck between cultural sensitivity and assessing client problems Treatment planning and accountability
08–What's a Supervisor to Do?	*Client(s):* F, unspecified *Worker(s):* F, unspecified	Christianity	Micro, macro	Field practicum Family violence, victim recovery	Private agency	Policies about proselytizing in the workplace Ethical use of the professional relationship; client vulnerability Spiritual and professional development of the worker Impact of agency auspice and mission	Supervision of students, developing abilities to handle value issues Agency's relations with community Self-determination, informed consent Appropriate self-disclosure Abortion

Case	Client(s)/Worker(s)	Religion	Level	Setting		Topics	Additional Topics
09–To Leave or Not to Leave	Client(s): M, Christian Worker(s): M & F, unspecified	Christianity	Macro, mezzo	Child welfare	Faith-based agency	Interaction between spiritual and religious values and professional social work values Relationships between faith-based agencies and various constituencies Private, faith-based agencies and public funding	Gay and lesbian issues Relative costs and benefits of taking action Legal rights of faith-based agencies, staff, and clients Conscientious disagreement with agency/administrator policies
10–Do We Have to Go Now?	Client(s): F & M, African-American Worker(s): F, unspecified	Christianity	Micro, macro	Child welfare	Public child protection	Interaction between spiritual and religious values and professional social work values	Foster care, adoption Cross-cultural issues Family violence
11–Helping the Homeless	Client(s): F, unspecified Worker(s): M, unspecified	Christianity	Macro, micro	Homelessness	Private shelter	Client compliance with religiously based policies Assessing and dealing with spiritual/religious strengths and resources, barriers	Rural social work Agency's relations with its community Impact of agency auspice and mission
12–I Will Not Be God's Entertainment	Client(s): M, unspecified Worker(s): M, Jewish	Judaism, spirituality, Christianity	Micro	Mental health	Community health center	Alienation from traditions of family of origin Spiritual journey of the client Assessing, dealing with spiritual/religious strengths and resources, barriers	Physically challenged persons Assessment Adolescent development Therapeutic alliances (teen/parent) Psychological trauma

(continues next page)

Case No.	Gender, Ethnicity	Central Spiritual/Religious Traditions	Primary Practice Level	Field of Practice	Practice Setting	Spiritual/Religious Issues	Other Practice Issues
13—Why Can't They Make This Place More Jewish?	Client(s): F, Jewish Worker(s): M, Euro-American	Judaism, Christianity	Micro, macro	Elderly	Public agency	Attending to spiritual and religious needs in public agencies Helping clients find or develop spiritually and religiously appropriate resources Spiritually and religiously "segregated" vs. "integrated" resources	Rural social work Community building, networking Intervention to foster systemic change Gerontological social work Dealing with life transitions and loss
14—These Things Happen	Client(s): F, Latina Worker(s): M, Latino	Christianity—Pentecostal, Hispanic	Micro, mezzo	Church-based social work	Congregation	Finding ethical balance between respecting and challenging cultural and spiritual beliefs and practices Dual roles of social worker and minister Assessing and using strengths, resources of client spirituality; dealing with barriers	Family violence Cross-cultural issues Values and ethics, resolving competing value tensions Interorganizational relationships Gender roles Collegial relationships Formal, informal helping networks
15—Reason to Believe	Client(s): F, unspecified Worker(s): M & F, Euro-American	Christianity—Branch Davidian	Micro, macro	Child welfare	Public agency	Finding ethical balance between respecting and challenging cultural and spiritual beliefs and practices Respect for religious diversity Distinguishing between what is ethical, legal, and a matter of spiritual/religious preference Potential oppression of diverse groups	Handling media attention Recording/documentation Ethics of literal honesty vs. "working the system" to buy time Laws and policies regarding child abuse and protection

Case	Client(s)/Worker(s)	Religion	Level	Field	Setting		
16–A Tale of Too Many Relationships	Client(s): F, Euro-American Worker(s): F, Euro-American	Christianity	Micro, mezzo, macro	Mental health	Private practice	Sexual misconduct of clergy and licensed or unlicensed therapists Professional boundaries, multiple relationships with colleagues, clients Dealing with legal, moral, ethical, and clinical issues	Ethical obligation to report professional misconduct Social worker's own anger and sense of betrayal Confidentiality vs. protection of otherss Value of supervision/consultation
17–A Cursed Child?	Client(s): F, Afro-Caribbean Worker(s): F, Jewish	Indigenous West Indian	Micro, mezzo	Mental health	Community mental health	Religious traditions as method of healing Respect for religious diversity Assessing and dealing with spiritual/religious strengths and resources, barriers.	Interdisciplinary teams Cross-cultural issues Worker's need to understand client's culture
18–Grace	Client(s): F, unspecified Worker(s): F, unspecified	Christianity	Micro	Field practicum	Faith-based family service agency	Religious culture in the workplace Spiritual journey of worker	Supervision of students Agency policies
19–Not in My House!	Client(s): F, unspecified Worker(s): F, Asian-American	Buddhism	Micro	End-of-life care	Hospice	Religion, spirituality in end-of-life care Religious group boundaries: belonging and exclusion Respect for religious diversity	Who is the client? Natural helping networks Welfare reform policies
20–Sugarland's Dilemma	Client(s): F, Euro-American Worker(s): F & M, African-American	Christianity—Protestant	Micro, mezzo, macro	Welfare	Congregation	Religious institutions as resource Faith-motivated volunteers	Self-determination

(continues next page)

Case No.	Gender, Ethnicity	Central Spiritual/Religious Traditions	Primary Practice Level	Field of Practice	Practice Setting	Spiritual/Religious Issues	Other Practice Issues
21–Seeking, But Not Finding	*Client(s):* F, Euro-American	Native American, indigenous spirituality	Micro	Child welfare	Residential treatment center	Religion, spirituality as resource Distinguishing psychiatric symptoms and religious experiences	Child abuse Psychological trauma Assessment
22–Developing Community in Truman Village	*Client(s):* Unspecified *Worker(s):* M, F, African-American, Euro-American		Macro	Community development, program administration	Community, faith-based and government-collaborative	Role of organized religion in community development Multiple roles; dual relationships in a faith-based context	Professional boundaries Effects of workers' race, gender, ethnicity, and sexual orientation

Introduction

Spirituality and Religion, Decision Cases, and Competent Social Work Practice

David A. Sherwood, Terry A. Wolfer, and T. Laine Scales

The vision for this collection of decision cases was conceived in February 1999, when the School of Social Work at Baylor University assembled a group of 12 scholars and 5 practitioners for a consultation on the integration of social work with spirituality and religion. The consultants, who included the editors of this book, represented a range of spiritual and religious traditions and have published or otherwise contributed to the knowledge base for effective social work practice with individuals, families, communities, and organizations for whom spirituality and religion are significant factors. The meeting focused on how we could work together to define and strengthen this knowledge base.

The consultants discussed the resources necessary for teaching students to work effectively with various dimensions of religion and spirituality. Because these topics commonly generate strong emotions and value conflicts for both students and faculty, several of us decided to create a collection of decision cases that would challenge students to consider the value dilemmas and complex decisions related to religion, spirituality, and social work practice.

Why Focus on Spirituality and Religion in Social Work Practice?

We want to start by emphasizing that this casebook is about everyday, competent social work practice. It is intended for all social workers in all settings. This not a specialized text about a particular

kind of practice for social workers who happen to be interested in "this sort of thing." All social workers will encounter the need for skills that enable them to work effectively with diversity, including spiritual and religious diversity, and the whole person-in-situation. Spiritual and religious issues come up in all sorts of ways in all sorts of situations. We are trying to fill a gap in traditional social work education.

Although social work has always held allegiance to the concept of working with the whole person-in-situation and developing competency to address all kinds of diversity, issues concerning spirituality and religion have often been similar to the proverbial pink elephant in the living room that we did not see or were afraid to mention because we were not sure what to do with it. This deliberate evasion occurred in spite of overwhelming evidence demonstrating that matters of meaning and purpose are central in the lives of clients, that spirituality and religion have great importance to many people, and that religiously based groups, congregations, and organizations are vital sources of social support.

As we discussed the integration of spirituality and religion in social work practice, we recognized that we had studied social work mostly under the old paradigm of modernism—positivist/empiricist/materialist/determinist. Social workers were supposed to be "value-free" except for certain privileged ideals, such as the dignity and worth of every person and a sense of social justice. Spirituality and religion were often perceived as illusions that had no future (and were often assumed to be pathological). Social workers were trained to engage in exhaustive psychosocial assessments that somehow never addressed issues of meaning, spirituality, or religion, unless their clients' "pathology" forced these issues to become targets of change. When spiritual concerns could not be ignored, clients generally had to be referred to someone else (we were social scientists and clinicians, after all, not pastors or priests).

We are still clinicians and social scientists, not pastors, rabbis, imams, priests, shamans, or curanderos, and we should not presume to be experts on spiritual issues. However, we now realize that our professional paradigms legitimize and even mandate the inclusion of spirituality and religion as integral aspects of competent social work assessment and practice. Because spirituality and religion are sources of meaning, values, life-direction, and substantive emotional and physical resources for so many, if we functionally ignore or marginalize spirituality and religion in our practice, we critically violate our fundamental social work concepts of persons-in-situation, systems, and holistic understanding.

One of the benefits of the increasing attention paid in social work to some sort of postmodern perspective is that we are regaining a vocabulary for taking seriously the search for meaning embodied in the stories people tell about their lives, in the narratives they inhabit, in the communities that sustain them, and in the possibilities for change that can come through respectful exploration of these meanings (Pardeck, Murphy, & Min Choi, 1994; Sands, 2001). Postmodernism questions whether strictly empirical or "objective" epistemologies and intervention strategies can do justice to these more subjectively and socially-situated perceptions and constructions of meaning, values, and purpose through which people understand who they are and where they are going (Freedman & Combs, 1996). Many of these stories about identity and meaning, many sustaining communities, and many overarching meta-narratives contain significant spiritual and religious elements (Abels & Abels, 2001). In order to work effectively with people, social workers must be able to explore these meanings with respect and sensitivity.

The last several years have seen a burgeoning of social work literature that bears witness to the profession's growing maturity (as we would see it) in addressing spirituality and religion as a normal part of social work practice. People like Alan Keith-Lucas (1972, 1985, 1994), Vincentia Joseph (1987), and Frank Loewenberg (1988) have kept the issue alive. Ed Canda and others have helped develop a commonly accepted vocabulary and frame of reference for thinking and talking about spirituality and religion in social work, and they have also documented the lack of appropriate preparation for dealing with spiritual and religious diversity in social work (Canda, 1988, 1998; Canda & Furman, 1999; Furman, 1994; Sanzenbach, 1989; Sheridan, 2001; Sheridan et al., 1992). Resources are being developed for social work educators and practitioners that provide helpful knowledge regarding spiritual and religious traditions (Canda & Furman, 1999; Canda, Nakashima, Burgess, & Russel, 1999; Van Hook, Hugen, & Aguilar, 2001;), spiritual assessment (Boyd, 1998; Hodge, 2001; Sherwood, 1998b; Van Hook, 1998), and spiritually sensitive intervention (Ellor, Netting, & Thibault, 1999; Garland, 1991; Hugen, 1998; Sherwood, 1998a, 2000).

The Challenge for Social Workers: Competent Practice Regarding Diversity

There are several consistent findings in the literature regarding social work students' and practitioners' readiness to deal with spiritual and religious diversity in their practice. First, students and practitioners recognize a need to develop competence in addressing spiritual and religious diversity to more effectively meet the needs of their clients. Second, students and practitioners frequently perceive spiritual and religious issues to be important in their personal lives as well as influential in their professional practice, which leads to a need for increased self-awareness and professional use of the self. Finally, they often report that their social work education did not sufficiently prepare them to deal with issues of spiritual and religious diversity (Bullis, 1996; Canda & Furman, 1999; Dezerotes, 1995; Furman, 1994; Sheridan et al., 1992).

The inclusion of issues of spirituality and religion in everyday social work practice can be understood to some extent as part of the idea of "cultural competence and social diversity," which is highlighted in both the National Association of Social Workers' (NASW) Code of Ethics (1999) and the Educational Policy and Accreditation Standards of the Council on Social Work Education (CSWE, 2001). In section 1.05 of the NASW Code of Ethics we find the following:

a. Social workers should understand culture and its function in human behavior and society, recognizing the strengths that exist in all cultures.

b. Social workers should have a knowledge base of their clients' cultures and be able to demonstrate competence in the provision of services that are sensitive to clients' cultures and to differences among people and cultural groups.

c. Social workers should obtain education about and seek to understand the nature of social diversity and oppression with respect to race, ethnicity, national origin, color, sex, sexual orientation, age, marital status, political belief, religion, and mental or physical disability.

The CSWE Educational Policy and Accreditation Standards underscores the importance of content in social work education to prepare students to deal effectively with diversity in the process of assessment and intervention:

Social work programs integrate content that promotes understanding, affirmation, and respect for people from diverse backgrounds. The content emphasizes the interlocking and complex nature of culture and personal identity. It ensures that social services meet the needs of groups served and are culturally relevant. Programs educate students to recognize diversity within and between groups that may influence assessment, planning, intervention, and research. Students learn how to define, design, and implement strategies for effective practice with persons from diverse backgrounds (2001, p. 10).

The Educational Policy and Accreditation Standards also specifies that graduates must be prepared to "practice without discrimination and with respect, knowledge, and skills related to clients' age, class, color, culture, disability, ethnicity, family structure, gender, marital status, national origin, race, religion, sex, and sexual orientation" (CSWE, 2001, p. 9; cf. Accreditation Standard 6, p. 16). Regarding human behavior and the social environment, standards further specify that social work programs must provide content on theories and knowledge of biological, sociological, cultural, psychological, and spiritual development across the life span. This requirement also includes content on the range of social systems in which people live and the ways that social systems promote or deter people in maintaining or achieving health and well-being (CSWE, 2001, p. 11).

Defining *spirituality* and *religion* is not easy, especially when we are looking for definitions that all social workers can understand and use, whether or not they consider themselves to be spiritual or religious. However, after substantial discussion of these issues in the social work literature, the profession seems to have evolved a general sort of consensus.

Spirituality is typically used in a fairly broad sense to refer to the human sense of and search for transcendence, meaning, and connectedness beyond the self. An example of this definition is provided by Ed Canda, who describes spirituality as the "basic human drive for meaning, purpose, and moral relatedness among people, with the universe, and with the ground of our being" (Canda, 1989, p. 573). The concepts of *transcendence, meaning*, and *connectedness* are inclusive enough to provide a basis for communication among persons with a wide range of beliefs and worldviews, including the nontheistic (Sherwood, 1998b).

Religion clearly relates to spirituality, but refers to a more formal organization and embodiment of spirituality into relatively specific belief systems, practices, and organizational structures. "A religion is a system of beliefs and practices that provides values to give life meaning and coherence by directing a person toward transcendence" (Corduan, 1998, p. 21). Transcendence takes us beyond our selves, and when it is embodied religiously it tends to encompass our whole lives. In Canda's language, religion is "an institutionally patterned system of beliefs, values, and rituals" (Canda, 1989, p. 573).

Instead of imposing our own values and beliefs on clients, addressing issues of spirituality and religion in social work practice means we admit the inevitable role that these values and beliefs play in our own lives as well as in our clients' lives. It also means that we must take responsibility for handling these issues with integrity, including being aware of our own beliefs and how they may affect our practice, respecting our clients' rights of self-determination, and not exploiting our positions of trust and power with clients. This has always been much more easily said than done, and the challenge does not occur only in regard to explicitly spiritual or religious issues. It happens anytime a social worker encounters clients with significantly different values, beliefs, or practices from themselves, especially when the social worker experiences the difference as a conflict.

Competence in addressing spiritual and religious issues does not mean that we practice unethically outside the areas of our own training and expertise. Dealing skillfully and ethically with religious diversity is not the same as providing specialized services of a spiritual or religious nature. We remain social workers, and for the most part, social workers in secular contexts.

We do not have to share our clients' culture or ethnicity to work with them respectfully and sensitively or to engage their cultural or ethnic resources constructively. However, we may have to be intentional about gaining relevant knowledge prior to engagement (whenever possible) and we must allow our clients to be our teachers as to what their culture or ethnicity mean for them (always). Competent social workers will approach issues of spirituality and religion in the same way.

The challenge is to treat issues of spirituality and religion just like any other potentially important (or unimportant) dimension of our clients' lives. However, the fact that spirituality and religion *may* be important does not mean that these issues will always have the same relevance for every client and social work helping context. This relevance can only be understood through sensitive listening as clients tell their stories, through appropriate questioning to help them tell the stories, and through

identifying all of the relevant issues, resources, and barriers in the particular case. In other words, everyday, competent social work practice.

Why Use Case Method Teaching?

Like practice in other professions (Schon, 1983, 1987), much of social work practice is messy and ambiguous. In that sense, issues of religion and spirituality are not unique but merely add to the complexity of social work practice and education. Although theory is necessary for practice, it is not sufficient. In actual practice, social workers must translate theory to the particularities of concrete situations, a process that is seldom neat and straightforward. For that reason, social work education will succeed best when it provides theory alongside opportunities for applying it.

Social work is one of several professions, such as law and business, which have long used cases in education for practice. Cases represent one way to present students with the opportunity to see how theory applies to practice. But the cases used in social work education tend to be primarily illustrative, that is, cases have most often been used to demonstrate theoretical concepts or to depict practice situations and the appropriate professional responses (Welsh & Wolfer, 2000; for example, see: LeCroy, 1992, 1999; McClelland, Austin, & Este, 1998; Rivas & Hull, 2000). As a result, students get to consider how a theoretical concept applies but they do not grapple with selecting and adapting a concept for an indeterminate situation. Furthermore, the cases used in social work education, especially those in textbooks, tend to be very short (a few sentences to a few paragraphs in length) composites that are somewhat oversimplified. As a result, interventions can seem rather straightforward, even obvious, and the cases therefore inadequately reflect the specificity and messiness of actual practice and appear false (or at least fabricated). Such cases are often less compelling. In addition, case authors often provide questions to guide student understanding and to help instructors structure brief class discussions of cases. Such questions may appropriately model helpful ways to approach case material but they do not challenge students to figure out how to approach situations themselves, as they must eventually do in actual practice.

In contrast, case method teaching uses somewhat longer, more complex cases for in-depth class discussions. Most significantly, case method teaching requires open-ended cases that compel decision making on the part of students, both to formulate problems and to choose courses of action. Case method teaching is frequently advocated as a means for promoting critical thinking skills and for better preparing students for professional practice because it provides them with opportunities to exercise judgment (Barnes, Christensen, & Hansen, 1994; Boehrer & Linsky, 1990; Christensen, Garvin, & Sweet, 1991; Fisher, 1978; Meyers & Jones, 1993). Rather than present information, case method teachers rely heavily upon a variation of Socratic questioning to facilitate in-depth discussion of cases (Lynn, 1999; Welty, 1989). First pioneered at the Harvard Business School, case method teaching has recently emerged in other professions (Barnes, Christensen, & Hansen, 1994; Lundeberg, Levin, & Harrington, 1999; Lynn, 1999) and has sparked renewed interest among social work educators (Cossom, 1991; Welsh & Wolfer, 2000).

Decision Cases

Case method teaching employs open-ended "decision" cases, a particular type specifically developed for this teaching approach. Such cases present students with the ambiguities and dilemmas of social work practice and require active decision making (e.g., Cossom, 1991; Golembiewski & Stevenson, 1998; Golembiewski, Stevenson, & White, 1997; Lynn, 1999; Rothman, 1998). Sometimes referred to as "teaching" cases, these decision cases describe in great detail actual situations practitioners have encountered. Although they are carefully edited, the cases depict situations that are often messy and ambiguous. Written from a particular practitioner's perspective, the case reporter, decision cases sometimes include conflicting statements from the various participants, time constraints, competing ethical values, extraneous details, and incomplete information. Because the cases are open-ended, however, they do not tell the reader what the practitioner ultimately did, nor how the case turned out. Case method teachers discovered early on that revealing the end of the story leads students to think that what actually happened

is "the right answer." Actual practice dilemmas require making complex judgments, which involve prioritizing competing values, choosing among plausible theoretical formulations, and taking concrete action under conditions of limited time and information. Competent professionals will not always agree on what the "right" answers are, and the way we teach practice should come to terms with this uncertainty.

Rather than simply critique a professional's behavior, the cases require that students use their analytic and critical thinking skills, their knowledge of social work theory and research, and their common sense and collective wisdom to identify and analyze problems, to evaluate possible solutions, and to formulate a preferred intervention (Welsh & Wolfer, 2000). Decision case discussions emphasize analysis, problem formulation, and decision-making processes. In addition, leaving the cases unresolved encourages students to continue thinking and talking about the case long after the class session has ended.

Writing as business educators, Barnes, Christensen, and Hansen (1994) argue that case method instruction helps students to develop an applied, "administrative point of view" (p. 50). In social work education, this can be referenced as simply a practitioner point of view, whether it involves primarily macro or micro practice. Barnes, Christensen, and Hansen (1994) suggest that an administrative or practitioner point of view includes the following elements:

1. a focus on understanding the specific context;

2. a sense for appropriate boundaries;

3. sensitivity to interrelationships;

4. examining and understanding any situation from a multidimensional point of view;

5. accepting appropriate personal responsibility for solving an organizational problem; and

6. an action orientation (p. 50-51).

Further, Barnes, Christensen, and Hansen (1994) describe this action orientation as having the following ingredients:

a. a sense for the possible;

b. willingness to make decisions on the basis of imperfect and limited data;

c. a sense for the critical;

d. the ability to combine discipline and creativity;

e. skill in converting targets into accomplishments; and

f. an appreciation of the major limits of professional action (p. 51).

The practitioner point of view concept redirects attention from what students know to how they use their knowledge in professional practice, in other words, "thinking like a practitioner" (Wolfer, Freeman, & Rhodes, 2001). This pragmatic application of knowledge distinguishes more experienced professionals from novices, and the decision case method promotes the use of theory and self-reflection necessary to accelerate this transition (Levin, 1999; Lundeberg & Fawver, 1994).

In general, we believe case method teaching represents a valuable approach for professional social work education. It is a particularly good fit for addressing issues of religion and spirituality in social work practice, which has the potential to become an example of educational process reflecting important aspects of competent practice. Further, the decision case method makes apparent how interconnected spiritual and religious issues are with many other issues in social work practice. For these reasons, we have developed this case collection to present actual situations from social work practice.

Writing Actual Cases

In order to present actual cases that meet a variety of teaching objectives important in social work education, including, but not limited to, addressing spirituality and religion in social work practice, we developed a case writing workshop to bring practitioners and educators together. The School of Social Work at Baylor University received a Millenium Grant from the Council on Social Work Education to facilitate a three-day workshop in Dallas, Texas in September, 2000. Authors assembled to learn how to write and teach decision cases and to begin drafting cases. The core of this collection is composed of the cases that emerged from the Dallas workshop with other cases added to expand the variety of religious traditions and fields of practice.

The majority of the cases in this text were researched and written using a process developed by Welsh (1999). We brought together case writing teams composed of two social work educators and two social work practitioners. After a training session in case teaching and writing, each team gathered for intense, concentrated meetings that produced two cases over a period of two days. In these work sessions, a practitioner reported a real case situation that he or she had experienced. These case reporters were encouraged to bring a brief written account of the problem or dilemma that they had faced and then describe in detail the story behind the issue. These discussions were tape recorded to collect quotes and detailed descriptions. Immediately after the first work session, the assigned case writers prepared a working draft of the case that included a title, an introductory "hook," and a story line with details, quotes, and descriptions. This draft was given back to the case reporter for further discussion at a follow-up session. Case writers used the clarifications and the further details that emerged from this second meeting to prepare the final draft of the case as well as the teaching note. Writers retained the terminology and classification of ethnic and religious traditions that the case reporters used (e.g., "Hispanic," "Native American," or "Pentecostal"). This process ensured that a case accurately reflected the practitioner's own experience and understanding of that particular challenging situation. Finally, the social work educators in each team piloted the cases in social work classrooms and used that experience to refine the case and the teaching note.

Selecting the Cases

Although no collection can include every religious tradition or form of spirituality, we were deeply committed to selecting cases that represented a variety of religious and spiritual beliefs that could be used in a number of diverse courses. We included cases from traditions such as Buddhism, Islam, Native American beliefs, Christianity, Curanderismo, and Judaism, but there is no presumption that these cases provide comprehensive content on the staggering diversity of spiritual and religious beliefs. The cases reflect a variety of issues that may surface with clients in micro, macro, or mezzo levels of practice, for example religious group identity, belonging and loyalty, religious freedom, ethical integration of spirituality and religion, or the interplay of biological, psychological, social, cultural, and spiritual dimensions. Cases may involve the religion or spirituality of clients, practitioners, or both and they illustrate how spirituality and religion are inseparable from almost any other dimension of social work practice. These narratives can be used to stimulate discussion on various content areas of social work education, including human behavior and the social environment, the values and ethics of professional practice, practice with individuals and families, practice with groups and communities, practice with organizations, social policy, and research. The cases balance attention between religion and spirituality as a resource for clients and social workers on the one hand, and as a source of challenges and ethical dilemmas for clients and social workers on the other.

The case studies were also selected to help social work students examine the different ways that social workers relate their own values, beliefs, and religious experiences to their professional identity and their ethical practice. Because of students' diverse perspectives, case discussions promote self-awareness about the effects of personal beliefs on perceptions of clients' spirituality and religion as well as on practice with these clients. In addition, the range of views typically revealed by case discussions helps students to better understand and empathize with diverse perspectives in cases and practice.

Each case that we selected potentially holds some emotional power for the reader, presents some uncertainty or problem with no clear answer, and is complex enough to generate discussion or disagreement. Issues of spirituality and religion often come to us entwined with (and sometimes inseparable from) other issues of great importance to clients and practitioners. The authors present a minimum of theoretical material, and instead of providing "pre-analyzed" vignettes, they focus on the "raw data" of the story, often with detailed description and dialogue. As raw data, the cases both allow for and invite application of theory during the classroom discussion. Faculty may be guided through this process by the teaching note that follows each case.

However, the primary leadership regarding theoretical discussion will come from the instructor leading the discussion, with input from the theoretical materials the students have studied. Presenting the raw data of the actual situation, without a preconceived theoretical framework imposed onto the case, allows students and faculty to draw theory from the particular course in which the case is used. For example, the case "Ya Me Voy" was used in an undergraduate HBSE class to discuss cultural diversity of clients, in a graduate course in international social work to illustrate social work with immigrants, and in a graduate course on macro systems to explore the dynamics of power within organizations. Although spirituality and religion became part of the discussion in each course, the instructor was able to require that students apply very different theoretical frameworks to the same narrative because theory was not embedded into the writing of the case. In short, these descriptive cases are extremely versatile and easy to use in a variety of courses.

A Resource for Social Work Education

We believe that this collection of decision cases will enable social work faculty members to better address the multifaceted topics of religion and spirituality as both resources and challenges for social work practice. This text also places these issues realistically in the context of exploring other areas of social work practice. Because all social workers practice with clients who are religious in diverse ways, and because many social workers are employed in faith-based settings, competence in dealing with religious and spiritual issues is critical for effective social work practice. In the next chapter, we present suggestions for getting the most out of case discussions.

References

Abels, P., & Abels, S. L. (2001). *Understanding narrative therapy: A guidebook for the social worker.* New York: Springer.

Barnes, L. B., Christensen, C. R., & Hansen, A. J. (1994). *Teaching and the case method* (3rd ed.). Boston: Harvard Business School Press.

Boehrer, J., & Linsky, M. (1990). Teaching with cases: Learning to question. In M. D. Svinicki (Ed.), *The changing face of college teaching* (pp. 41-57). San Francisco: Jossey-Bass.

Boyd, T. A. (1998). Spirituality sensitive assessment tools for social work practice. In B. Hugen (Ed.), *Christianity and social work: Readings on the integration of Christian faith and social work practice* (pp. 239-256). Botsford, CT: North American Association of Christians in Social Work.

Bullis, R. K. (1996). *Spirituality in social work practice.* Washington, DC: Taylor & Francis.

Canda, E. R. (Ed.). (1988). Spirituality, religious diversity, and social work practice. *Social Casework, 70*(9), 238-247.

Canda, E. R. (1989). Religion and social work: It's not that simple. *Social Casework, 70*(9), 572-574.

Canda, E. R. (1998). *Spirituality in social work: New directions.* Binghamton, NY: Haworth Pastoral Press.

Canda, E. R., & Furman, L. D. (1999). *Spiritual diversity in social work practice: The heart of helping.* New York: The Free Press.

Canda, E. R., Nakashima, M., Burgess, V., & Russel, R. (1999). *Spiritual diversity and social work: A comprehensive bibliography with annotations.* Alexandria, VA: Council on Social Work Education.

Christensen, C. R., Garvin, D. A., & Sweet, A. (Eds.). (1991). *Education for judgment: The artistry of discussion leadership.* Boston: Harvard Business School Press.

Corduan, W. (1998). *Neighboring faiths: A Christian introduction to world religions.* Downers Grove, IL: InterVarsity Press.

Cossom, J. (1991). Teaching from cases: Education for critical thinking. *Journal of Teaching in Social Work, 5,* 139-155.

Council on Social Work Education. (2001). *Educational policy and accreditation standards.* Alexandria, VA: Author.

Dezerotes, D. S. (1995). Spirituality and religiosity: Neglected factors in social work practice. *Arete, 20*(1), 1-15.

Ellor, J. W., Netting, F. E., & Thibault, J. M. (1999). *Understanding religious and spiritual aspects of human service practice.* Columbia, SC: University of South Carolina Press.

Fisher, C. F. (1978). Being there vicariously by case studies. In M. Ohmer & Associates (Eds.), *On college teaching: A guide to contemporary practices* (pp. 258-285). San Francisco: Jossey-Bass.

Freedman, J., & Combs, G. (1996). *Narrative therapy: The social construction of preferred realities.* New York: Norton.

Furman, L. E. (1994). Religion and spirituality in social work education: Preparing the culturally-sensitive practitioner for the future. *Social Work & Christianity, 21*(2), 103-117.

Garland, D. R. (1991). The role of faith in practice with clients. *Social Work & Christianity, 18*(2), 75-89.

Golembiewski, R. T., & Stevenson, J. G. (1998). *Cases*

and applications in nonprofit management. Itasca, IL: F. E. Peacock.

Golembiewski, R. T., Stevenson, J. G., & White, M. J. D. (1997). *Cases in public management* (5th ed.). Itasca, IL: F. E. Peacock.

Hodge, D. R. (2001). Spiritual assessment: A review of major qualitative methods and a new framework for assessing spirituality. *Social Work, 46,* 203-214.

Hugen, B. E. (Ed.). (1998). *Christianity and social work: Readings on the integration of Christian faith and social work practice.* Botsford, CT: North American Association of Christians in Social Work.

Joseph, M. V. (1987). The religious and spiritual aspects of clinical practice: A neglected dimension of social work. *Social Thought, 13*(1), 12-23.

Keith-Lucas, A. (1972). *Giving and taking help.* Chapel Hill, NC: University of North Carolina Press.

Keith-Lucas, A. (1985). *So you want to be a social worker: A primer for the Christian student.* Botsford, CT: North American Association of Christians in Social Work..

Keith-Lucas, A. (1994). *Giving and taking help* (Rev. Ed. ed.). Botsford, CT: North American Association of Christians in Social Work.

LeCroy, C. W. (1992). *Case studies in social work practice.* Pacific Grove, CA: Brooks/Cole.

LeCroy, C. W. (1999). *Case studies in social work practice* (2nd ed.). Pacific Grove, CA: Brooks/Cole.

Levin, B. B. (1999). The role of discussion in case pedagogy: Who learns what? And how? In M. A. Lundeberg, B. B. Levin, & H. L. Harrington (Eds.), *Who learns what from cases and how? The research base for teaching with cases.* Mahwah, NJ: Lawrence Erlbaum.

Loewenberg, F. M. (1988). *Religion and social work practice in contemporary social work practice.* New York: Columbia University Press.

Lundeberg, M. A., & Fawver, J. E. (1994). Thinking like a teacher: Encouraging cognitive growth in case analysis. *Journal of Teacher Education, 45,* 289-297.

Lundeberg, M. A., Levin, B. B., & Harrington, H. L. (1999). *Who learns what from cases and how? The research base for teaching with cases.* Mahwah, NJ: Lawrence Erlbaum.

Lynn, L. E., Jr. (1999). *Teaching and learning with cases: A guidebook.* New York: Chatham House.

McClelland, R. W., Austin, C. D., & Este, D. (1998). *Macro case studies in social work.* Milwaukee, WI: Families International.

Meyers, C., & Jones, T. B. (1993). Case studies. In *Promoting active learning: Strategies for the college classroom* (pp. 103-119). San Francisco: Jossey-Bass.

National Association of Social Workers. (1999). *NASW code of ethics.* Washington, DC: Author.

Pardeck, J. T., Murphy, J. W., & Min Choi, J. (1994). Some implications of postmodernism for social work practice. *Social Work, 39,* 437-448.

Rivas, R. F., & Hull, G. H. (2000). *Case studies in generalist practice* (2nd ed.). Pacific Grove, CA: Brooks/Cole.

Rothman, J. (1998). *From the front lines: Student cases in social work ethics.* Boston: Allyn & Bacon.

Sands, R. G. (2001). *Clinical social work practice in behavioral mental health: A postmodern approach* (2nd ed.). Boston: Allyn & Bacon.

Sanzenbach, P. (1989). Religion and social work: It's not that simple. *Social Casework, 70*(9), 571-572.

Sheridan, M. J. (2001). Defining spiritually sensitive social work practice: An essay review of *Spiritual diversity in social work practice: The heart of helping. Social Work, 46,* 87-92.

Sheridan, M. J., Bullis, R. K., Adcock, C. R., Berlin, S. D., & Miller, P. C. (1992). Serving diverse religious client populations: Issues for education and practice. *Journal of Social Work Education, 28,* 190-203.

Sherwood, D. A. (1998a). The relationship between beliefs and values in social work practice: Worldviews make a difference. In B. Hugen (Ed.), *Christianity and social work: Readings on the integration of Christian faith and social work practice* (pp. 107-126). Botsford, CT: North American Association of Christians in Social Work.

Sherwood, D. A. (1998b). Spiritual assessment as a normal part of social work practice: Power to help and power to harm. *Social Work & Christianity, 24*(2), 80-99.

Sherwood, D. A. (2000). Pluralism, tolerance, and respect for diversity: Engaging our deepest differences within the bond of civility. *Social Work & Christianity, 27*(1), 1-7.

Schön, D. A. (1983). *The reflective practitioner: How professionals think in action.* New York: Basic Books.

Schön, D. A. (1987). *Educating the reflective practitioner: Toward a new design for teaching and learning in the professions.* San Francisco: Jossey-Bass.

Van Hook, M. P. (1998). Incorporating religious issues in the assessment process with individuals and families. In B. Hugen (Ed.), *Christianity and Social Work: Readings on the integration of Christian faith and social work practice* (pp. 187-206). Botsford, CT: North American Association of Christians in Social Work.

Van Hook, M. P., Hugen, B., & Aguilar, M. A. E. (2001). *Spirituality within religious traditions in social work practice.* Pacific Grove, CA: Brooks/Cole.

Welsh, M. F. (1999). A technique for cross cultural case research and writing. In H. E. Klein (Ed.), *Interactive teaching and the multimedia revolution: Case method & other techniques.* Madison, WI: Omni Press.

Welsh, M. F., & Wolfer, T. A. (2000, February). *Making a case for case method teaching in social work education.* Faculty Development Institute presented at the Annual Program Meeting of the Council on Social Work Education, New York, NY.

Welty, W. M. (1989). Discussion method teaching. *Change, 21*(4), 41-49.

Wolfer, T. A., Freeman, M. L., & Rhodes, R. (2001). Developing and teaching an MSW capstone course using case methods of instruction. *Advances in Social Work, 2*(2), 156-171.

Case Method Teaching in the Social Work Classroom

T. Laine Scales

Case discussion is an excellent method for integrating issues of spirituality and religion into the social work curriculum. As demonstrated in chapter 1, case method teaching is based on a pedagogy that is student-centered and requires a different set of skills from the traditional lecture. In this form of instruction, the teacher facilitates the student's work rather than simply delivering information or providing answers. In this chapter, I will draw from the literature on case method teaching, as well as from my own experiences, to provide practical suggestions for preparing and leading the case discussion.

What Is Case Method Teaching?

According to Boehrer and Linsky (1990), use of the case method to teach professional practice has its roots in nineteenth-century legal and medical education, when actual cases were used to illustrate general principles and specific content. These professions, like social work, also used the traditions of apprenticeship and internship to promote learning through supervised practice. In fact, case discussion is an abstraction of the apprenticeship process that is removed from the field and placed in the classroom for students to consider together. The Harvard Business School pioneered this classroom approach in the early twentieth century and the case method is now used to train professionals in a variety of fields and professions, including accounting, engineering, nursing, teaching, and social work (Boehrer & Linsky, 1990, p. 44).

As noted in chapter 1, the cases in this collection are decision cases. As Lynn (1999) points out, this format is one of the most popular for teaching cases because it facilitates the development of professional skills. The decision case requires students to do what social workers must do every day: make difficult decisions in trying circumstances. Decision cases also require students to consider complex information in a systematic way, which increases their awareness of "the emotional, intellectual and procedural complexity of deciding in the real world"(Lynn, 1999, p. 107-8).

In order to produce a uniform collection of decision cases, authors for this volume were instructed to create cases with specific characteristics. Each case

- Is based on the actual experience of the social work practitioner who reported the events and signed a release form giving the author(s) permission to publish the case.

- Identifies one or more protagonists who are social workers or social work students facing some sort of dilemma with no single "right" answer.

- Requires students to formulate and analyze the problem and generate possible solutions.

- Is written for teaching purposes, with pedagogical goals in mind.

- Disguises identifying information to protect confidentiality, as determined in collaboration with the practitioner who reported the case.

- Is accompanied by a teaching note written by the authors.

- Has been piloted in a social work classroom in order to test the effectiveness of both the case and the teaching note.

The teaching note that accompanies each case guides the instructor through the preparation for each case. In this chapter I will draw from the established case method literature, as well as from my own experiences as a learner of this method, to offer tips and suggestions for using the case method.

Preparation for a Case Discussion

The instructor's preparation for an effective case discussion is very different from preparation for a lecture, and in my experience, may take more time. Contrary to common assumptions, the case discussion does not provide an opportunity for the instructor to show up unprepared or to relax and let students run the class. Case method teaching requires thorough preparation and careful facilitation by the instructor.

It may seem like a paradox to plan for a class discussion that one imagines will spring forth spontaneously. However, many experienced case method instructors have found that the more they prepare, the more they are able to let the discussion flow in a spontaneous way:

The magic of being prepared is that I can either leave all the preparations behind or draw from them at will. The thorough preparation gives me the confidence I need to be creative and improvise as needed to challenge my students and involve them in a topic (Erskine, Leenders, & Mauffette-Leenders, 1998, p. 116-117).

What Discussion Do You Want to Have?

When preparing for a case discussion, you will need to carefully consider what learning objectives you wish to address and what the students might contribute to the discussion. This is very different from preparing for a lecture when preparation is centered around what you, the instructor, will say. (Lynn 1999, p. 68). How can instructors prepare for a discussion when they do not know for certain what the students are going to say? First, the instructor must be completely familiar with all of the elements of the case. In my experience, this requires at least two or three readings, marking the text or taking notes. The instructor must continually ponder the question, "What discussion do you, the instructor, want to have?" The specific issue here is purpose: One must identify learning objectives and decide what the students can gain from the discussion (Boehrer, 2000).

After carefully considering the ideal discussion, prepare a teaching note for use during the class. In this text, teaching notes are included for each case, written by the case authors and based upon their experiences teaching the case. These can provide a starting point, but you may need to adapt them to the particular learning objectives that you had in mind when you chose the case. Some of the questions will be more relevant than others for your specific class at this particular time in the semester. You may wish to add questions that highlight certain issues you want or need to address (Boehrer, 2000).

As you read the case and prepare the teaching note, think about your audience and consider again the principle preparation question: "What discussion do you want to have?" Additional questions to take into account include the following: Can you predict some likely responses to the questions you have prepared? What reactions do you expect students might have to the case? Are students likely to fall into several camps during the discussion? Is there a predictable line of reasoning that students may take?

Students amaze me every time I teach a case. They always come up with something new and unpredictable, such as an answer that never occurred to me, even though I was well-prepared. I make sure to vocally acknowledge the originality and uniqueness of such answers, and I tell the students that I am always learning from them. On the other hand, many student responses are expected, which can help you prepare. If the discussion is likely to be one-sided, you may need to think through ways that you could play the "devil's advocate." Imagining what students may say in advance can help you move the class into the discussion that you want to have (Erskine, Leenders, & Maufefette-Leenders, 1998, p. 87-88).

As noted in chapter 1, the purpose of case method discussion is to provide opportunities for students to use their analytic and critical thinking skills, their knowledge of social work theory and research, and their common sense and collective wisdom to identify and analyze problems, to evaluate possible solutions, and to formulate a preferred intervention (Welsh & Wolfer, 2000). To accomplish these learning goals, the cases must be open-ended, that is, they should not describe what the practitioner ultimately did, nor how the case turned out. Therefore, students and instructors must remember that there is not one "right" answer and as the instructor, you must resist the temptation to steer students to specific answers that you consider to be correct. Instead, you must be willing to let students navigate around a topic, while facilitating their exploration. One experienced case instructor notes,

> I think a [new] instructor's problem is that he or she has worked out an analysis of the case from a scientific point of view that is totally exhaustive, mutually exclusive, and gives a clear and penetrating breakdown; and that he or she wants to make sure the class gets there. If you start trying to force students into your assumptions and your framework, you wind up with a "dog and pony show" sooner or later (Erskine, Leenders, & Mauffette-Leenders, 1998, p. 96).

Assigning the Case

When assigning a case, the instructor must be very clear about what the students are to do with it. If the students have little or no experience with decision cases, the instructor must provide guidance about how to begin case analysis. Let the students know why you are assigning the case by sharing your objectives with them. Anticipate any problems that may be caused by incomplete or faulty information. If you are grading students on the skills they demonstrate during the discussion or on any related written assignments, it is only fair that you share with them the criteria upon which the grade will be based.

Instructors may assign supplementary readings on topics related to the case and ask students to integrate those readings into the discussion. Some case instructors recommend assigning questions for students to ponder before the case discussion. Students may be asked to write out and turn in their responses, or to meet in small groups outside of class to work on a collaborative response.

Erskine, Leenders, and Mauffette-Leenders (1998) recommend three standard assignment questions that can be used for almost any case:

1. If you were in the position of…(the decision maker) in the case, what would be your analysis of…(this decision, problem, issue, challenge or opportunity)?

2. What decision would you take and why?

3. What would be your action/implementation plan? (pp. 100-101)

Instructors may assign various formal or informal writing assignments to be completed after the class discussion has taken place, with students summarizing the main arguments and taking a position. Some instructors may prefer to assign a full case report. Students begin the report on their own, use the case discussion to try out their arguments, and complete the report following the discussion. Another model, used successfully in MSW capstone classes at the University of South Carolina, is to assign a written executive-summary style case analysis to be completed in advance of the case discussion. Students are encouraged to exchange and critique the drafts of their classmates, and the case discussion provides an opportunity for them to present the work they have already done.

Student Preparation

Instructors have a variety of expectations for student preparation and it is important for you to clarify what you expect from students before the first case discussion. At a minimum, instructors may ask that students read the case at least once before the class, think about the decision dilemma, and jot down some notes. As mentioned above, instructors may choose to create some questions for the students to consider before class or they may require students to meet in small groups to begin discussing the case before class. Alternatively, you can begin the class with small groups and later move to a discussion involving the whole class. The amount of preparation students engage in before the class will greatly affect the extent and quality of their involvement during the discussion. Those who have spent time reading, answering questions, and meeting in small groups will be able to engage the issues and dilemmas at a deeper level.

Class Size and Physical Arrangements

Some variation of case method teaching can be used in any size class, but in my experience, the ideal size for case discussion is between 15 and 25 participants. Social work classes are often small enough to fit these ideal parameters, and teachers must keep in mind that a smaller group of 10 participants may require extra effort to produce a variety of perspectives, while a large class with many vocal participants may force the instructor to referee. Larger classes also permit more students to stand on the sidelines without entering the discussion.

The ideal setting would allow all participants to see one another, with desks arranged in a semi-circle or U-shape. Movable tables and chairs will allow for small groups or spontaneous role plays. The instructor should have space to move around as the discussion proceeds and have access to a board for recording key points.

Managing the Discussion

Once you are prepared, the next step is to begin the discussion. Although instructors may be spontaneous and alter their plans in the midst of the class, it is recommended that the first question or statement, "the discussion starter," be carefully planned and written out. I suggest starting with questions that are fairly simple and for which non-debatable answers can be found in the text. The teaching notes in this text advise the instructor to begin with questions surrounding the facts of the case because it is important to identify the organizations and participants involved. A creative instructor may elicit from students ecomaps, genograms, organizational charts, or other visual diagrams to help identify how participants relate to one another. With

these starter questions, students can answer with confidence, they can look back at the text if they are unsure, and there should be little disagreement at this point. Starting with the facts of the case gives the students and the instructor a chance to warm up, and it also illustrates one way of beginning to analyze a real practice situation in social work: stating the known facts. This method also helps to clarify possible misunderstandings, especially in complex cases.

After a few minutes of talking about the stated facts, the instructor can lead the class deeper into the case by asking questions that require analysis, which are categorized by that heading in the teaching notes. Students who are experienced with case discussions may move in this direction without any prompting. Sometimes, during the fact-based phase of questioning, one student may ask a question that moves the group toward analysis and the discussion leader will have to decide if the class is ready. If not, you can simply say, "That's a great analytical question and let's hold onto it for a minute while we establish a few more facts." Otherwise, if the class is warmed up and ready to go, you can presume that the rest of the facts will come up later in the discussion and you can allow the class to begin analysis.

Once sufficient analysis has been completed, I recommend opening the action phase of the discussion in which students recommend a course of action for the protagonist, based on the prior analysis. The instructor must assess the appropriate time for the class to move into this phase. It is not useful to recommend actions too early, before analysis has been done. Students must learn to support their recommendations with reasons, and spending time in the analysis phase of the discussion will provide them with a foundation for articulating their reasons for recommending particular actions.

Sometimes, instructors may want to take the class in a different direction by shifting the line of discussion with a more deliberate transition. Lynn (1999) recommends phrases such as "I want to ask you a different question now," or "let's look at the problem from a different perspective" to make sure the discussion is proceeding in the intended direction. An "interim summary" also allows the students and the instructor to track the discussion by asking "What conclusions can we draw at this point?" (Lynn, 1999, p. 85).

Once you teach a few cases using this method, you may recognize that the linear process of establishing the facts, moving to analysis, and proposing possible actions is somewhat artificial, and actual case discussions are messier than this neat outline may suggest. The class may begin with the facts and move to analysis, but sometimes, during analysis, the discussion must return to establish a different set of facts. Or, while formulating a plan of action, the discussion may need to revert back to the analysis or even all the way back to the facts. The process is recursive and the "back and forth" nature of the discussion simulates real-life decision making and enlivens the classroom. The well-prepared instructor should be able to start with the linear outline in the teaching note and guide the spiraling movement of the class toward the discussion's conclusion. Being well-prepared is necessary so that you are not afraid to allow the discussion to weave back and forth among the various stages of inquiry, in the same way that a practitioner's thoughts flow when making a decision.

Skills for Leading Discussion

In order to effectively use the suggested strategies, the instructor must develop and practice a skill set conducive to the case teaching method. Many instructors may have developed these skills and will only need to apply them in the case discussion. Others may find they need to learn new abilities or sharpen other skills for use in a new and different context. As the class gets underway, the instructor's responsibility, as discussion leader, is to listen and to guide.

Listening

Listening is a skill that social workers cultivate and constantly use in practice. Active listening is one of the most important roles for the instructor at the opening of the discussion. This is where your thorough preparation will pay off because instead of worrying about what questions to ask, or struggling to remember facts of the case, the well-prepared instructor can carefully listen to student responses. Communicate that you are listening by making consistent eye contact with the speaker and by offering verbal and nonverbal indications that you are engaged with the speaker's words. You may need to occasionally provide one-sentence summaries of the discussion. It is also important to keep in mind the learning objectives while listening. The class has a particular purpose, so careful, critical listening will help you guide students toward the discussion you want to have.

Taking Notes

Taking notes on the board accomplishes several purposes. First, instructors can communicate that they are listening attentively as they selectively write down what students say. By choosing what to write, instructors can influence the course of a discussion, moving it toward the learning goals. In addition, keeping a record of the discussion helps both instructors and students to track the flow of the analysis and prevents confusion or repetition of comments. Notes on the board also provide visual reinforcement for the discussion and may facilitate recall. Many who are experienced with case method teaching recommend that the instructor include the recording task as part of the teaching role, rather than delegating this responsibility to a student (Erskine, Leenders, & Mauffette-Leenders, 1998, p. 103).

Guiding

It is essential to guide the discussion by continually asking yourself, "What discussion do I want to have? Will the route we are on get us there, or are we following a path that is too divergent?" If you find the class wandering away from your objectives, you may gently pull it back with a few prompts, such as "We are moving into a little different area and I want to bring us back," or "That is a different area of discussion, and I'm going to jot a note on the board here in case we have time to come back to it." Often, simply asking the right question will turn the discussion in the direction that you want.

Linking Student Comments

Once students are talking, the instructor must manage the flow of the discussion by linking the contributions. Instructors provide not only the connections between points of the current discussion, but also the links between the case, the course objectives, and previously discussed cases. Asking appropriate questions can facilitate these linkages. The instructor may ask a student to repeat a comment, explain further, or ask, "How is that important from the standpoint of social work ethics, human diversity, social policy, or human behavior?" (Erskine, Leenders, & Mauffette-Leenders, 1998, pp. 157-59).

Fostering Cooperation

As you plan and conduct the discussion, encourage students to learn from one another in a spirit that is cooperative, rather than competitive.

Students can build on as well as critique each other's statements. A general lesson they can draw from their participation is that they can advance the discussion without having to outsmart each other, that in the process of collective inquiry the product of the class as a whole improves and the learning of each member increases (Boehrer & Linksy, 1990, p. 48).

Bringing the Discussion to a Close

With experience, an instructor will become more adept at knowing when and how to end the discussion. Lynn (1999) recommends three skills that instructors must develop for a good closing. *Auditory memory* helps the instructor summarize by recalling what points were made and by whom. *Withholding your opinion* allows students to develop their own analysis, but requires patience, especially when students ask for your perspective. However, Lynn warns, "you can undo all the good you have done by either deliberately or inadvertently providing 'the answer'… Your students must recognize the inevitability of living with ambiguity and the necessity of making up their own minds, rather than have an answer provided by an expert authority." The third closing skill is *synthesis,* in which the instructor assists students in relating parts to the larger whole, seeing patterns, and looking at the bigger picture (Lynn, 1999, pp. 97-100).

Case Discussion and Cultural Diversity

Case discussion is more natural for students who are accustomed to classroom norms that value participation, intellectual argument, reward for individual efforts, and respect for knowledge itself over the authority of the teacher. Students from cultures that value consensus over argument, and who defer to the authority of the teacher may find it difficult to challenge views presented by other students or by the instructor (Erskine, Leenders, & Mauffette-Leedners, 1998; Lynn, 1999). In classes where the majority of students are from non-Western cultures, the instructor may alter the format. For example, one experienced case teacher has found that his Chinese students are often reluctant to offer any solutions publicly. However, it may be more acceptable for these students to generate solutions in small groups and appoint a spokesperson. (Erskine, Leenders, & Maufette-Leenders, 1998, pp. 283-86). In addition, instructors must recognize that cases are always culture bound. For example, when assigning a case about a social worker in a rural town in Texas, the instructor may falsely assume that readers have some cultural knowledge of that setting, if not from experience, from books, television, movies, or other cultural material. However, all students will not have the same cultural references, and working in small groups or with a partner before the larger discussion may give these students opportunities to ask about the cultural context.

As Lynn (1999) points out, the multicultural classroom presents opportunities as well as challenges. You may make an effort to draw out individual participants to discover how their cultural background influences their response to the case. However, this should be done without tokenism and without implying that a person is being asked to represent his or her entire culture.

Using Activities to Increase Participation

Role Plays

Students remain engaged when they identify with the characters of the story. One way to highlight the characters and the dilemma is by staging a role play. The instructor can assign different groups of students to represent various perspectives.

Small Group Activities

Students may work in small groups to recommend an action, to explore a particular viewpoint assigned to them, or to share written work representing their own prepared analysis. Group work may be used either before, during, or after the larger discussion.

In-Class Writing Assignments

After the discussion has reached the analysis stage, instructors may ask students to write a page in class recommending an action. Additionally, students may take the perspective of the practitioner and address the dilemma by drafting a memo to an imaginary supervisor or by writing case notes. Students can share their responses by trading with each other, by discussing their responses in small groups, or by turning them in for the instructor to read.

Follow-up Activities

In my experience, a powerful case discussion will become a part of a shared class experience, which students and instructors will recall and continue discussing throughout the rest of the semester. Instructors may require that students link the case to new theoretical material at a later time, either in discussion, in writing assignments, or on a test.

Using the Teaching Note

The teaching note that follows each case is intended to assist you in preparing for the discussion. The authors have written these as a guide based on their own experiences with teaching these particular cases. They emphasize questions related to spirituality and religion, but also suggest other potential lines of inquiry. If you wish to use these cases to focus on other topics, you can simply alter the questions. You may prefer to write your own teaching note or add to the one provided in the blank space at the end of each note.

The Construction of the Teaching Note

Each note begins with a case synopsis and learning outcomes. The authors have listed first the outcomes related to religion and spirituality, though each case is richly textured and useful for teaching additional topics. Reading the synopsis and the objectives will help you choose which cases might be appropriate for your course. In addition, the authors suggest levels of experience (BSW or MSW) and list a variety of classroom topics for which the case might be used. In general, the recommendation for levels and topics are related to the skills necessary for effective practice in the situation presented by the case.

The discussion questions in each teaching note are organized into three categories: facts, analysis, and action. As suggested above, I like to begin the discussion with questions to elicit factual answers. Students can easily report facts of the case and there is generally little disagreement. The next questions move the discussion toward analysis, which may comprise the majority of the discussion time. Finally, students are asked in the next set of questions to recommend an action. The goal of the application section is for students to grapple with the question, "What would I do if I were in this situation?"

Instructors may find that they do not ask every question listed in the teaching note. Choose your questions in advance, but be ready with alternative questions if the discussion takes you in unexpected and productive directions. After many of the questions, the authors have provided comments, which are designed to stimulate the instructor's thinking during the preparation stage, but are not meant to represent the "right" answers. In case teaching, there are many answers that could be considered valid and the authors' comments, offered for the more complex questions, suggest particular points that may prove relevant.

Your Notes

Additional space has been left for you to write notes and reminders for yourself after you have taught the case. You may find it helpful to record any surprises, any questions that flopped or discussion threads that were unproductive. Additionally, you can list items that were particularly productive, or exercises or role plays that emerged as a natural part of the discussion. You may want to create a timeline documenting the length of the discussion and the points at which the discussion naturally moved from facts to analysis to action. These notes will be useful for you the next time you teach the case and will help you develop your own unique approach.

Problems and Pitfalls of Leading the Discussion

I believe you will find case method teaching to be a wonderfully productive pedagogical technique. It is important to note, however, that everything may not go as smoothly as you might have imagined because this method is less safe and less predictable than the traditional lecture. Students may not participate, due to confusion or lack of interest, or the logic of the discussion may not flow as you had hoped. In spite of these potential problems, in my opinion this risk is worth taking because of the great potential for real critical thinking and analysis. In addition, if the first discussion does not progress as you might have liked, I believe that, with planning and practice, you will be able to develop the skills to facilitate a smooth case discussion. Below are a few problems I have seen or experienced and some suggestions for addressing them.

A Chaotic Discussion

Managing a lively discussion requires that instructors have good listening skills, an ability to see where the discussion may be headed, and an ability to relate a variety of points and arguments to the whole discussion. Additionally, the instructor must maintain order in the classroom, without which it is nearly impossible to have a fruitful case discussion. To prevent chaos, in the first class establish ground rules about interruptions, raising hands (or waiting your turn to speak), and respecting others' comments. As you talk about these issues, inform your students that they are responsible, along with you, for monitoring the class. When students hold themselves accountable for respecting each other, waiting their turn, and generally following the established guidelines, they will begin to feel ownership for the discussion, which will lead to a greater investment in the class.

A Few Participants Dominate

It is the instructor's responsibility to prevent a few individuals from dominating the discussion and to ensure that everyone has a chance to participate. To achieve this goal, you may need to elicit responses from the more reticent students. Let them know that you are seeking balance by setting ground rules from the beginning: "Ideally, everyone will have a chance to comment; I ask that you not interrupt each other and that you listen respectfully to what each person has to say." If two or three students are monopolizing the discussion, you can postpone their comments by saying, "Let's hear from someone who has not spoken yet, and we will come back to you." Other instructors will simply call on a student who has not yet spoken.

Students Do Not Respect the Opinions of Others

When discussing topics that are emotionally charged, such as spirituality and religion, students may forget to demonstrate respect for one another's views and beliefs. The successful instructor will draw upon social work values and ethics to create and maintain a climate in which diversity of opinion is valued. If students insist on being disrespectful, the instructor may ask a student to sit out of the discussion by noting, "We have heard your viewpoint, now let's hear from someone else."

Students' Participation Is Inadequate

Students are motivated by a variety of stimuli.

Some students will not speak unless asked, some will start once the discussion is underway, and others are more than happy to start the discussion themselves. On occasion a talkative student will comment, even when it is clear she or he has not prepared for the case, or a student may make a comment that is shallow or off the topic. The instructor must remind the class of the quality of preparation and participation that is expected and push the students to meet these expectations. For example, if students make uninformed, irrelevant, or inappropriate comments, the instructor may ask the student about her or his preparation, may request that the student address the point at hand, or may suggest that the class might come back to that point at a later time. Accepting poor quality discussion brings the whole class down to a level of mediocrity (Erskine, Leenders, & Maufette-Leenders, 1998, pp. 143-45).

Getting Stuck

Occasionally you may feel that you are not sure where to go next; after all, it can be quite difficult to listen, talk, and strategize at once. If you feel stuck, you might ask the students, "Where do you think we should we go from here?" Stop and reflect with the class, saying something like "We want to get to the point where we can recommend an action. Let's stop and think for a moment about how we will get there together." Meanwhile, as the students are focused on the question "Where do we go from here?" it will probably become clear to you what needs to happen next.

The Discussion Ends Too Soon

Sometimes students reach consensus before a variety of perspectives have been considered. The group may all agree on the first solution that is offered because of a lack of energy, preparation, or interest. In this situation, Lynn recommends playing the role of devil's advocate and presenting alternative points of view. Additionally, you might suggest other solutions or perspectives and work to ignite further interest in the case (Lynn, 1999, pp. 88). Careful preparation is extremely important here.

You Run Out of Time

Ideally, the experienced case method instructor should be able to manage the timing of the discussion in such a way that the climax and wrap-up occur before the class ends. However, if you do find that you are running out of time, there is no reason to panic. In contrast to a lecture, in which the instructor must convey a certain amount of information, a case can continue to elicit reflection from a student even after the bell has rung. In fact, sometimes it is better if all the loose ends are not all neatly sorted out. Instructors should be prepared to assign activities that will help students bring closure to the case. Here are some suggestions:

- Ask students to write responses to an assigned question in the last five minutes of the class.

- Encourage students to continue their discussion by email on the class electronic mailing list.

- Assign students a question to write about and turn in at the next class period.

- Require students to meet in small groups and continue the discussion before the next class.

- Resume the discussion for a short period at the beginning of next class, but be sure to assign some task that will require students to continue thinking about the case in the meantime.

The Discussion Does Not Go as You Planned

If the discussion does not progress exactly as you had hoped the first time you try it, you may take comfort in the fact that, unlike the lecture, a case discussion is a shared venture between students and instructors. With practice, you are likely to improve, and with experience, students may improve their ability to carry the discussion.

As Boehrer and Linsky (1990) point out, each particular case discussion is a unique event. You have a chance to start with a clean slate on the next occasion and to make that discussion different. Students bring their own perceptions and experiences to the event, which means that what matters most about the case is what that particular group of students makes of it. "The discussion is the fulfillment of the case's purpose; until that event occurs, the case, however simple or elaborate, is mere potential" (p. 46).

Using This Text

The first two chapters of this text have been developed as a guide for instructors who want to gain more experience with case method teaching. Although most social work educators have used cases or vignettes in their teaching, the skills required of an educator who uses decision cases go beyond simply illustrating didactic teaching with case examples. Instead, this technique encourages an experiential, inductive approach to learning that facilitates active engagement on the part of students with knotty practice issues.

I believe that the decision case method is ideal for addressing content on spirituality and religion, which involves the complex issues of respect for diversity, personal ethics and attitudes of the professional, and clients' values and beliefs. I hope that you will find this book useful in your social work courses and that your experience of teaching these cases will be as productive as mine has been.

References

Boehrer, J. (2000, August). *Enlivening teaching: Using disciple-based cases and classroom research to improve learning and teaching.* A working conference for college faculty, Vancouver, BC.

Boehrer, J., & Linsky, M. (1990). Teaching with cases: Learning to question. In M. D. Svinicki (Ed.), *The changing face of college teaching* (pp. 41-57). San Francisco: Jossey-Bass.

Erskine, J., Leenders, M., & Mauffette-Leenders, L. (1998). *Teaching with cases.* London, Canada: Ivey Publishing.

Lynn, L. E., Jr. (1999). *Teaching and learning with cases: A guidebook.* New York: Chatham House.

Welsh, M. F., & Wolfer, T. A. (2000, February). *Making a case for case method teaching in social work education.* Faculty Development Institute presented at the Annual Program Meeting of the Council on Social Work Education, New York, NY.

01.

This Work Is My Religion

David A. Sherwood

"This work is my religion." These measured but passionate words burned in Sharon Dolan's mind as she sat alone in her office late one evening. They had been delivered by Lena Sefera, an ethnic Albanian immigrant and one of Sharon's most valued staff members at Helping Hands, the refugee resettlement program she directed.

Sharon knew that no matter what she said or did in their meeting the next morning, Lena's "religion" was going to be shaken.

Helping Hands Refugee Resettlement Program

Helping Hands was one of several programs under the auspices of Inter-Faith Community Ministries in Rochester, New York, a private, nonprofit social service agency which had begun modestly in 1951 as a cooperative approach to providing basic emergency food and clothing needs. It had evolved to include a major housing rehabilitation program, a VISTA coalition, a community outreach and youth mentoring program, an Older Adult Connection program, a Commission for the Homeless, and the Helping Hands Refugee Resettlement program. A faith-based but widely ecumenical agency, Inter-Faith Community Ministries defined its mission as twofold:

- Building relationships of trust through affirming relationships, accepting all people, and encouraging a deepening of spirituality within the community; and

- Building relationships through action by initiating actions that encourage the creativity and gifts of our members for attaining a just and compassionate society.

Funding came from a wide variety of sources including contributions from cooperating churches, synagogues, and mosques, private contributors, the United Way, grants, and government contracts.

Helping Hands worked with the U.S. State Department's Office of Refugee Resettlement through Catholic Charities and Church World Services to help resettle about 200 refugees in the Rochester area each year. The program did not have much funding to offer incoming refugees—about $200 per person to assist with finding housing, health care, and jobs—but was able to provide crucial assistance with vital needs by joining its resources with those brokered from other parts of the community. Nevertheless, for most of the refugees arrival in the American "promised land" inevitably fell disappointingly short of their dreams.

Although the Helping Hands caseload included refugees from Sudan, Pakistan, Iran, and West Africa, at the time about 60% of their clients were Eastern European, mostly Serbs and Croatians. However, the troubles in Kosovo were already on Lena Sefera's horizon.

Lena Sefera

Lena had said "this work is my religion" to Sharon in an intense after-hours conversation 12 months before, in April 1998, when Sharon had found Lena again scouring the Internet on the office computer, downloading information and names from contacts in Kosovo, her native land. Although it would be almost a year before Kosovo would break into American headlines, Lena could be found evening after evening gathering scraps of information about who was the latest person to disappear or to be killed.

"This work" was refugee resettlement, something Lena Sefera discovered through painful experiences. As an ethnic Albanian in Kosovo, she had lost her job as an administrator with the electric power company years before when Serbian dominance grew. After the Peace Corps arrived in Kosovo, her fluency in English, Albanian, and Serbo-Croatian had made her an invaluable translator. She had been forced to become a refugee herself when she became engaged to one of the Peace Corps workers. Both of their passports were confiscated and they were "advised" that they had 24 hours to leave the country. Lena had quickly found her place in Rochester, New York, with her new husband and, soon enough, her new job. She came to Helping Hands first as a client, but soon as a volunteer, and finally as a staff member. Lena was a refugee who had the passion, skills, and personality to speak tenderly to the most fearful refugees about their concerns and to advocate boldly to board members, community supporters, and television cameras about their needs.

Lena filled or assisted with several vital roles at Helping Hands. Her language skills made her almost indispensable in facilitating communication between the agency's caseworkers and the Eastern European refugees, during both the initial flurry of activity when they were being resettled and in the follow-up support activities the agency provided. Lena's contagious passion for social justice and the cause of refugees, her articulate speech, and her charismatic presence made her an effective spokesperson for the agency to the community, to media representatives, and to the many churches and church groups that supported Helping Hands financially. She made it her mission to sensitize and educate the agency about the troubles in Eastern Europe. "Here, read this," became a familiar refrain. She led in organizing candlelight prayer vigils "for peace."

As an ethnic Albanian, Lena Sefera was Muslim, but most of her religious faith had evaporated in the flames of her life experiences. This faith had been transmuted into her commitment to refugee resettlement and she had developed strongly egalitarian views about social justice.

"It doesn't matter who you are or what your religion is; if you are a refugee I want to help you," Lena had said. "I don't trust any of those religions. In fact, I despise them. This work is my religion."

A Beautiful Blue Poster and Clouds on the Horizon

Some time earlier, almost as soon as she moved into her office, Lena had put up a beautiful blue poster on the wall. Sharon loved to look at it. It was a travel poster, a large striking photograph of Kosovo taken in better times. The sky was blue, the sun was shining, and the countryside was lovely. It had deep meaning for Lena. It had been her home. And the poster had only one word on it, the name of the province. What could be more appropriate?

Sharon soon learned otherwise. As the number of Serbian refugees grew and was joined by a trickle of ethnic Albanians, caseworkers began relaying to Sharon rumblings of suspicion and discontent about the agency and its staff from the Serbian clients. These caseworkers reported that it was becoming increasingly difficult to convince the Serbians to accept their services. The agency tried to be proactive in dealing with the deep ethnic and religious differences among the clients, attempting to foster communication and understanding through small groups, but got nowhere. They organized a community-league soccer team involving refugees from every ethnic group, which seemed to be a great success for five weeks but quickly unraveled when U.S. and NATO bombs began to fall in Serbia and Kosovo at the end of March 1999.

Some Serbian refugees had even formally complained to their caseworkers, stating that they did not trust Lena Sefera. The caseworkers felt they were caught in the middle, but some expressed their own frustration. One said, "Yeah, the Serbs say they see her fingerprints all over this program," and another declared, "I don't think she's prejudiced, but I do think she's a hypocrite sometimes. Here she doesn't even believe in God and yet she's out there leading prayer vigils for refugees and peace and she's going around asking all these churches and synagogues and mosques for money."

This stunned Sharon, who was shocked that everyone could not see how much Lena cared and how dedicated she was to justice for all.

When Sharon assembled a group of the English-speaking Serbs and asked about the source of their distrust, the Serbs gave each other knowing looks. One spoke for the rest. "Just look at that poster in her office."

"It's a beautiful picture from your homeland," Sharon replied. "It's not political."

"Don't you see how the name is spelled? *Kosova.* That's the Albanian spelling." As far as the Serbians were concerned, the case was closed. Lena was obviously biased.

What Now?

When Sharon had tried to share with Lena these growing problems, Lena had become quite offended. "I do everything to be fair. If anything, I work harder for the Serbs. I live for justice and this feels very unjust to me."

The time when she usually left for home had long since passed, and Sharon still sat in her office, staring at the draft of the memo on her desk that she had just written. She could not decide whether to tear it up or give it to Lena during the meeting Sharon had arranged with her for the next morning.

The memo began, "It has been brought to my attention that your poster is creating tension for some of our clients and staff. Although I understand that the poster is very important to you personally, it is necessary that our agency remove as many barriers to service for our clients as we can . . . ."

Sharon shook her head. "But is it fair? Lena's whole identity as an Albanian and as a person of justice is at stake. And what will we do if she quits? The Serbians may be suspicious of her, but she is the only one here who can really speak their language. Am I just giving in to their religious and ethnic prejudices? And what will the media say when they hear about this? Or our supporters? And if she stays, how am I going to rebuild the trust among my staff and our clients? No matter what I do, it could really cost a lot. And I do believe her when she says she is fair in her work."

"Well, I guess the buck stops with me."

01.teaching note
This Work Is My Religion
David A. Sherwood

Case Synopsis

Sharon, the Director of the Helping Hands refugee resettlement program, confronts several micro and macro practice and value dilemmas as she tries to decide what to do in response to complaints from Serbian refugee clients about Lena Sefera, an ethnic Albanian Muslim originally from Kosovo, who is now one of her most valued and respected staff members. Lena, a refugee herself, has come to despise religions and ethnic divisions, channeling her faith and passion for justice into her refugee resettlement work, saying "this work is my religion." Lena's language skills in English, Albanian, and Serbo-Croatian have made her almost indispensable in assisting the agency's caseworkers to communicate with the Eastern European refugees, and her charismatic presence has made her an effective spokesperson to the community, the media, and the many church groups that support the agency financially. The Serbians' justification for their suspicions and fears of discrimination is embodied by a seemingly innocuous and beautiful travel poster hanging in Lena's office—a large, striking photograph of Kosovo during better days.

Learning Outcomes Relating to Religion and Spirituality

Case discussion will facilitate the work of students as they

1. Understand the complexities of identifying

and achieving what constitutes justice in conditions of religious and ethnic diversity.

2. Develop the capacity to engage in ethical and professionally competent assessment and problem solving when legitimate personal, spiritual, religious, and professional values come into tension with each other.

3. Practice developing spiritually and religiously sensitive social work interventions on micro, mezzo, and macro levels.

4. Develop alternative approaches for bridging deep divisions among people that are rooted in ethnic, religious, political, and class differences.

Other Learning Outcomes for Which This Case Could Be Used

Case discussion will facilitate the work of students as they

5. Develop critical thinking skills in understanding micro-, mezzo-, and macro-system implications of agency policy decisions.

6. Identify and prioritize costs and benefits of alternative policy and practice decisions.

7. Explore the limits of personal expression in the workplace.

8. Develop administrative skills in resolving staff and client conflicts.

Courses and Levels for Which the Case Is Appropriate

This case is most appropriate in a master's level micro/macro advanced practice course to highlight the interaction among values and ethics, diversity issues, social justice, and micro and macro practice skills. However, the case may also be useful in undergraduate programs or in the foundation year of graduate programs in practice or field seminar classes.

Discussion Questions Related to Religion and Spirituality

Establishing the Facts

1. What kind of agency is Helping Hands? What are its funding sources?

2. What is Sharon's position in the agency? What responsibilities and powers does she have?

3. What qualifications does Lena have for her job? What *is* her job?

4. What do we know about the Serbian clients' complaints and what do we not know that might be relevant? About possible staff dynamics? About how Helping Hands fits into the larger agency and its mission, governance, board, or supporters?

5. Who, if anyone, has Sharon consulted with regarding the situation, the issues at stake, the process to be followed, or the options available? Who might she consult with?

6. Where do staff members stand regarding Lena's role and functioning in the agency?

Analysis

7. What social work values and ethics are at stake and in some tension in this situation?

    Lena's rights to self-determination and self-expression in the workplace. Respect for her passion for jus-

tice. Understanding and respecting diverse religious and ethnic identities, values, and cultures on the one hand, but not enabling religiously and ethnically connected prejudices and biases on the other. Integrity in the manner with which the agency and its representatives address the public and engage in fund-raising (e.g., Is Lena being dishonest in organizing prayer vigils and "mining" the religious groups for resources when she "despises all these religions"?).

8. To what extent can the "right" action in a case like this be decided on the basis of utilitarian ethics (e.g., harm reduction, maximizing desirable consequences) and to what extent can the "right" action be decided on the basis of deontological ethics (e.g., telling the truth, upholding justice) in spite of the consequences?

    Utilitarian (consequentialist or teleological) ethics attempts to calculate the costs and benefits of an action and judges it ethical or "right" if the benefits outweigh the costs (the end justifies the means, the greatest good to the greatest number). An act is "good" if it has "good" consequences. A major limitation of utilitarian ethics is that it contains within itself no standard for what would constitute a "good" result or benefit, and instead assumes the benefit is self-evident or can be deduced from the "facts" of the situation. However, this is precisely what is often under debate.

    Deontologists would argue that even utilitarians require at least one nonutilitarian value judgment in order to define "good" or understand the benefit. Facts alone have no particular ethical meaning and they must always be interpreted in the context of values not derivable from the facts themselves. "Is" alone does not lead to any particular "ought." Another major limitation of strictly utilitarian approaches to ethical decision making is that calculating hoped-for benefits is immensely complex, fraught with unintended consequences, and never better than a prediction.

    Deontologists believe that ethical actions are grounded in some sort of moral principles that have validity independent of purely consequential considerations (e.g., truth telling is a prima facie moral obligation, minorities cannot be treated unjustly simply because it may have some benefit for the majority). Deontologists do not necessarily say that consequences have no relevance to ethical decision making, but that ethical actions must be based on more than purely consequential considerations.

Basic values of the social work profession are more accurately described as deontological than utilitarian, but most ethical decisions are based on both deontological and utilitarian considerations (cf. Reamer, 1990; Sherwood, 1999).

9. Is Lena's leadership of prayer vigils for peace ethical in light of her own views about spirituality and religion? Do her public-relations and fund-raising appeals to churches, synagogues, and mosques utilizing religious motivations constitute an unethical exploitation or "strip-mining" of these groups for resources? What responsibility does the agency have for taking advantage of her skills in this way?

10. What does the agency stand to lose if this situation "blows up"?

For example, the valuable, and very difficult to replace, skills and qualities Lena brings to the agency, public-relations difficulties, and possible loss of financial support if Lena leaves and takes her case public, major conflict among client groups and the agency if the poster stays or becomes a "cause."

11. What organizational issues does this case raise? What kinds of organizational cultures, structures, communication patterns, or policies and procedures might help agencies deal with issues like this better?

Action

12. What alternatives does Sharon have in dealing with Lena and her poster? What would you do if you were in Sharon's place and why?

13. If Sharon asks Lena to take down the poster, how can she try to explain this to Lena in a way that Lena can understand?

14. If Sharon asks Lena to take down the poster and Lena quits her job in pain and protest, how should Sharon respond? To Lena, to the staff, to the board, or to the community? (Lena has become a highly visible spokesperson for the agency in the community and in the media since the trouble in the Balkans has become prominent.)

15. What should Sharon do if she decides not to ask Lena to take down the poster? How and what should she communicate to the caseworkers and the clients?

16. What can Sharon do to rebuild the trust between Lena, the agency, the caseworkers, and the refugees?

17. How can Sharon, her staff, and the agency confront and overcome religious and ethnic animosity among the clients? How can they find a balance between being careful about ethnic sensitivities without feeding into and rewarding ethnic and religious animosity?

The over-simplicity of the logic of "respecting" or "celebrating" religious, ethnic, or cultural differences without judging their content or consequences is exposed in situations like this one. Social work rhetoric to the contrary, social workers find they sometimes do have to make both deontological moral judgments about religious, ethnic, and cultural differences and consequentialist judgments about how purely they can hold to their deontological values under the circumstances. Legitimate prima facie values come into tension or conflict with each other in case situations and some sort of prioritizing of values or compromise must be found. A fundamental ethical responsibility for social workers is to be highly aware of how their own values and beliefs interact with the issues cases present and to make that an intentional part of the professional decision-making process in a way that has integrity for both themselves and for their clients. In this case, part of the challenge is sorting through how much of the Serbians' concern about Lena is just and how much is unjust. But even after that task is complete, there is still the need to consider both intended and unintended consequences of any agency action or policy in response to the Serbians' concerns. How can the agency and staff model religious tolerance in a way that does not trivialize real and perhaps legitimate religious differences (Sherwood, 2000)?

18. What would be a fair and ethical policy for an agency like Helping Hands regarding individual freedom of expression by staff in the workplace? What sorts of limits can or should be placed on what social workers display in their offices that has political, ideological, moral, spiritual, or religious significance? Would there be any difference if the agency were a public agency rather than a private, faith-based agency?

Again, we are faced with balancing legitimate prima facie values that come into tension or conflict (e.g., individual freedom of expression and not exploiting a position of power). Even if an agency so desired, it is probably impossible to avoid communicating political, ideological, moral, spiritual, or religious messages on some level, either organizationally or by individual staff members. Lena's picture illustrates that even a beautiful travel poster may carry political and ideological meanings. New Age platitudes on posters, Bibles on desks, flyers for political rallies, notices for legislative lobby days, and even personal jewelry may all send messages of some sort. However, all agencies and staff have the responsibility to consider how self-expression affects clients. It is probably true that private agencies, including faith-based agencies, have greater freedom with regard to communicating political, ideological, moral, spiritual, or religious messages, but they also have a responsibility to do so in a way that enables client self-determination and avoids exploiting the helping relationship. Public agencies and staff should not think that this is not an issue for them as well. Even though their messages may not be overtly spiritual or religious, they may indeed be political, ideological, moral, or even spiritual. Agencies should not think they have solved the problem by simply banning either individual self-expression generally or spiritual and religious expression specifically. It is likely that the appropriate level of individual or agency expression is always going to be a judgment call that takes into account as many of the relevant values and practical considerations as possible. These judgments are usually best not made by one individual alone.

19. What should Sharon do if she suspects that caseworkers are jealous of Lena's fast rise and prominence in the agency and that this envy influences what the caseworkers report and how the agency's personnel dynamics have developed?

20. What kind of consultation or process should Sharon go through in order to arrive at her decision? Who are the stakeholders, responsible persons, and available resources that could or should be mobilized and involved? Can these resources include Lena, the caseworkers, or the Serbian clients? Why or why not?

Teaching Suggestions

Open the class with a 10-minute writing exercise. After students have read the case, have them take 10 minutes to jot down phrases in response to each of these questions (tell your students that you will want to collect their answers later, but that they will not be graded):

1. What is going on here? What are the social work practice and value issues that Sharon must address?

2. What alternatives does Sharon have?

3. What would you do, and why?

Begin a class discussion based on these questions, drawing out as many different issues and alternatives as you can from the students. Then, based on your own goals and the focus of the class, develop selected areas to explore in depth. Be sure to collect the written responses at the end of the class, if you said that you would.

References

Reamer, Frederic G. (1990). *Ethical dilemmas in social service* (2nd ed.). New York: Columbia University Press.

Sherwood, David A. (1999). Common ground and conflict: Exploring professional ethics and worldviews. *Social Work & Christianity, 26*(2), 81-100.

Sherwood, David A. (2000). Pluralism, tolerance, and respect for diversity: Engaging our deepest differences within the bond of civility. *Social Work & Christianity, 27*(1), 1-7.

Additional Notes

02.

Good Medicine
Diana R. Garland and Karen Grubb Gilbert

It was August 15, 2000, and for less than four months, Meguen Dancing Feather had been director of Good Medicine Indian Health Services, a program of Community Health Care of Minot, North Dakota. Recently graduated with a BSW degree, Meguen knew she must fit into the professional community, and at the same time, maintain her credibility with the Native American community she served. Yet here she was, being publicly accused by the chief of police of "neglecting your responsibility to serve our community."

Growing up Hidatsa

To be asked to serve as director of Good Medicine Indian Health Services in her first job while she completed her social work degree had been the fulfillment of Meguen's dream. Meguen's parents were from different tribes and reservations and had not been able to establish a stable home for their children. Her maternal grandmother was a traditional Hidatsa woman. The Hidatsa were peaceful American Plains Indians of Siouan ancestry who lived in semi-permanent villages on the upper Missouri River. This grandmother raised Meguen and her four brothers and sisters and instilled in Meguen her long-held values: "Treat all people well; be generous. Be good to older people; they have been on the earth longer than you and they know more than you do." Meguen remembered the smells of the healing ceremonies in her grandmother's home, with the

healing water, the tobacco, and the herbs, and she remembered the songs that the healing people sang to her grandmother.

When she reached age five, social services from the reservation sent Meguen to a Catholic boarding school. The school staff cut off her beautiful long braids, cropped her hair very short, and, assuming she had lice, doused her with "bug juice." They stripped her of her clothes and gave her a uniform to wear. She was taught Catholic behavior, learning Latin and participating in Mass in Latin three times a day. Meguen remembered thinking "This is not my way."

After high school, she struggled to find her own way. She tried the Lutheran Church for a while, then the Assemblies of God, and for a time she was a Jehovah's Witness. Finally, her quest led her to talk with an elder of her people, who asked only a few questions but seemed to understand her struggles. He suggested that Meguen undergo a cleansing ceremony, what the Native people call "a sweat." The purpose of this ceremony, conducted in a lodge heated by fiery stones, is to purify the mind, body, spirit, and heart. Gathered with others in the sweat lodge, she smelled again the healing water, the tobacco, and the herbs she remembered from her preschool years and she sensed her grandmother's presence. It was a significant healing experience for her; she had found her way back to her traditions. Further, Meguen came to believe that other Native people could be healed the same way.

At the same time Meguen was reconnecting with the traditional ways of her people, she decided to pursue a college degree, possibly in nursing. During her first year, a friend suggested that she look into social work, to which Meguen responded, "I hate social workers, they're so nosy."

"But you don't have to be that way," the friend persisted.

Meguen listened and decided to see for herself by enrolling in an introductory social work course. She changed her major when she began to imagine how she might connect Native American traditional practices and her concern for her people with the profession of social work.

The Work of Good Medicine

Over the door of her office in an old renovated house, Meguen hung sage wrapped in a red cloth, a symbol of the protection and care Good Medicine Indian Health Services tried to provide to Native people. Good Medicine served persons from the many tribes who came to Minot after migrating from reservations 75 miles away or more. Despite the distance, coming to Minot was a much wider cultural leap than it was a geographical move. Good Medicine helped Native families with everything from eyeglasses to low-cost medical care, because many had no medical insurance. Meguen provided over-the-counter pharmacy items, funds for prescription drugs, and referrals to public clinics. She also handed out personal hygiene products for the many Native American men and women who lived on the streets—those who she realized had not been able to adapt to the cultural transition.

According to the program brochure, the mission of Good Medicine, one of several programs of Community Health Care, was "to provide a holistic approach in addressing the health care needs of Native American people in the area in a culturally sensitive manner." The Minot United Way supported the work of the agency with funding which was supplemented by small grants from several local foundations. The board of Minot United Way expected outcome measures and accountability from all funded agencies and their programs. Meguen had heard that some members of the United Way board had raised questions about funding Good Medicine because of the program's use of elders

and pipe bearers, rather than licensed mental health professionals, to address family crises.

Although Meguen was new to professional social work, she had a long history in the community. She was married to the only Native American police officer in town, and together they were raising six children and were the guardians for another six year old. Meguen had fought for custody of this child, who was from her own tribe, under the Indian Child Welfare Act, when he was being placed for adoption at age six months. She knew her people and their problems. She also knew that Minot was a relatively small city and that the white community leaders worked together in informal social networks. She had to establish her credibility with them as a new program director because they funded her program. But she also wanted to continue the program's practices of using Native healing methods.

Launching of the Street Smart Program

The previous winter, the town had been shaken when a homeless Native woman had frozen to death under a downtown bridge. Agencies pointed fingers at each other and no one wanted to take responsibility. With the coming of spring, the business community launched a "beautification" program for the downtown area. The recently appointed chief of police, a newcomer to the community from Ohio, brought his own agenda of ridding the streets of homeless people to the beautification project, which matched well with the concerns of the business community.

In support of the chief of police's agenda, the program was named the Street Smart Program. Many of the homeless people in Minot were alcoholic and Native American, and their presence was troubling to business owners who feared that they discouraged shoppers from coming downtown. The chief of police vowed to move all homeless people out of the downtown area and his officers began threatening "trouble-makers" with arrest. The unspoken sentiment was that Native people did not belong here; if they had troubles, they should go back to the reservation where they belonged.

Because the police officers were preventing homeless persons from sitting or sleeping in public view, they began to congregate in the safety of Good Medicine's front porch. Meguen knew many of these people, and she listened to their stories. One man told her, "I was just drinking a coke. The officer came and took it away from me and poured it out on the grass. That coke cost me a dollar!" The more she heard about the city's approach to beautification, the angrier Meguen became.

In June, Meguen had been the director of Good Medicine for two months. After consulting with and gaining the permission of the executive director of Community Health Care, Meguen decided to attend the meetings of the Street Smart Program. At the first meeting, the chief of police described his police activities as "case management" with homeless persons. Meguen was furious, but at the same time she was intimidated. Quietly, she rose to her feet and said, "I'm wondering if you are violating these people's civil rights." She sat down and no one responded. When no one spoke to Meguen after the meeting either, she thought to herself, "I'm really in hot water now."

Later that week, a police officer and longtime friend cautioned her, "You're going to get your husband in trouble."

Some homeless people had built themselves small shelters along the riverbanks of the town, where they kept family photos, blankets given to them by churches, and spare clothing. A week after the June Street Smart meeting Meguen had attended, the police conducted an unannounced sweep of the riverbank area, demolishing the shelters and confiscating and destroying their contents. Meguen was outraged: "These are *my* people. I can defend them, and I will." She talked the situation over with a colleague and described the homeless as "a people who have lost their spirituality." In contrast to the police's approach of moving the homeless out of sight, Meguen dreamed of helping reconnect them to their spiritual heritage. She began planning a ceremonial place for them to experience the cleansing and strength that can come from a sweat and she considered how she might develop an agency program to address their spiritual needs. Meguen also knew that her approach might raise even more criticism among the community leaders who funded the agency.

The Second Street Smart Meeting

For the August Street Smart Program meeting, Meguen brought reinforcements from several church congregations and from Native American Ministries. Tension mounted quickly as the meeting began. A Native American community member stood and tearfully declared, with trembling voice, "These people are my brothers and sisters." Although Meguen appreciated the woman's feelings, she decided that she could not become emotional, but had to remain professional.

"I'm going to be totally logical. I can't let them shake me up."

Now on the defensive, the chief of police started: "It is our job to keep the city safe. These are violent and dangerous people. They're on drugs and they have weapons. I was hired by the city to do this job, and I'm going to do it."

Meguen slowly rose to speak. She hesitated only a moment and then began with a studied strength in her voice. "These people are powerless. They aren't welcome anywhere because they are chronic alcoholics. If they don't drink, they'll die. If they drink, they'll also die. These are the people that nobody cares about." With all the assertiveness she could muster, Meguen continued, listing incident after incident of harassment: the officer pouring out the soda, the threats of arrest made to people simply sitting on public benches or walking on public sidewalks, and the destruction of property without warning. She ended her speech by stating that "you are violating their civil rights!"

"Stop telling these horror stories!" Angrily, the chief of police jumped to his feet. "Sometimes you have to step on a few civil rights for the good of the community," he continued, glaring at Meguen. "You are neglecting your responsibility to serve our community."

The meeting ended quickly, and with no resolution. Meguen left as soon as she could, but realized when she reached her car that she had left her purse in the meeting room. After she went back to get it, she ran into a colleague, the director of Homeless Health, another program under the Community Health Care umbrella.

"Hey, Meguen, the police chief came up to me and asked who you are. I told him your name. He asked if you are married to a police officer, but I told him I didn't know."

The tension had caught up with Meguen; she was now shaking. "Tell him that you don't pry into the private lives of people. Tell him it's none of his business."

"You've got to be careful," he responded. "You're stepping on toes." Another social service professional joined them.

"Watch out, Meguen, you're biting the hand that feeds you. He can make things hard for you with United Way."

02.teaching note
Good Medicine
Diana R. Garland and Karen Grubb Gilbert

Case Synopsis

The new director of Good Medicine Indian Health Services, Meguen Dancing Feather, found herself advocating for the civil rights of homeless and alcoholic Native Americans in her community. The chief of police, her husband's employer (Meguen and her husband had seven children together), was harassing these vulnerable people with the support of the business community. Meguen quickly found herself in an adversarial position with the chief of police and other powerful community members who indirectly provide the funds to support her agency. Meguen was deeply concerned that these homeless Native people had lost their spirituality. Therefore, she wanted to use traditional Native American spiritual practices to address their needs, an approach that additionally provoked the community members who provided for her agency.

Learning Outcomes Related to Religion and Spirituality

The case discussion will facilitate the work of students as they

1. Identify ways spirituality can be both the passion that drives us into practice, as well as the source of some of the challenges we confront.

2. Describe how religion and spiritual practices can both support and conflict with social work values and ethics.

Other Learning Outcomes for Which This Case Can Be Used

The case discussion will facilitate the work of students as they

3. Understand how the communities we serve are multiple and sometimes conflicting.

4. Identify both the short- and long-term consequences of decisions, and consider how long-term goals may influence immediate decisions.

5. Appreciate how the work can take us in many different directions, and how the mission of our agency or program (and our own governing group) can help make those decisions.

Courses and Levels for Which the Case Is Intended

Written for the bachelor's level, the case may also be useful for graduate foundation-level content on racism and ethnicity; health care; alcoholism and homelessness; advocacy; spiritual and religious diversity; organizational governance, mission, and funding; and the relationship between law enforcement and social work practice.

Discussion Questions Related to Religion and Spirituality

Because of the focus of this book, some possible responses are given for those questions that relate to religion and spirituality. These responses and questions, however, are relevant also to the broader context of the case. These broader implications are also briefly considered, but it is expected that the instructor will develop them more fully.

Establishing the Facts

1. What decisions has Meguen made that brought her to this point?

2. Who are the persons and organizations to whom Meguen must relate concerning her actions in response to the homeless Native Americans? Who else could be involved?

3. What do we know about the spirituality of Native people, based on Meguen's experience? How is her spirituality connected to her motivation as a social worker?

   It is connected through her experiences in a Catholic boarding school, her own spiritual wandering and forays into various Protestant Christian practices, and the powerful connection as an adult of the sweat experience with early childhood memories of her grandmother. She believes that traditional Native practices have been healing for her. She is committed to serving her people, and she is invested personally and culturally in this community as the wife of the only Native American police officer in town and mother of seven children. Her commitment has expressed itself in her pursuit of professional education in order to serve as a healer for her people, initially via nursing and then through social work. In her social work, Meguen uses traditional practices, such as the sage over the door for protection.

4. How did Meguen become involved as an advocate for homeless people?

   These are "her" people. She knows many of them personally because the front porch of her agency became a safe haven for them and because she also provides health services for them. Consequently, she heard the stories of harassment. Her advocacy also grows out of the early religious teaching of her grandmother that emphasized being kind and generous to all people. Meguen is therefore motivated not only professionally, but also spiritually.

Analysis

5. What do Meguen and the chief of police each mean when they refer to "community?"

   Meguen thinks of the Native American population, but the chief of police sees her as serving the broader community, including the business people downtown. We do not know, however, how the middle-class Native community feels about her advocacy for homeless and alcoholic persons, beyond the tearful support of the volunteer in the Street Smart program meeting.

6. What has led Meguen to conclude that these homeless people have lost their spirituality? What is the empirical evidence for her conclusion? What kind of assessment did she use? Could she use?

   In her own mind, Meguen has somehow connected the experience of these homeless, chronic alcoholics with her own experience of spiritual wandering. There is no evidence of any further assessment on her part, but she has listened to their stories, and it may be that she has concluded from those stories that their lives are directionless and "meaningless." A content analysis of qualitative interviews might indeed document spiritual crises, which entail a sense of emptiness or loss.

7. How is Meguen's assessment that these people have lost their spirituality connected to her advocacy for them?

   This seems to be the point at which Meguen most identifies with them as "my people." She has experienced this loss of spirituality and has found her way again. It is this experience, as well as their shared ethnicity, that drives Meguen's passion to be the advocate for these homeless and alcoholic Native Americans.

8. What are the social work values that Meguen is expressing in her practice? What are the values that may be in conflict with Meguen's work?

   She is confronting oppression and social injustice. Her plan to address the spiritual needs of her clients may be both respect and support for religious and cultural diversity, but if it becomes a condition for service, it may also be a violation of self-determination.

9. What is the role of the police in contemporary society and what powers do they have? Because they serve the majority, how do you protect the rights of the minority? In what ways is this a spiritual issue for Meguen?

10. In what ways are the issues that confront Meguen religious and spiritual as well as cultural? How does this case relate to the experiences of other minority groups?

    Discuss minority groups relevant to the class: African Americans, Southeast Asians, or Bosnian refugees, etc.

Action

11. What are the decisions that Meguen must make soon? What decisions does she *not* have to make?

12. Is it appropriate for Meguen to use and promote Native spiritual practices in her agency? How is your opinion affected by the fact that :
    - She serves a vulnerable population group experiencing discrimination.
    - They represent a distinct, endangered minority culture.
    - The agency is funded with private instead of public funds.
    - Clients appear to have no other service options in town.

Additional Notes

- Meguen's spiritual beliefs and practices are similar to or different from your own.
- The situation involves adults who can make choices, not children.

What additional factors can you identify that influence your understanding of Meguen's promotion of a religious approach?

13. How would your response be different if Meguen were a conservative Protestant Christian advocating the use of prayer?

14. What should Meguen do next in response to the continuing Street Smart program? What should she consider as she plans to address *all* the needs of the population she serves?

Teaching Suggestions

Start with a question about how Meguen finds herself confronting the community power structure less than four months after becoming a program director. Help them begin by tracing Meguen's own motivation for becoming a social worker and by examining the passion with which she addressed the needs of homeless Native people. To explore these dynamics further, work groups, or the class as a whole, could analyze the extent to which the variables in this case affect the decision to employ Native spiritual practices in response to the health needs of this vulnerable population.

03.

Loss and Faith

Ann Fleck-Henderson and Michael P. Melendez

While the woman in his office spoke urgently, Roberto Martinez recognized a feeling he had not had in years: the desire to "stop the action" of this clinical session and get a consultation. His attention wandered from the anguished words of his client, Janice, to his own uncertainty about how to respond. After 15 years as a clinician, he had rarely felt the flow of a session break in quite this way. There were about five minutes left in Janice's clinical hour. Roberto was not sure what to do.

The Past

Roberto had first met Janice Shapiro over a year ago in 1995. She had been referred for child guidance to the mental health clinic where he practiced. Her second child, Joseph, was experiencing difficulties in school and was subsequently diagnosed with a learning disability. Joseph was 9 at the time, with a 3-year-old brother and two sisters, 7 and 12. Janice was a college-educated entrepreneur with her own prosperous editing business, and her husband was a successful lawyer. Roberto recalled that Janice was a devoted parent and a cooperative and intelligent client who had benefited quickly from the consultation. One of her family's strengths, he had noted at the time, was their long-term membership in a tight-knit Orthodox Jewish community that Janice and her husband had joined when they married. The synagogue was actively supportive and welcoming of all the family members. Until this month,

Roberto had not seen or heard from Janice since their earlier short clinical relationship.

The Current Crisis

Janice had found out from the clinic how to reach Roberto's private practice and had called, asking urgently for an immediate appointment.

"It's not about my children—they're fine. It's me," she had said. "I can't explain on the phone. I need to talk to someone neutral, and you were so helpful before." Her voice was panicky. "I need to talk to someone now, as soon as you can… I don't even care what it costs."

Roberto had given her an appointment for the next day, although it meant missing lunch, something he always tried to avoid.

When she arrived the following day, she started right away.

"I've just visited my brother, Seth," she said. "He is very, very sick, with some kind of horrible infection. I knew he had been sick a lot for the last couple of years. I just had no idea it was this serious. They say he has AIDS. I—I guess he does. He is gay." She glanced at Roberto, assessing his reaction, and then went on, "which I knew, but no one else in our family does. He and I are very close. We have a big family, but he and I have always been the closest."

She paused. "I think he is going to die," her voice became quiet. "I love him, Roberto. I don't want him to die. I never expected this—he is too young."

Roberto knew a lot about AIDS. In addition to the years of professional practice and considerable training for working with HIV-positive clients, he had developed a deeply personal understanding of the disease. He was a Latino man of approximately Janice's age, and he was gay. However, he did not know if Janice was aware of his sexual orientation. Roberto had recently experienced the deaths of several close friends from AIDS and Janice's grief and sorrow moved him greatly. Additionally, he was forced to make an effort to avoid being distracted by his own close relationship with his sister. He wanted to be professional in his response and stay fully focused on Janice's current distress over her brother's life-threatening illness.

While dealing with her grief, Janice also tried to be responsible to her family. "I can tell my husband, but he is not going to want to hear a lot about this, and he will want me to keep it quiet, but I need to know what to say to my kids. How do I tell them their Uncle Seth is so ill without telling them everything?" It seemed to Roberto that she expected him to have all the answers.

The first session went by quickly, and Janice claimed to be relieved. She appreciated having this environment for talking and crying and she felt clearer about what to say to her children. They needed to know that Uncle Seth was very ill, and she could honestly say he had a bad infection. From there on, she decided she would respond to her children's questions, but would not volunteer anything else. The only child likely to want more information was her eldest daughter. Roberto agreed to continue to meet with her weekly for the coming month, and then they would reassess the situation.

"How Can I Pray?"

During the next couple of weeks, Janice often visited her brother. She watched him getting weaker and thinner. He had trouble breathing, and the medications did not seem to work because he just seemed to be getting worse and worse. Janice desperately wished that a miracle would occur, that her brother would at least live long enough for new treatments to be developed.

"I assume you're not Jewish," she said to Roberto at her third session. "Maybe you don't know, but for Orthodox Jews, homosexuality is an abomination." Roberto acknowledged that he understood.

The urgency returned to Janice's voice. "How can I pray for my brother? In my congregation we pray publicly for the sick during the worship service, but I am afraid people will ask questions, and then they will condemn Seth. That would be worse than not praying at all, but it seems wrong to exclude him and my love for him from the community which I also love."

As Janice shared her conflicted feelings, Roberto reflected on his own Catholic background. He thought perhaps he could understand and relate to what Janice was experiencing. Roberto recalled participating in a Gay Pride parade in New York, when he watched a small group of Orthodox Jewish men standing on the sidelines and yelling, "Die from AIDS! Die from AIDS!"

"Can You Help Me?"

This morning, Janice arrived angry and upset for her fourth session. In the synagogue, she had overheard a conversation about the evils of homosexuality and about how AIDS was a punishment from God. Throughout the session she wept about her brother's worsening condition and the conversation she had heard. She had never thought of her brother as sinful, but now she wondered if "maybe I just couldn't face it."

Roberto listened, saying very little, as Janice articulated her conflicted feelings. It was painful to hear her good friends say these things and it made her wonder if she was betraying her own faith by loving her brother. Did she doubt the Torah? How could Jehovah be so punitive? Seth was a good man and it did not seem right that her community would condemn him for how he was born. How could her friends say those things and unknowingly abandon her?

She paused in her questioning and looked at Roberto with some resolve. "I know now I cannot tell them about Seth's illness or his lifestyle. I want to pray for him during the service, but I cannot." Roberto acknowledged the loss this decision involved.

Janice looked at Roberto. "Yes," she said, " It's too much. I can't get through this without my faith and my community. What can I do? Homosexuality is wrong, but do you think the Lord would do this to him? Could AIDS really be a punishment?"

Roberto did not immediately respond and Janice began to sob deeply. "I need to be able to pray with my community. Time is running out and he is going to die. I don't know if you can help me."

Minutes passed with only the sound of her sobbing. Roberto silently reflected on his options. He truly wanted to provide solace to Janice and a sense of God's love for both her and her brother. But he was not part of her religious tradition, and in any case he was not trained as a spiritual counselor. Roberto wondered, "Maybe I am out of my field of expertise and I should suggest she talk with the rabbi. But I truly believe that AIDS is not a punishment and that God would not damn Seth for his homosexuality. Isn't God merciful? Janice needs hope and spiritual encouragement. What should I do?"

03.teaching note
Loss and Faith
Ann Fleck-Henderson and Michael P. Melendez

Case Synopsis

Roberto, a clinical social worker and a gay man, was counseling Janice, an Orthodox Jew who was in anguish over her beloved brother's diagnosis of AIDS and his failing health. Her grief was compounded by her fellow congregants' recent discussion of homosexuality as "an abomination" and AIDS as a punishment from God. Janice was feeling uncertain about her own religious convictions and felt abandoned by her spiritual community, with whom she could not safely share her grief. Janice asked Roberto to respond to her theological questions and her need for spiritual support. Roberto was unsure how to proceed.

Learning Outcomes Related to Religion and Spirituality

The case discussion will facilitate the work of students as they

1. Consider the boundaries between clinical social work and spiritual counseling, and consider the different roles of the clinician, as opposed to a rabbi or a pastor, with a client whose faith is in doubt.

2. Identify guidelines for sharing one's own religious convictions with a client.

3. Increase knowledge of some aspects of Orthodox Jewish belief and practice.

Other Learning Outcomes for Which This Case Can Be Used

The case discussion will facilitate the work of students as they

4. Clarify their positions about self-disclosure of sexual orientation.

5. Consider the implications of informed consent in a situation where the social worker has invisible characteristics that might affect a client's consent to a therapeutic relationship.

6. Clarify the behaviors required by the responsibility to provide culturally competent practice.

Courses and Levels for Which the Case Is Intended

This case could be useful at the BSW or MSW foundation level. It may be useful for discussing content on generalist practice methods, ethics, spirituality, cultural sensitivity in practice, or gay and lesbian issues.

Discussion Questions Related to Religion and Spirituality

Establishing the Facts

1. What is the nature of Roberto's contract with Janice?

Roberto agreed to meet with Janice weekly for one month before reassessing their situation.

2. What are the issues with which Janice is struggling when she makes her first appointment?

    Grief about her brother; whether or not to discuss the situation with her children.

3. What other issues emerge for Janice during the weeks she meets with Roberto?

    Doubts about her own faith; alienation from her faith community; whether or not Roberto can help.

4. What aspects of Janice's religious tradition and practice contribute to her conflict?

    The belief that homosexuality is sinful; the public nature of prayer; the importance of the congregation as a primary social group in her life.

5. What evidence is there concerning Janice's perception of Roberto's religious affiliation? Is this a positive or negative factor for her?

    Janice sees Roberto as "neutral" and says she assumes he is not Jewish. As she is unable to speak about her grief within her community, this is initially a positive factor.

6. What is revealed about Roberto's religious beliefs and background?

    Roberto was raised Catholic. He has struggled with his own church's stance toward homosexuality. He affirms a merciful and loving God.

7. What is the issue facing Roberto at the end of the case?

    He has been asked direct questions about his religious beliefs. Does he answer them?

Analysis

8. Roberto's own personal experiences and memories are evoked by Janice's story. Is this likely to be a hindrance or an asset in his work with her?

    It can be either or both. His empathy and compassion may be deepened, but he must be careful to separate his own thoughts and feelings from his client's.

9. Generally, should a clinical social worker in a secular setting provide help to a client struggling with doubts about her faith?

    A social worker can help the client sort out her own beliefs and conflicts, and consider possible resources which fit the client's faith tradition. It is not usually within the social work role to provide answers to explicitly religious questions. On the other hand, questions of faith, personal meaning, and existential despair are involved in any serious life issue. Therefore, one might argue that clinical social work of any profound nature inevitably involves faith and doubts about faith.

10. If a client's religious beliefs conflict with a social worker's personal and professional values, should the social worker say so? Is this a factor in the present case?

    There are clinical and ethical implications of this question. Clinically, if a social worker is personally offended by a client's religious beliefs, these feelings may impede his or her ability to be empathic. Ethically, there is a point where a social worker may feel obligated to at least note her or his difference of opinion if the client's beliefs contradict social work values. In this case, Roberto does not seem to be personally offended by Janice's beliefs, although they do conflict with his personal values and the values of the social work profession. Perhaps he is not ethically required to say anything.

11. When it becomes clear that beliefs about homosexuality are central to Janice's concerns, should Roberto make his sexual orientation known to her?

    Roberto's sexual orientation and religious beliefs are separate from his role as a clinical social worker. Janice and he need to focus on her situation and her struggles. Raising the issue of the social worker's sexual orientation would be an unnecessary and distracting interruption to a person trying to get help in a crisis. On the other hand, you could argue that Janice would feel betrayed should she learn about Roberto's sexual orientation, given the salience of the issue to her, and that therefore his silence might be problematic.

12. In general, should therapists make personal characteristics such as sexual orientation known? If so, how and when?

13. Is it important for Roberto to know more than he does about Orthodox Jewish beliefs and practices? Can he be a culturally competent practitioner with his level of knowledge? If not, what should he have done about it, and when?

   It might be helpful, although perhaps not ethically required, for Roberto to have more knowledge. On the other hand, particular rabbis and particular congregations vary enough to prevent him from knowing what Janice was facing. At this point in the narrative, however, Roberto himself feels his lack of knowledge. He might share this with Janice and ask if she thinks it would be helpful to her if he learned more about Orthodox Judaism. In many ways Janice, an upper middle-class educated business woman, shares a culture with Roberto, an educated middle-class Latino man.

Action

14. At the end of the case, Roberto considers what to do next. Outline his options.
   He can say something about his own beliefs.
   He can refer to the rabbi.

Additional Notes

He can seek more information (e.g., ask Janice what meaning his answer would have for her, or ask her about the issues for her in consulting her rabbi).

15. Consider the values promoted and the risks incurred with each of the options.

Teaching Suggestions

The instructor may begin by asking: What are the issues that Roberto is facing at the end of the case account? This will elicit quite a few responses and areas of discussion, addressing many facets of the case. Once those are on the board, the instructor may ask about the issues Janice was facing. From that point, there are many possible directions, depending on the instructor's goals and the students' interests and concerns.

As the instructor moves toward the action question, she or he may ask what options were available to Roberto. Once these are elicited, the instructor may ask about the risks and benefits for each option and about the values that underlie the choice of one option versus another.

04.

Dying to Talk About Death

Terry A. Wolfer

Medical social worker Cynthia Smith felt shaken as she sat in her office trying to decide how to respond to the events that had just transpired. An hour ago she had been paged about problems with a cancer patient, Becky Ingram, with whom she had worked for some time. The message had only said, "Becky really needs to talk with you."

Arriving on Becky's floor, Cynthia had stopped at the nurse's station to ask about the message. Nurse Anne Brown reported, "Dr. Cresswell was just in there, and dropped a bomb on Becky. He wants to stop her dialysis."

Stunned, Cynthia asked, "He—he just said that to her?" From the nurse's station, Cynthia could hear Becky screaming. Without dialysis, Becky could likely live no more than two weeks.

When Cynthia had arrived in Becky's hospital room, Becky was screaming and hysterical. "Dr. Cresswell just came in here," she cried, "and he said that he wants to stop dialysis. He just said it like it was no big deal!" Becky sobbed, "I'm gonna die, I'm gonna die, I'm gonna die! I don't know what I'm gonna do. Nobody wants to save me; there's no other way to go. I'm so scared."

Nearly overwhelmed by the force of Becky's emotion, Cynthia responded, "Calm down, calm down. Tell me what he said. Let's go back and let's figure this out." Cynthia hugged Becky and sat down on her bed.

Becky confronted Cynthia: "Why didn't you tell me this was a possibility?"

"Becky, the doctor never talked to me about this."

"What does the chart say?"

"It's never been mentioned in the chart." Cynthia tried to explain that doctors were concerned about the pain Becky experienced, and about her quality of life. While trying to answer Becky's questions, Cynthia resented that she had been placed in this situation. Professionally, there were limits to what Cynthia could say, but Cynthia also saw herself as Becky's friend, and she wanted to help Becky understand the severity of her medical situation.

Cynthia's First Encounter with Becky

As Cynthia sat pondering the situation in her office, she recalled her first contact with Becky about four months before, in July 1997. After graduating with a master's of social work in May, Cynthia had only been on the job for six weeks at Roanoke Medical Center, a major regional hospital in southern Virginia, when she heard about a patient readmitted in serious condition. Upon first seeing Becky, Cynthia felt disturbed, even "grossed out," by the extent of the woman's physical deterioration. Her body had been ravaged by childhood-onset diabetes mellitus. Though not overweight, Becky's body was bloated from water retention and her square face was puffy. Her fair skin was yellowed with jaundice and her teeth were crooked and brown. Poor blood circulation had bent and stiffened her fingers, and had hardened their tips with cracked skin.

Becky's Medical History

From the hospital's records, Cynthia had learned that Becky had assumed personal responsibility for daily peritoneal dialysis several years before. This form of dialysis required expensive medical equipment but was less invasive and had fewer side effects than hemodialysis, and could be self-administered at home. Despite the regular dialysis, the illness caused cumulative deterioration and Becky's lower left leg had to be amputated in May 1997, an operation known as *below knee amputation* (BKA). After her discharge from the hospital in early June, Becky was sent to an extended care facility for rehabilitation.

Cynthia had met Becky when she was readmitted to the hospital for a left *above knee amputation* (AKA), which was necessitated by an infection in the recently created stump. Cynthia suspected the health care facility was inadequately staffed or poorly managed because Becky's dressings apparently had not been changed for several days (these dressings should be changed up to four times per day to prevent infection). Consequently, Becky's stump was severely infected and inflamed, and as Cynthia recalled, "the stench was horrible." Cynthia knew that Becky would never have been readmitted to the hospital if the stump had been given proper care, and she thought that Becky might have been able to sue the facility for negligence.

In July 1997, Becky signed the standard consent form and was given a general anesthesia for the left AKA. Because her foot had already been amputated, the medical personnel viewed this operation as nonmajor. However, when the surgeon, Dr. Jackson, observed the extent of the damage to both lower extremities, he reportedly decided in the operating room to also remove Becky's right leg, making the operation a bilateral AKA. Because the surgeon had been involved with Becky for a long time and because he had a close relationship with her family, he felt justified in making this unilateral decision. Becky regained consciousness to find both of her legs amputated above the knee and, not surprisingly, had an extremely difficult time adjusting to this unexpected reality. Cynthia disagreed strongly with Dr. Jackson's decision to amputate Becky's second leg without her knowledge or consent, but she felt unable to do much about it after the fact.

As a medical social worker, Cynthia understood that she was expected to defer to physicians on medical matters. As hospital policy dictated, Dr. Cresswell, the nephrologist and Becky's primary doctor, did not want Cynthia talking with Becky about her prognosis, particularly after the bilateral amputation. But Cynthia felt concerned that Becky was not getting the information she deserved, and she had suggested several times to Dr. Cresswell that he talk with Becky about the seriousness of her condition. Although she worried about Dr. Cresswell's bedside manner, Cynthia knew that his decision was realistic. Physicians and nurses alike were losing hope for any type of future for Becky, and Cynthia recognized that further information could undermine Becky's currently robust will to live. Once, Cynthia had confided to a colleague that Becky's will to live was "so strong and so amazing, it gives me chills."

Relating to Becky

Cynthia realized that this willfulness exerted a powerful pull on her, and she reflected that it influenced their relationship, as did the absence of other relationships in Becky's life. Following her first hospitalization, Becky had been living at the extended care facility for nearly two months with the goal of returning to live with her father. Becky's father was confined to a wheelchair because of polio, and therefore he could not provide physical care for his daughter in their home and was unable to visit her while she was away from home. Becky's mother had died of cancer some 20 years ago, when Becky was 11 years old. Becky had one brother who was married with three children. Like her father, her brother lived more than one and a half hours away from both the hospital and the extended care facility, but despite this distance and a full-time job, he visited Becky almost every week.

In the months following Becky's second operation, Cynthia had established a strong relationship with her. Cynthia's job was to provide family-support counseling, primarily to Becky and her brother, and she had discovered that she and Becky had some important things in common. Close to the same age, they had both experienced the loss of a parent and substantial hardship in their lives. Cynthia felt that Becky just needed someone to care for her, but she also realized that her limited experience as a novice social worker made it easy for her to over-invest in particular clients. Becky was certainly one of those clients who elicited an especially strong response from her.

Dealing with Death

As Cynthia sat in her office and pondered what action to take, her thoughts briefly shifted to her own experiences. Cynthia had lost her own father less than two years before. He had died of pancreatic cancer, an illness that in his case developed rapidly. To Cynthia, it seemed that the doctors had responded almost nonchalantly, giving him false hope about his chances for recovery even when his death was imminent. Cynthia had nursed her father and had provided hospice-type care for him. Although they did not talk about it, Cynthia knew her father was dying and believed he recognized that they both knew. Cynthia felt that her father was not afraid to die but did not want to give up. At the time, she feared that talking about dying would have damaged his will to live, and to her, "bringing it up would mean giving up." In retrospect, however, Cynthia wished that she had talked to her father about death, to help them both achieve greater closure.

Cynthia knew that Becky, unlike her own father, was terrified of death. She was angry and frightened by the unknown. Sometimes Becky would lie screaming in her room at the hospital, and the nurses complained that she was a "pain in the neck." But Cynthia recognized that Becky had good reasons to be angry and scared. She had a hard life. Physically she was ravaged by the disease, and mentally she struggled every day. Cynthia had wanted to help ameliorate this fear by talking with her about dying, but did not. Instead, she recruited a psychiatrist to prescribe medication and involved the hospital chaplain. One day, while sitting on the edge of Becky's bed, Cynthia finally raised the topic herself by simply asking, "Have you thought about dying?" With this permission, Becky opened up and talked freely. Although the ensuing conversations were emotionally difficult, Cynthia felt gratified by them.

At times, it seemed there was nothing Cynthia could do but sit with Becky and hold her hand. At one point, Cynthia had given Becky her pager number, but she feared that Becky was becoming too dependent on her; whenever she needed to talk, Becky would call on Cynthia first. Although she felt pressured by other responsibilities, receiving up to 40 pages a day, Cynthia tried to show Becky how much she cared for her. Once she had even told her that "this is not my typical case, and I am really connected with you. This is really hard for me, too, but I want to be a part of this because it means so much to me and I don't want you to be so afraid."

Spirituality played a large role in how Cynthia handled her father's death, and Cynthia found herself "tiptoeing into that" with Becky, too. Cynthia tried to reassure Becky that she had done nothing wrong, that death was not something to fear. To Cynthia, it seemed as though Becky felt "suspended over the pit of hell in some eighteenth-century vision." In contrast to her brother, who appeared to be religious and was a regular church-goer, Becky did not identify with any religion.

Cynthia encouraged Becky, telling her how proud she was of her efforts to struggle with the illness. Cynthia wanted Becky to understand the magnitude of her journey, and she had told her that she had never known someone who had been through what Becky was experiencing.

How to Help Becky

Sitting alone in her office, Cynthia pulled herself back to the present situation. Doctor Creswell had finally, and without warning, suggested that Becky stop dialysis, and Cynthia thought that Becky was falling apart mentally and emotionally. Today's confrontation had left Cynthia feeling shaken and inadequate. She now knew that she faced Becky's imminent death, and more importantly, working with Becky to accept it. She had never done anything like this before and she wondered whether and how she could help Becky now.

04.teaching note
Dying to Talk About Death
Terry A. Wolfer

Case Synopsis

Novice medical social worker Cynthia Smith was responsible for providing services to Becky Ingram, a young adult patient who was severely disfigured by childhood-onset diabetes mellitus and terminally ill. When a physician had abruptly advised Becky to stop dialysis, ensuring that she would die within two weeks, Becky "fell apart" mentally and emotionally. Confronted by Becky's overwhelming anxiety and dependency, Cynthia wondered how best to help Becky.

Learning Outcomes Related to Religion and Spirituality

The case discussion will facilitate the work of students as they

1. Recognize that death and dying may bring spirituality and religion to the forefront of attention for clients, social workers, or both.

2. Understand that competent social work practice sometimes requires practitioners to deal with the religion and spirituality of our clients.

3. Understand, further, that religious and spiritual competence requires that social workers consider multiple factors, such as the client's spiritual and religious history, the client's current religious affiliation, auspices of the social worker's professional organization, the dynamics of the helping relationship with that particular client, and their own spirituality.

Other Learning Outcomes for Which This Case Can Be Used

The case discussion will facilitate the work of students as they

4. Identify how a social worker's personal history may alternately contribute to or detract from therapeutic relationships, especially when this history involves emotionally intense experiences.

5. Identify ways to manage intense helping relationships.

Courses and Levels for Which the Case is Intended

Although written for a master's level capstone course in social work, this case may also be useful at the graduate-level for specialized courses on religion and spirituality, death and dying, medical social work, mental health services, or social work practice with individuals.

Discussion Questions Related to Religion and Spirituality

Various combinations of the following questions can be used, depending on what aspects of this case the instructor wishes to explore or emphasize.

Establishing the Facts

1. What exactly happened to precipitate this crisis?

    Without collaborating with or warning Cynthia, a physician informed Becky that her situation was imminently terminal and advised her to discontinue dialysis. When Cynthia arrived on the scene, Becky was severely distraught. The medical information raised numerous questions for Becky, and she demanded Cynthia's help. But Cynthia's ability to help was impaired by her inexperience, the nature of their relationship, and her own history of loss.

2. What is known about Becky's spirituality? What are the metaphysical or spiritual issues in this case?

    This case provides very little information about Becky's spirituality. The case mentions that Becky did not identify with any religion, in contrast with her brother who was "religious and a church-goer." Cynthia perceived that Becky was terrified by her impending death, but there is no direct evidence that dying has any religious significance for Becky. When Cynthia raised the issue of dying, Becky talked freely. Further, this case indicates that Cynthia "tiptoed" into talking about spirituality but gives no indication of what Becky had to say. Nevertheless, spiritual and religious issues related to dying would not be surprising. In a hospice setting, for example, such issues may be dealt with much more directly and proactively than they appear to be handled in this hospital setting. Much of the limited religious and spiritual content in this case reflects Cynthia's experience rather than Becky's. For example, it is Cynthia's perception that Becky felt "suspended over the pit of hell in some eighteenth-century vision." But the case provides no information about which aspect of Becky's experience this characterization is based upon.

3. How has Cynthia, the social worker, addressed religion and spirituality thus far? Has this been sufficient?

    To this point, Cynthia has referred Becky to the hospital chaplain but she has only "tiptoed" into discussions of death and dying herself. If Becky were a client of a hospice, such issues would likely be dealt with more explicitly, but because she is dying in a hospital there may be less precedent or structure for professional social work intervention based around spiritual issues.

Analysis

4. What expectations do various participants in this case have for Cynthia? How can Cynthia respond to these conflicting expectations?

    The participants in this case have widely divergent, often contradictory expectations for Cynthia. For example, Becky wants a friend and a professional willing to listen, provide information, and advocate on her behalf. Physicians expect Cynthia to not intrude upon their own relationships with Becky and to support their medical decisions. Nurses expect Cynthia to keep the patient quiet. Becky's family members may expect information about Becky's medical condition. As a professional social worker, Cynthia has fundamental obligations to her client and her client's family. For example, Cynthia must be especially considerate of and prepared to advocate for Becky's right to self-determination. In this case, Becky's right has been infringed upon by unilateral decisions made by physicians and a lack of timely information. But as a medical social worker, Cynthia must also consider how her actions in this case will affect her ongoing interdisciplinary professional relationships, which will influence her ability to help subsequent patients. In addition, Cynthia must try to protect herself, both emotionally and professionally.

5. How can Cynthia manage her relationship with Becky? What is appropriate about their relationship? What is not? What would be best for Becky, or for Cynthia?

    As a recent graduate and new employee, Cynthia apparently poured herself into her first job, and Becky was one of her most challenging early cases. Cynthia and Becky shared several things in common: both were single, young adult women, and both had lost a parent. Because of health problems and distance, Becky's family provided limited support for her. As a result, Cynthia felt special concern and affection for Becky. Becky demanded and Cynthia provided more than the usual attention, and as a result, this relationship became more friendly than professional. There is no mention in this case of Cynthia's supervisor as a re-

source for helping her manage over-involvement in this situation. Becky needed someone to take her side in the hospital setting and to be a steady presence but she also needed someone who could challenge her. She would not benefit from having Cynthia removed from her case. For her part, Cynthia needed someone to help her to talk through her own feelings and thoughts, to help her clarify her personal boundaries and responsibilities, and to help her balance support and challenge with Becky. This case may be pivotal in her development as a professional social worker.

6. How does Cynthia's relationship with Becky help her efforts to address religion and spirituality? How does it hinder these efforts?

   The blurred boundary between these two women complicates Cynthia's efforts to help Becky deal with spiritual issues by making it hard to ensure that Becky can respond freely. On the other hand, the intimacy of this relationship may increase Becky's comfort in terms of expressing and discussing deeply personal thoughts and feelings. From a strengths perspective, Cynthia cares about Becky enough to push herself into new and difficult territory in their relationship.

7. How would this situation be different if Cynthia knew Becky came from a church-going family? How would this influence your understanding of Becky's spirituality?

   Because Becky does not currently identify herself as religious, this situation might be significantly different if Cynthia knew that Becky came from a church-going family. For example, this refusal to identify as religious could mean that Becky had rejected the faith of her childhood and her family, that she felt disillusioned about religion, or that she felt angry with God for her illness. If Becky no longer endorsed religion, knowing that she came from a church-going family might suggest the need for further exploration of religion and spirituality. It might also provide a starting point for exploring possible resources in the family or in the community.

Action

8. Should Cynthia address Becky's spiritual or metaphysical concerns? Why or why not? If so, how? What are her qualifications for doing so?

Earlier, Cynthia appropriately referred Becky to the hospital chaplain. But it also seems appropriate for her to have raised the topic of dying with Becky herself, because Becky's death was imminent and inevitable. Obviously, dying may elicit profound spiritual and religious concerns for a client. As a social worker, Cynthia probably has no special training in handling spiritual issues, and for that reason she must be especially tentative and sensitive to Becky's responses. Nevertheless, Cynthia need not avoid the matter, given the potential relevance of spirituality in this situation and Becky's apparent comfort with Cynthia. Because of the relationship dynamics noted in the response to question 6, Cynthia must be particularly careful in trying to help Becky address spiritual issues, probably more than she is aware she needs to be. Also, it is important that Cynthia seek support and advice from her supervisor.

9. As a professional social worker, what is appropriate for Cynthia to say or do regarding religion and spirituality? Does the imminence and inevitability of Becky's death give Cynthia greater freedom in this area?

   Becky's impending death creates both the opportunity and the obligation for Cynthia to address religion and spirituality. But it is important that Cynthia elicits Becky's interests and concerns rather than assume her own experience applies to Becky's situation. As a result of dealing with her father's recent death, Cynthia may be sensitized to these issues in a helpful way. But if these issues are personally unresolved for Cynthia, it is likely that her efforts to understand and to help Becky will be impeded by her own experience. In short, Cynthia's ability to help Becky accept dying will be contingent, in part, upon how completely she has resolved the issues surrounding her own father's death.

10. Should Cynthia be an advocate? If so, for whom, how, and at what system level?

    Physicians have apparently failed to respect Becky's right to informed consent and to self-determination, and little time remains for rectifying this problem. Consequently, Cynthia should consider adopting an advocacy role, but she must decide whether and how she can assist Becky, her family, or any future patients. For example, she can help Becky die with dignity, elicit support for Becky from her family, or help

Becky talk with her physician. Alternately, she may challenge the medical decisions in this case, to attempt to prolong Becky's life. Further, she could try to prevent similar situations in the future by working to change hospital or social policy regarding renal patients. At each system level, she must consider the consequences of working inside or outside of the hospital structure.

Teaching Suggestions

The instructor could begin with questions about the known facts of this case and the exact circumstances of the incident that precipitated the crisis and use this to raise questions about the interpersonal dynamics in this case. To more deeply explore this issue, groups of students (or the class as a whole) could systematically discuss possible expectations for Cynthia held by Becky, Becky's family members, Dr. Creswell, nurses, and by Cynthia herself. Group reports (or a whole class discussion) could provide a starting point for asking how Cynthia might respond to these conflicting demands. To probe further, the instructor may ask about places for Cynthia to get help deciding and acting, about immediate versus longer-term responses and possible consequences, and about who needs protecting. Further, the instructor may ask for whom Cynthia should advocate in this situation and how she should do so.

Additional Notes

05.

To Tell the Truth

Leola Furman and Roger Aker

In November 1999, Sue Johnson, the newly appointed Executive Director of Mankato Christian Housing (MCH) in Mankato, Minnesota, received a phone call that left her stunned. The caller reported, "Yesterday afternoon Mary kicked Ron [her husband] out. Then Kurt [her boyfriend] moved in with her and the four kids before the sun went down." If true, this anonymous tip would change everything for Mary, one of Sue's housing clients who was waiting for final possession of a newly built home that she and her husband were already renting. Without Ron's income, Mary would not meet the financial qualifications necessary to purchase the home on her own. Sue reluctantly faced the question: "Will I have to evict this family?"

As Sue hung up the phone, her heart sank. "Oh, no!" she thought. "This is going to be a nightmare! How did I miss this? And Calvary Lutheran Church? They built the house, they'll be devastated! It was the first time they had really sunk their teeth into a project like this. It had done so much for the members of the congregation."

How Did We Get Here?

Sue sat at her desk and recollected her relationship with Mary and Ron over the past several months. Selecting the couple for home ownership had not been without some difficulties.

MCH is an organization that uses several strategies to fulfill its mission of meeting the housing needs of lower-income families. Mainly it assists with home rental costs and supports graduated home ownership. Similar to Habitat for Humanity, MCH organizes church volunteers to build homes with and for selected families. In this successful program, each year volunteers typically finish eight houses by early summer and eight more before winter. To select the new owners of these homes, every year a volunteer committee sifts through over 300 applications submitted by low-income families. Families are chosen based on their level of need, their willingness to become partners in the program, and their ability to repay the no-interest loan.

At first, Ron and Mary's application for a new home was not approved because their debt-to-income ratio was too high, making eventual loan repayment problematic. But some of the members of the volunteer selection committee, taken with the couple's sincerity and perseverance, helped them find a way to legitimately meet the guidelines for acceptance into the program. The committee then appealed to the board to reconsider Ron and Mary's application. After lengthy deliberation, the board ultimately approved them as one of the eight families to receive a new home in the spring of 1999.

Following their approval, Ron and Mary were matched to a house being built by Calvary Lutheran Church. Calvary had agreed the previous year, 1998, to provide the volunteers to build the home, their first effort. It is the policy of MCH to introduce the selected family to the church congregation that will help build the new home in order to help celebrate and cement the partnership. Though not required, families sometimes began attending and participating in the church that was helping build their new home. Such was the case with Ron and Mary.

The family, always arriving just a few minutes late, would file up to the front pew. The spectacle of the children crawling on, over, and under the pew did not deter the congregation from embracing this family. Likewise, Mary and Ron did their best to participate in the church worship services, though they did not always understand the meaning of what they were doing.

When she visited the job site, Sue learned of Ron and Mary's involvement at Calvary from the church volunteers. Along with the volunteers, Sue mused about Ron and Mary's motivation: Was it gratitude, reciprocation, spiritual need, or opportunism? Sue agreed with several of the volunteers who noted that Mary, larger than her undersized husband, appeared to be submissive to him. Both at church and at MCH, Mary was the one who responded to questions, but she would always seek Ron's approval, waiting for him to nod his head in agreement. If Ron was absent during a conversation, she would regularly add to her comments, "I think Ron would agree to this, too." Though Sue had her doubts about Mary's actual submissiveness, she did not reveal them to the volunteers.

Before construction began on the new house, an old home on the property had been torn down. Even though the deed had not yet been altered to reflect the change, a quick-claim deed was granted to MCH by the city so that the construction could begin. The attorney for MCH expected that the change to the deed would be completed long before construction was finished. But, as occasionally happens, the deed had not been set straight before the house was ready and as a result, Ron and Mary could not complete the purchase until the deed was clear.

Because Ron and Mary had no responsibility for the delay, the board agreed to rent the house to them so they could move in on the target date. MCH arranged to apply the monthly rent to the amount of the loan while MCH remained as the deed holder. When the anonymous tip was received, Ron, Mary, and their four kids had been living in the new house for just one month.

Bubbling Up

Beginning with that fateful phone call, new information seemed to keep bubbling up periodically. On a tip from Ron's sister a few weeks later, MCH checked new sources of information about Mary's background. A Mankato Police Department report indicated several misdemeanors and one felony count for the embezzlement of $7,500 from a retail store where Mary had been employed five years before. The MCH application form requires applicants to disclose felony records, but Mary had indicated that only $100 had been embezzled, which would have been a misdemeanor.

In December, the pastor of Calvary Lutheran Church mentioned offhandedly to Sue that Ron was not the father of the younger two children. He assumed that Sue knew that Ron had a vasectomy after the couple's second child was born, and that Kurt had fathered Mary's two younger children. Ron, though keenly aware of the relationship triangle, was unable, or unwilling, to leave the marriage.

One day in early February, after three months of living with his sister following the separation, Ron himself called Sue. His voice quivered and he sounded confused and frightened. "Mary filed for divorce. I don't know what to do." He confirmed that only the older two children were his, and that Mary had agreed that they should live with him, at least until everything was settled. To remove all doubt, Sue asked a staff person to search for the divorce petition at City Hall and, if it existed, to make a copy of the document for the file.

Fallout

Sue regularly fielded questions about Ron and Mary from board members, from staff, and from the church congregation, but she always measured her answers carefully. The board recommended that if eviction seemed necessary, legal counsel should be sought. Certainly there were legal issues stemming from the false information that Mary had given on the application. In addition, Mary no longer met MCH homeowner financial guidelines without Ron's income, and if only two children were to live with Mary, her need for housing was also decreased. This house had been built for six people, not four.

Aside from these considerable organizational issues, Sue struggled even more with spiritual questions. Though more than a few volunteers had expressed concern about the divorce, most were even more animated about what they viewed as the "sustained adulterous relationship" of Mary and Kurt. Sue shared the dilemma represented by the conflicting sentiments of the volunteers who had called.

One volunteer had exhorted, "Why can't MCH work out any differences and let Mary and her younger two children stay and purchase the home? We built the house for this family. Everyone makes mistakes. Aren't we supposed to forgive? Our church needs to continue ministering to them."

But some volunteers were convinced otherwise. As one put it, "She kicked her husband out. He has two of the kids. By allowing Mary and her boyfriend to stay, MCH is saying marriage and commitment aren't all that important. It also sends a message that dishonesty is tolerated at MCH. Is that what we really want?"

"And what about us here at MCH?" Sue wondered about office morale. Staff members were clearly being affected, as conversations often contained phrases of bewilderment such as "How could she...?" or resolute declarations like "We've got to make sure nothing like this ever happens again!" Sue consoled those around her by reminding them that "this is a very special ministry. But sometimes it hurts, because we can't help but get attached to these families... our families. Sometimes they make mistakes."

Looking for Answers

Although Ron and Mary's application was approved before Sue was hired as the director, she felt responsible. She was certainly responsible for what happened next, and being new, she especially wanted a good outcome for this situation with Ron and Mary. Should the family suffer the consequences because the staff had not discovered this information earlier? Was the screening process adequate? Sue also remembered the 350 hours of labor that Ron and Mary had given to the construction of the home. And what would happen to the children? Though a long shot, perhaps Mary might rethink her decision to file for divorce, and with some counseling, perhaps the marriage could yet be saved.

The MCH board trusted Sue to manage the dilemma. Board members listened and offered advice, but did not pressure Sue for a quick decision. Sue's few meetings with Mary during this four-month period had been short, tense, and cautious. Sue was finding it harder and harder to trust any of Mary's responses. But the time had now come for a resolution, and Sue had invited Mary to her office to discuss Mary's plans.

During the interview, Sue asked Mary about the divorce, "I've received information that you have filed for a divorce. Is it true?"

Mary blinked a few times, but she seemed prepared for this moment. "No, I have not. But I suppose it's crossed my mind."

Sue produced the photocopy of the divorce petition that the staff person had brought from City Hall. "Is that your signature?" she asked.

Mary took the document and studied it closely for nearly half a minute. "Maybe," she said. "But I don't remember signing anything like this." With little emotion, Mary continued, "I don't see how that makes any difference in all this."

"Come on, Mary," Sue replied.

The two stared at each other for a long moment. Finally, Mary asked, "So where do we go from here?" Her words hung in the air as she stood and slowly left the office.

"I don't know yet, Mary," Sue answered as Mary closed the door behind her.

The conversation had not gone the way that Sue had hoped. Ron and Mary's situation was without precedent and it revealed gaps in MCH policies. Clearly MCH had not been thorough enough in gathering information about the family. On the other hand, Mary was brazenly deceitful. Who could have known that she was only waiting to get into the house before separating from Ron? And now the board, the staff, and the church were looking to Sue for a recommendation about how to best resolve the situation and move on.

To Tell the Truth

Leola Furman and Roger Aker

Case Synopsis

Mankato Christian Housing (MCH) in Mankato, Minnesota, organized church volunteers to build homes for low-income families. Applicants were approved through a screening process based on eligibility criteria such as debt-to-income ratio, need, and recommendations based on responsibility and reliability. Discrepancies in the already approved application of a couple, Mary and Ron, and changes in their marital status called into question the couple's future ownership of the MCH house that they were already renting. In their housing application, Mary had failed to disclose that she had been arrested for several misdemeanors and one felony count of embezzlement. Also, within the past few months, Mary had asked her husband to leave the home, had moved her boyfriend Kurt into the house, and had filed for divorce, which she subsequently denied. The paternity of Mary's four children had only recently been revealed: the older two children were fathered by her husband and the younger two by Kurt. Ron had then been forced to take custody of the two older children.

Sue Johnson, the newly appointed Executive Director of MCH, faced the possibility of evicting Mary and her children. The church sponsoring Mary, Ron, and their children was divided between continued support and ministry for this family and evicting them from the house they helped build.

Learning Outcomes Related to Religion and Spirituality

The case discussion will facilitate the work of students as they

1. Identify ways that religion may shape organizational policy.

2. Describe the role of religion in human service delivery.

3. Identify the ethical dilemmas that religion can create in human service delivery.

4. Describe the personal feelings and professional responsibilities a director faces when attempting to integrate a faith-based organizational mission and social work codes of ethics with organizational policy.

Other Learning Outcomes for Which This Case Can Be Used

The case discussion will facilitate the work of students as they

5. Consider the mission and values of an organization when making decisions about clients.

6. Better appreciate the difficulties of balancing organizational structure with client welfare.

7. Understand the interactions and transactions of multiple systems.

8. Grasp the impact and the use of the law in organizational practice.

9. Understand the influence of organizational policy on practice.

Courses and Levels for Which the Case Is Intended

This case is intended for MSW students who are enrolled in macro practice and HBSE courses and can be used in an MSW capstone course. It may also be useful in a BSW capstone course or in courses that deal with social and economic justice, social work and legal processes, organizational policy and procedures, and faith-based volunteer organizations.

Discussion Questions Related to Religion and Spirituality

Establishing the Facts

1. Who is the client?

At first glance students will naturally assume that Mary, her ex-husband Ron, and the children are the clients. Further discussion might elicit the concept that the sponsoring church, the volunteers, and the board are all clients or constituents. These different groups create one of the dilemmas that Sue faces. She might truly wish to help Mary keep her housing situation, yet the church, through their volunteer efforts for the agency, might have expectations about families conforming to the rules that MCH has established. This case could clearly impact future volunteer home-building efforts for this organization.

2. What do we know about the rules and expectations for prospective housing recipients? What do we *not* know?

We know that most organizations like MCH develop applicant acceptance policies within certain financial, legal, ethical, and nondiscriminatory parameters. Also, most organizations are generally geared to local economic and community practices. As a lending institution, MCH must follow certain guidelines in approving prospective homeowners, including

adequate background checks and character or professional references. Conversely, we do not know the history of policy development at MCH, nor to what extent they have relied on the experiences of a larger organization like Habitat for Humanity. We are not told if this crisis is an isolated event or one of many in a troubled organization.

3. What legal issues affect policy in this story?

Mary had been charged with embezzlement, a felony, and had not informed MCH about it on the application form. Felony questions appear on most low-income housing application forms, including the one for MCH. Additionally, the house was built and sold to the family on the basis of Mary and Ron's joint income and on the number of family members who would ultimately live in the house. Their individual incomes will not likely meet the minimum income requirements. In addition, there would now only be three family members instead of six (Mary and her two younger children or Ron and his two children) living in the house. If she were newly applying to MCH, these factors would make her ineligible for participation in the program. The complication is that Mary is currently living in the house. Since Mary is a renter, will legal issues and rights regarding the eviction process be relevant? Additionally, Ron may have certain legal claims to the home.

Analysis

4. What might Sue be feeling throughout this experience?

Sue would most likely have conflicting emotions. In all likelihood, she would be feeling very angry and betrayed because Mary has conned her, MCH, and the church. On the other hand, Sue might be very worried about the emotional welfare and alternative living arrangements for Mary and her two younger children.

5. What issues are of concern to Sue as Executive Director of MCH?

Obviously, Sue is concerned about her staff members who are also feeling duped and betrayed. Staff members may be struggling with the realities of human frailty and error. They are probably curious to know whether Mary's actions were premeditated. Is she a con artist who should be punished, or is she a victim of her own vices who should receive counseling and care? Does either situation entail her staying in the house?

Sue also would be concerned about the reaction of the community at large, who ultimately are organizational stakeholders, when the details of this case are brought out. Trust issues between MCH and the community will likely be raised.

This case will also impact other churches that are interested in working with MCH, because church volunteers constitute an essential workforce involved in the building of each house. As the Executive Director of MCH, Sue realizes that she will ultimately be held responsible for this dilemma and its resolution. The reality is that some members of the community will disagree with the final decision.

6. What confidentiality issues are involved?

The pastor of the church that is sponsoring this family casually revealed to Sue that Mary's boyfriend, not her husband, had fathered her youngest two children. Most clergy have a code of ethics or a professional understanding that would prevent this type of disclosure. Additionally, there was a great deal of gossip about Mary in the church.

7. How would this dilemma be different if MCH was not a faith-based organization but a federal agency such as HUD?

Mary had clearly broken housing rules: she had not admitted her felony charge on housing application forms, her income level had dropped below the minimum requirement for making house payments, and now there were fewer people in the household than had been stated on the application. HUD, therefore, would have evicted her without hesitation.

8. How might an earlier closing on the house have changed this situation?

If MCH had been able to achieve the deed to the land immediately, the house would have been sold to Mary and Ron already. Therefore, nothing could have been done after Mary divorced Ron. MCH would have felt that they had been exploited, but would not have had the dilemma about what they should do about it. The experience, however, would probably have motivated them to rework their policies and procedures for accepting applicants and to make provisions for a thorough background check.

Action

9. What are the decisions that Sue must make?

Sue may have to evict Mary and her two children. If so, Sue may decided to invite Mary to reapply for a smaller MCH house. Likewise, she might have to give the same offer to Ron. Both of the names can be put on the list for separate housing applications.

10. What policy changes will Sue and her staff need to make at MCH?

A new policy will need to be developed that requires the staff to conduct a more thorough background check, including searching both local and state police records to determine whether a housing applicant has been found guilty of a felony. MCH may also consider a policy to better manage any future irregularities that arise before the closing of a mortgage with a new homeowner.

11. What key factors will Sue need to consider in dealing with Mary and her children?

Because Mary and her children are still living in the house, Sue must consider several options if she evicts them. First, Sue will need to help Mary connect with alternative housing sources so that she and her children will have a place to live. Sue also will need to refer Mary for personal and financial counseling. In addition, Sue can develop a contract with Mary that will act as a transition plan to help Mary meet certain pre-established goals and guidelines so that she can provide for her children and possibly become eligible for home ownership.

12. What type of public relations tactics should Sue use to address the church that has sponsored Mary and the other churches in the community?

Sue should honestly and openly inform the sponsoring church clergy about the procedures that MCH took in this case and about how these procedures are intended to resolve the situation. Next, Sue should obtain the sponsoring church's consent to discuss this with its congregation. Sue would need to discuss the process of the case in general terms, not mentioning the details of the felony or the parentage of Mary's children. The congregation needs to have resources to use in order to determine what support they will give Mary and Ron, and what concerns they will need to address in future sponsorships. It will be up to the clergy and the congregation to determine whether the church will continue to minister to Mary, Ron, and their children. Additionally, Sue should contact the Clergy Alliance Association for that community and request a chance to speak about the issues in this case to halt misunderstandings that might prevent other churches from becoming involved in the work of MCH.

Teaching Suggestions

The instructor could begin with questions about the concrete facts of the case and move to more analytical questions about the interplay between multiple client systems. Students can explore the variety of options open to Sue. The case may be used to emphasize micro or macro levels of practice, depending on the instructor's objectives. Students may be divided into smaller groups to discuss various action alternatives.

Additional Notes

06.

Ya Me Voy! (I'm Going Right Now!)

Linda B. Morales and T. Laine Scales

Ruben Garcia had been a social activist for most of his 48 years. In 1999, he finally graduated from the University of Texas at Arlington with a BSW, realizing his lifelong ambition to earn a college degree and become a professional social worker. Now he was facing one of the most challenging situations of his professional career. Ruben had always been intensely proud of his Mexican American heritage, but the most highly respected physician in Traylor, Texas, had just challenged both Ruben's heritage and his professional competence. "Doc Hutch," who inspired both awe and fear in his patients, had told Ruben, "It's my way or the highway!" If Ruben failed to comply with the doctor's request, he might as well start job hunting.

Ruben's Background

Ruben Garcia grew up in *el Valle de Tejas*, the fragrant South Texas valley, but his childhood was filled with wanderings and digressions as his family frequently relocated for employment as migrant farm workers. The Garcia family traveled throughout the western half of the United States, picking lettuce, cotton, onions, and eventually working Wisconsin mint fields. Because the family had to follow the crop seasons, Ruben's schooling was inconsistent; he was nearly 20 years of age when he graduated from high school in Mission, Texas.

Ruben was reared in the Catholic church, his mother insisting that he attend Sunday masses regularly. During his childhood, Ruben had a par-ticularly close relationship with his mother's people. When the family would "light" for the winter in South Texas, Ruben would find himself under the strong influence of Don Miguel Salinas, his maternal grandfather. Every winter there were long walks in the fields and orange groves when Ruben helped his *abuelo* (grandfather) search for herbs for his special potions, lineaments, and teas. His grandfather was a *curandero*, a traditional Mexican healer.

Curanderismo is a type of healing deeply rooted in spiritual and supernatural traditions and practiced widely in southern Texas and in Mexico. In some parts of the Texas Valley, the work of the *curandero* (or female, *curandera*) is incorporated into the work of modern medical clinics. The *curandero* becomes the "Dear Abby," the individual people seek when romance sours, when family relationships suffer, and when the body is plagued with aches and pains.

Ruben watched his grandfather practice his natural healing ways with villagers who came for help for all sorts of ailments. In many ways his grandfather was a spiritual mystic; he could touch and talk to people and their troubles seemed to disappear. Ruben's family, like many Mexican families, easily mixed Catholicism with belief in the power of the *curandero*.

Ruben regretted that he had never taken the time to learn his grandfather's spiritual ways—the brewing and mixing of his teas and concoctions that led to miraculous healing. Don Miguel died when

Ruben was following farm work with his parents, as they tried to carve out an existence from the land.

One of the things that Don Miguel used to tell Ruben regularly was *no hay mal que por bien no venga*. Roughly translated, this means that something good comes out of everything that may happen to you. Little did Ruben know how difficult it would be, years later, to apply his grandfather's advice.

Ruben Becomes a Professional Social Worker

As a young man, throughout the 1960s and early 1970s, Ruben worked in federal manpower development and training, specifically in relocation programs for migrant farm workers and their families. He moved from the valley where he grew up to East Texas to work as a paraprofessional in these programs. He began to take courses part-time at Arlington, and after attending school for six years he finally earned his BSW. In 1999, he passed his Texas licensing exam and became a practicing social worker.

Fulfilling his lifelong dream, Ruben got a job right after graduation in a hospital in Traylor, an East Texas town of 30,000 people. Traylor is a farming community which had managed to show steady growth over the past 30 years. Its economy was based on poultry production and the timber industry, with the paper mill and the two chicken processing plants being the largest employers in the county. At the center of Traylor was a sleepy town square, surrounded by two hardware stores, a seed store, a variety store, and the bank. Concerts in the downtown plaza were held twice a month, led by the banjo and fiddle maestros who also owned the string shop just off the square.

Chickasaw Memorial Medical Hospital was the only facility in the region and served the medical needs of three East Texas rural counties. It was an 80-bed inpatient facility that had resisted becoming part of a corporate medical system, instead operating under a Board of Directors made up of Traylor community leaders, including members of the medical profession. The hospital employed three social workers: one BSW social worker specifically handled obstetrics and pediatrics, Ruben handled most other cases, and Glen Harris, a seasoned MSW social worker, supervised them both. Glen had complained to the hospital's chief administrator on

occasion that Ruben became "overly emotionally involved" with his clients, and that he should somehow tame his "passion" for his work with rational detachment. This had been an extremely difficult process for Ruben.

Jessie Cantu and His Doctor

Ruben's current dilemma involves Jessie Cantu, a 38-year-old green-carded Mexican national who was injured on his job at a large chicken processing plant nine days ago. Jessie had a wife and two small children living in Zacualtipan, a village in Central Mexico about 800 miles away. His family's survival was dependent on the money he regularly sent home. Jessie had found some stability in Traylor and had been employed by the plant for two years when he seriously injured his back. He had a herniated disc in the lumbar region, as well as a bulging disc to the left side of the sciatic nerve. The herniated disc was removed in surgery, but the bulging disc was still intact and excruciatingly painful.

Dr. Morris Hutchison was Jessie's surgeon. Known as "Doc Hutch," he was highly regarded in the community for his long-term medical care for the community's older population. In fact, his grandfather was one of the founders of the hospital. Doc Hutch was a personal friend of the owner of the chicken processing plant where Jesse Cantu worked, and as a favor, he agreed to perform the surgery on the injured employee. The post-surgery instructions suggested that Jessie should remain in the hospital a minimum of two weeks with physical therapy added during the second or third week, and that he should not engage in jolting movement, pick up heavy weight, or engage in sexual relations until healing was complete.

Jessie had grown increasingly impatient with the recovery process since his back surgery eight days earlier. On the eighth day, he told Ruben, in Spanish, "I have to go home. I need to be with my wife and babies." He said he was planning to leave the hospital to return to Zacualtipan to visit with the village's *curandera*. Jessie's family had visited the *curandera* throughout his life, and Jessie fully expected that his back would be healed. He told Ruben that he had also mentioned to "Mr. David," the male charge nurse on the floor, that he was planning to just "take off."

On Tuesday morning, nine days after Doc Hutch performed the back surgery, Mr. David walked into the hospital room to find Jessie fully dressed with his cardboard suitcase packed, sitting on the side of the bed bent over with pain.

"*Ya me voy!*" Jessie told the charge nurse. "I am going right now!"

David told Jessie that traveling could cause serious complications and that he should not even consider leaving the hospital until further healing had occurred. One bad bump could cause permanent damage to his back, and could even lead to paralysis.

Within five minutes Dr. Hutchinson had been notified of the patient's intent to leave the hospital *against medical advisement* (AMA). Ruben received a page the moment he walked into Chickasaw Memorial Medical at eight in the morning. Dr. Hutchinson requested an urgent social work consultation. He called Ruben to his office immediately.

Doc Hutch Versus Ruben Garcia

Dr. Hutchinson and Ruben Garcia had disagreed on several occasions over patients' rights to make their own choices. Doc Hutch never hesitated to draw up orders for his patients on issues that Ruben thought were a matter of personal choice. Nurses feared Doc Hutch, ward clerks trembled when he passed, and even Ruben's supervisor rarely stood up to the physician. Now Ruben had received the page that all employees feared.

"Ruben. This Jessie Cantu in 211B is packed and ready to leave. Says he's going to see this curah-churah-that mumbo jumbo medicine woman healer back in Mexico. He would be putting himself in grave danger if he even attempted to ride the bus all the way to central Mexico. And for what? For nothing. *Nada!*" *Nada* was the one Spanish word Doc Hutch knew. "I want you to go to his room right now and talk him out of leaving."

Ruben was not surprised by the doctor's direct order. He retained his composure as he tried to engage Doc Hutch in a dialogue about the situation. Perhaps if he helped Doc Hutch understand Jessie's spiritual beliefs, he might be more open-minded about the situation.

"I'm not sure that's really the best thing to do, Doc," Ruben countered cautiously.

"That's what you will do. I'm liable for his safety and it's too soon for him to travel. And you know how crowded and rough those Mexican buses are. It's up to you, Garcia. Go on down there and talk him out of going AMA. I insist."

Ruben looked at Doc Hutch. He did not know what to say.

The doctor began to walk away, but turned and shouted over his shoulder, "Look, Garcia, if you want to continue to practice social work in Chickasaw County, you do what I say. Now!"

What Am I to Do?

A range of thoughts and emotions—anger at Doc Hutch, nostalgia for his old way of life, compassion for Jessie—washed over Ruben as he briskly walked toward Jessie's room. He was really torn about what to do. "Doesn't Jessie have a right to practice his own spiritual beliefs?" he asked himself. "And as his social worker, don't I have an obligation to advocate for his rights?"

"On the other hand," Ruben considered, "what if Doc Hutch is right? What if Jessie is re-injured en route? As an employee of this hospital, I am obligated to ensure that Jessie follows the doctor's orders. And as a professional social worker, I should promote his physical well-being and safety. The long and rough bus ride may really jeopardize his health."

Ruben knew that traveling to Mexico would be taxing on Jessie's body. But what about Jessie's spirit? Could the *curandera* really heal Jessie? Ruben believed it was possible. He had seen his own *abuelo* heal people who were in worse shape than Jessie.

When Ruben opened the door to 211, there stood Jessie Cantu, his cardboard suitcase in his hand. The pain in his face was mingled with rigid determination.

"*Ya me voy*, Ruben. Right now. *Ya me voy!*"

Ya Me Voy! (I'm Going Right Now!)

Linda B. Morales and T. Laine Scales

Case Synopsis

Ruben Garcia was a new social worker in a hospital setting. His client, Jessie, was a Mexican American factory worker with a green card who had been injured on the job. Jessie believed strongly in *curanderismo*, a Mexican spiritual tradition of healing. Against the orders of Dr. Hutchison, Jessie intended to return to Mexico right after surgery to find a *curandera*. The doctor insisted that it was Ruben's responsibility to keep Jessie away from the *curandera* and in the hospital. Ruben, the grandson of a *curandero*, empathized with Jessie and quickly found himself disagreeing with the doctor.

Learning Outcomes Related to Religion and Spirituality

The case discussion will facilitate the work of students as they

1. Identify ways in which spirituality can be a resource for clients dealing with health issues.

2. Describe the tensions social workers may encounter when a patient's spiritual beliefs and practices are different from what is understood rationally about health and physical safety.

3. Determine under what circumstances it may be appropriate for a social worker to advocate for a client's right to practice his or her religious or spiritual beliefs.

4. Understand that social workers may be caught off guard by their own deeply held spiritual convictions when working with clients of similar backgrounds.

Other Learning Outcomes for Which This Case Can Be Used

The case discussion will facilitate the work of students as they

5. Consider alternatives available to social workers who have differing opinions from those in power.

6. Examine the social work values and ethics that influence this case.

7. Assess the risks to a social worker of countering a supervisor or other person in a power position.

8. Appreciate how cultural elements may influence the actions of new immigrants.

9. Identify the power differences among client, social worker, supervisor, and doctor.

Courses and Levels for Which the Case Is Intended

This case involves a bachelor's level social worker and is most appropriate for bachelor's level courses or graduate foundation courses. The case provides the opportunity for discussion of religious diversity, race and ethnicity, health care, organizational policy, and the appropriate use of supervision, advocacy, and skills in engagement, assessment, intervention, and termination.

Discussion Questions Related to Religion and Spirituality

Establishing the Facts

1. Who are the persons and organizations to whom Ruben must relate concerning this case?

2. What is known about Jessie's spirituality? What is known about Ruben's spirituality? In what ways are they similar or different?

Analysis

3. Why does Jessie's case cause Ruben to become so emotionally involved?

    Ruben grew up a culture similar to Jessie's and his family faced poverty, just as Jessie's family does now. In a town where Mexicans may face racism and prejudice, Ruben may feel a connection to Jessie through their common experiences of poverty and oppression. In addition, they both speak Spanish, a language which most of the hospital staff do not understand. Although they come from similar backgrounds, Ruben has made his success in "the Anglo world," and in some ways, Ruben may feel that Jessie needs him to serve as an interpreter of culture and language.

4. What types of power does Doc Hutch hold? Does Ruben hold? Does Jessie hold?

    Doc Hutch holds a great deal of power because, as a doctor, he sits at the top of the hospital hierarchy. He also has the advantage of being well-respected in this rural town, whereas Ruben is a newcomer and therefore an outsider to the established community. Doc Hutch is a member of the dominant ethnic group in power, whereas Ruben and Jessie are Mexican Americans and therefore members of an oppressed ethnic group. Ruben does have the power of speaking Spanish, the language of his client, and Doc Hutch needs him to interpret. Ruben is also in the position of social worker, which gives him some credibility in the arena of the social

needs of the client. Jessie has a green card and therefore has certain rights as a legitimate worker in the economy of the United States. He also has the "spiritual power" of strong belief in his traditions.

5. What are the social work values that Ruben is expressing in his practice? What values may present tensions or conflicts for him?

    Self-determination of the client is particularly relevant here, as well as the values underlying advocacy for oppressed persons.

6. What are the values that Doc Hutch is expressing in his practice? Are there points of conflict with social work values?

    Doc Hutch is thinking about client safety, duty to protect, and the Hippocratic oath. There are also some issues concerning dual relationships related to Doc Hutch's friendship with the factory owner.

7. What is the role of the supervisor in this case?

    The supervisor is obligated to assist Ruben in making a good decision with the best possible short- and long-term outcomes. The supervisor must honor social work ethics, must be concerned for Ruben's development as an employee, and must consider the credibility and standing of the social work profession in this hospital setting.

Action

8. What decisions must Ruben make now?

9. What should he say now
    *   To Doc Hutch?
    *   To Jessie?
    *   To his supervisor?
    *   In his written notes about the case?

        Here the instructor may want to divide students into groups to respond to different aspects of the question. Or, a writing assignment could be formulated around Ruben's different options. For example, students may be asked to take on the role of Ruben and write up case notes to be turned into the supervisor about the actions that Ruben took and why he chose them. Or students may be asked to create a process recording detailing Ruben's conversation with Jessie.

10. How would your response be different if Jessie was a Jehovah's Witness born in the United States who refused a blood transfusion?

   Here students must ask themselves whether a spirituality that is unfamiliar to them and lacks an organized religious framework may be "legitimate." Does the fact that Jessie's spirituality is unfamiliar to the hospital staff make a difference? Does it make a difference that curanderismo *is not an organized religion like the Jehovah's Witnesses? Does it make a difference that he is not a U.S. citizen and does not speak English fluently?*

11. How might Ruben's response be different if he was White and did not speak Spanish?

   Much of this case's intensity for Ruben stems from the fact that he is one of the few people in the hospital who can understand Jessie in terms of experience, culture, and language. Would a social worker who was not Mexican American respond differently?

Teaching Suggestions

The instructor could start the discussion with a factual question about the persons and organizations involved in the situation. Help students move to a deeper level of analysis by asking questions related to power in the organization and to values and ethics. Probe issues of diversity in terms of race, nationality, and spirituality. To move the class to consider the action dilemma, the instructor may divide the class into work groups to consider a variety of possible actions, or assign written responses that require students to place themselves in the role of the social worker.

Additional Notes

07.

Some Day…

Nancy K. Brown and Terry A. Wolfer

The couple was one of the most attractive that Emma Pickard had seen in her many years of social work practice. The husband, Khaleefa Massoud, was an unusually handsome man. At six feet tall and 31 years old, he reminded her of the actor Omar Sharif in his youth. His clothes, along with his demeanor, had a European quality that made Emma wonder if he had been educated in England. He appeared polished and well put together. Michelle, the wife, was 27 years old and also attractive. Not, Emma thought, on the same scale as Khaleefa, but certainly very good looking and sophisticated in her bearing.

Michelle had initiated the request for treatment at Family Resources, Inc. (FRI). During the first session, she had told Emma that she wanted a divorce because her hopes for the marriage were dashed, and she felt betrayed and manipulated. She stated that the only reason Khaleefa had agreed to come to counseling was his need for her to sign his green card papers. Khaleefa, on the other hand, pointed out that there were many avenues open for him to obtain a green card, and he argued that he had come to the counseling because he wanted his marriage to work. Michelle said that they were overwhelmed with interpersonal conflict and cultural differences, but she was devastated by the idea of a second divorce. Khaleefa appeared calm during the interview; Michelle was emotional and distraught. Later sessions revealed that Michelle did not really want a

divorce and that she was trying to drive Khaleefa into a course of action that would ultimately save their marriage. It seemed quite clear to Emma that divorce was not what either of them wanted.

Emma Pickard and Family Resources, Inc.

Emma met with the couple at FRI, a private for-profit agency owned by a psychiatrist and his wife, a psychiatric nurse. FRI contracted with several businesses in the Columbus, Ohio area, including Ameritech and Wendy's, to provide their employee assistance programs. FRI employed nearly 20 consultants, all of whom were social workers and clinical psychologists in part-time private practice. The consultants provided various forms of individual and family therapy, and the psychiatrist provided medical supervision. Only three administrative staff members worked for the agency full-time.

Emma had been a consultant with FRI for two years, soon after beginning full-time work as a school social worker at Harvell Alternative School. Previously, she had worked for 5 years as a therapist for a therapeutic foster-care program, her first position after earning a MSW. Emma enjoyed moonlighting with FRI, especially because she had no administrative responsibilities. Like other consultants, Emma typically worked two or three evenings per week for an hourly fee, and the agency handled the billing. However, most FRI clients, including the Massouds, came with medical insurance that required consultants to periodically request that the insurance company approve the treatment.

In the Beginning

Over the course of the sessions the story of the couple's relationship unfolded. They had met at a dance club. Khaleefa, the dark and exotic stranger, was extravagant and he made Michelle feel like a princess. She was a competent American woman who adeptly managed her complex life. Expensive dinner dates and romantic evenings were routinely part of their courtship. It was pure chemistry and after dating for 6 months, they were married. The ceremony took place in a Muslim mosque, but for the sake of her parents, Michelle and Khaleefa consented to a second ceremony at her parents' church. Michelle had a 6-year-old biracial daughter, Monique, from a previous marriage and Michelle felt lucky that such a prince had come her way. She looked forward to family life, to buying a house and having more children, and Khaleefa agreed that this was his ultimate goal as well. At the time of the first session, they had been married for one year.

While they were dating, Michelle noticed Khaleefa's devotion to his family back in Egypt and loved his commitment to them. He sent money every month to help support his mother, his father, and his two sisters, who all depended on him for extra money while his father recovered from an illness that kept him out of work. All together, he sent about $400 to $500 each month to help his family with expenses. Prior to his marriage to Michelle, he had made enough money working as a waiter in an exclusive, upscale restaurant to meet his commitments to his family in Egypt, dress impeccably, maintain the apartment he shared with his older brother, and drive an expensive car.

Family Comes First

Michelle assumed that this dedication would transfer to their new family as the newlywed couple settled into their life together at Michelle's apartment. Michelle worked hard, but the first year of their marriage had not brought the changes to her circumstances that she desired. She continued to struggle with a car payment, day-care costs, and the rent. Khaleefa could offer little help with the finances, giving Michelle only a limited amount of money each month due to his commitments to his parents and his sisters. Michelle saw her dream of a home and a family fading as Khaleefa's focus failed to shift from his family in Egypt to Michelle and Monique.

Khaleefa was confused and angered by Michelle's lack of patience with his familial obligations. He told Emma early in the sessions that as a Muslim, he was not only obligated by a cultural and religious mandate to care for his parents and his sisters, but that he did so willingly because they were very important to him. Khaleefa explained, "I came to this country four years ago with my older brother to find jobs to help my family back home." He reiterated again and again throughout the sessions, "She knew all this before we were married." Khaleefa bristled at the distinction Emma made between his family of origin and his newly constituted family. He asserted that Michelle was impatient and that her demands were unrealistic.

Khaleefa's brother was a source of irritation and conflict. At 33, Mohammed enjoyed an energetic nightlife. He dated very young girls, and there were regular parties at his apartment. When Mohammed lost his place, Khaleefa invited him to move in, and the parties relocated to Michelle's apartment. Michelle was angry and hurt that Khaleefa simply offered this solution to his brother without consulting her. As a parent with a young child, she felt that this was completely unacceptable. Khaleefa made it clear that Mohammed was his family and that he could not ignore his responsibility.

Mohammed eventually found a new place to live but his lifestyle, which included significant alcohol and drug use, left the responsibility for sending money back to their family to Khaleefa alone, even though Mohammed was the oldest. Michelle intensely resented this discrepancy. She did not think it was fair that Khaleefa held so tightly to his idea of family obligations, while Mohammed lived a free and easy life, knowing that his brother would always be willing to bail him out. In the beginning, it was Khaleefa's commitment to family that attracted Michelle, but now it proved to be an impediment to their marriage.

It Will Get Better, *InshaAllah*

Khaleefa continued to reassure Michelle that

they would eventually have what they had dreamed about before their marriage, *InshaAllah* (if God wills). He had faith that his brother would eventually outgrow his ways, that his father's health would improve, and that his sisters would eventually marry and transfer their dependency to their husbands' families, as was done in Egypt. Khaleefa remained baffled by Michelle's impatience, and intractable in his commitment toward his Egyptian family. To Emma, Khaleefa seemed sincere, yet immovable.

Khaleefa acknowledged that he had not been able to actively work toward their shared goals, but he was adamant about his commitment to Michelle and Monique. Emma believed that his loyalty was sincere, but had nagging doubts about his ability to deliver on that commitment.

It's Not All Me

Despite his own family beliefs and obligations, Khaleefa complained that Michelle's parents did not do enough to help them. He believed that because they were well off financially, they could give Khaleefa and Michelle the down payment for a house, or at least pay their rent or their car payment. He stated during one session, "This is the United States and they should do it [pay our rent]." Michelle's parents had paid for her first church wedding, but not the second (the Muslim wedding was free), and Khaleefa offered this fact as proof that her family was not generous. He saw no contradiction between the long hours that Michelle worked in her position as an administrative assistant and his sisters' jobless lives because it was not expected for women to work in Egypt. In the United States, he pointed out, custom made it reasonable for Michelle to work.

Maybe You Are Not Who I Thought You Were

The relationship had other problems. Michelle wanted Khaleefa to be more active in his role as stepfather to Monique, whose own father was distant and uninvolved. Michelle was willing to accept household chores, such as cooking and cleaning, as hers alone, but she was annoyed by Khaleefa's lack of attention for her daughter. Khaleefa often left Monique at the day-care center until 6 p.m., even though he left work at 3 p.m., because he felt that this time belonged to him and he deserved to relax.

Despite his assurance that he would act no differently with his own children, Michelle grew concerned about the emotional impact of his detachment from Monique. Khaleefa maintained that he genuinely cared for the little girl and that Michelle's fears were unfounded.

Emma saw Khaleefa and Michelle as emotional opposites. He was, it seemed to her, aloof and very controlled. His feelings were as neatly maintained as his fine clothes. Michelle was much more emotional and dramatic. At times, during a heated session, Khaleefa would look toward Emma as if to say, "See, see what I have to put up with?" Yet, he remained calm and seemingly unaffected by his wife's tears and pleading. Emma suspected that at the heart of their relationship was a match between Khaleefa's need to control and care for someone and Michelle's wish for a prince who would take her away from "all this." Despite making little progress in their treatment, Khaleefa and Michelle both reiterated their desire to stay together and avoid divorce.

Over the next five weeks, Khaleefa and Michelle continued to attend the sessions, sometimes together, sometimes alone. Almost nothing was achieved during this period, which was occasionally punctuated by either romantic interludes when Michelle's parents would baby-sit while the couple had weekends with lavish dinners, or separations when Khaleefa would leave for several days to live with his brother.

This Is All Too Much for Me

During the sixth session, Khaleefa sat unsmiling, his arms resting on his thighs with his palms turned upward. "I am *not* going to abandon my family back home," he said. Emma caught the edge of anger that threatened to crack Khaleefa's meticulously maintained veneer.

He continued. "What you are saying is, 'Take care of *this* family,' and if I do that, I abandon my family back home. This is an impossible situation. How can I say, 'I love you more than my mother or my father?'" Emma watched as Michelle crumbled and broke into tears. Khaleefa did not move to console her. He sat silently, unable to respond.

As the session came to an end, Khaleefa said aloud what he and Emma were both thinking: "This

counseling is not helping us." It seemed that neither Khaleefa nor Michelle were able to consider
any compromise that could lead them to their
shared goals of a house and a family. Khaleefa held
rigidly to his belief that it would all eventually work
out as the situation in Egypt improved. Michelle
would not make current financial sacrifices in order
to achieve at least some of their long-term financial
goals. She continued to feel betrayed by Khaleefa's
other obligations. Distressed and impatient,
Michelle now returned to her earlier position that
the marriage could not work, and she insisted that
she simply would not go on like this. Emma was not
hopeful. She did not know what to do next.

07.teaching note
Some Day...
Nancy K. Brown and Terry A. Wolfer

Case Synopsis

Michelle and Khaleefa Massoud came for marriage counseling to Emma Pickard, a social worker with several years of experience. They had been married for a year and were experiencing difficulties due to conflicting family obligations. Among their difficulties was the substantial sum of money that Khaleefa gave monthly to his family back in Egypt, which Michelle believed was preventing the couple from reaching their shared goals. While expressing commitment to their marriage, neither spouse seemed able to compromise. Therapy appeared ineffective, and Emma and the Massouds ended the sixth session with little hope for the relationship.

Learning Outcomes Related to Religion and Spirituality

The case discussion will facilitate the work of students as they

1. Recognize how religion and culture are often intertwined with family and individual dynamics and how difficult it may be to distinguish their separate effects.

2. Recognize the importance of understanding clients' religious and cultural backgrounds and current involvement when interpreting their behavior.

3. Understand how religion and culture can both complicate and contribute to family formation and functioning.

4. Understand how a social worker striving to be culturally sensitive and competent may be stuck when facing a family's conflicting religious values.

Other Learning Outcomes for Which This Case Can Be Used

The case discussion will facilitate the work of students as they

5. Understand the importance of clearly specifying treatment goals and objectives.

6. Understand the difficulty and importance of maintaining bilateral relations with spouses experiencing marital conflict.

Courses and Levels for Which the Case Is Intended

This case is intended for master's level courses. Originally developed for a social work capstone course, it was designed to integrate human behavior and practice theory into practical applications. This case could also be used in courses on culture, human diversity, family systems, and family and couples therapy.

Discussion Questions Related to Religion and Spirituality

Establishing the Facts

1. What do we know about the history and the nature of Michelle and Khaleefa's relationship?

   Michelle and Khaleefa have been married for 1 year after dating for 6 months. Their courtship was characterized by romantic and extravagant dates. Michelle had been married before and has a biracial daughter, aged 6.

2. What obligations did each bring to the marriage?

   Prior to the marriage, Michelle was a single parent whose primary obligation was to her daughter. Khaleefa is financially obligated to his parents and his sisters who remain in Egypt. He also feels an obligation to his older brother who resides in the United States.

3. What evidence is there for culturally or religiously based motives for Khaleefa's position? For Michelle's position? What evidence contradicts this?

   At the beginning of the therapy, Khaleefa made his cultural and religious obligations clear. Aside from his strong Muslim beliefs, he willingly participated in a Christian marriage ceremony to please Michelle's parents. It is possible that this participation stems from a sense of obligation to Michelle's family. While Khaleefa says that culture and religion are important forces that motivate his behavior, there is one important contradiction in his actions. His brother's use of drugs and alcohol is specifically mentioned, and although this behavior is clearly prohibited by Islamic law, Khaleefa apparently tolerates it.

   Michelle is Christian, but the denomination is not identified in this case. There is no evidence that her personal religious commitments are a source of conflict for the couple. She also may have participated in the Christian ceremony to please her parents.

   Although Michelle does not share Khaleefa's religious beliefs, she participated in the Islamic marriage ceremony and admires his values and commitments.

4. What are the apparent emotional dynamics in their relationship?

   Khaleefa reveals little of his inner emotional life. Aloof and stoic, he is unbending in his commitment to family life and his responsibilities. At other times, he is romantic and indulgent, as evidenced by extravagant dinners and entertainment. He seems frustrated and resentful of Michelle's repeated demands to change in ways he believes are unwarranted at this time.

   Michelle was attracted to Khaleefa's devotion to his family, but now demands that Khaleefa turn his attention as well as his resources to their new family. She believes that he places their family lower in his priorities than his Egyptian family. Michelle is angry about Khaleefa's unwillingness to compromise.

   Their relationship seems very unstable. They are intensely in love one moment and then distant and angry the next.

5. What are the couple's expressed goals?

   Both Khaleefa and Michelle say that they would like to eventually have a house and additional children of their own.

6. What other factors in the social environment impact this couple?

   Michelle has a daughter, Monique, from her first marriage. Both Khaleefa and Michelle work, and they each have commitments outside the home. Although they appear to have adequate income, they have not made any changes to how they manage their money in order to reach their joint goals, and they do not seem to be making financial progress as a couple.

   Michelle believes that she is no better off than before she was married. She continues to be responsible for the same things as before: meeting her own financial obligations, caring for her child, and maintaining her home.

Analysis

7. What are some ways of expressing the couple's problems?

   Initially, students may focus on the individual and couple levels of explanation, which may include the following:

   - *Khaleefa has taken on the role of "family hero." He seeks the approval of his Egyptian family to the detriment of his newly constituted family.*
   - *Michelle is unreasonable in her expectations re-*

garding their mutually agreed upon goals. Khaleefa's obligation to his family has been clear since the beginning of their relationship.

- *There is a clash of culture and religion. Khaleefa is obligated to his Egyptian family, and Michelle believes, as is common in American culture, that his primary duty is to his new family.*

8. What does Islamic culture and religion require of adult children in their duty to their parents?

   In Islamic religion, obligation to parents is a sacred duty. The Quran specifically addresses the duties of adult children toward their parents:

   Your Sustainer has decreed that you worship none but Him, and that you be kind to parents. Whether one or both of them attain old age in your life-time, do not say to them a word of contempt nor repel them, but address them in terms of honor. And, out of kindness, lower to them the wing of humility and say: My Sustainer! Bestow on them Your mercy, even as they cherished me in childhood (17:23-24).

9. What dichotomies are evident in this case?

   Culture and religion versus family dynamics; cultural behaviors versus personal behaviors; marital expectations versus cultural responsibilities; individual needs versus family concerns.

10. To what extent can the actions of Khaleefa and Michelle be attributed to their respective religious and cultural backgrounds as opposed to their individual psychology?

    Khaleefa is steeped in his religion and his culture and driven by their mandates; yet, he is also a son within the context of his Egyptian family and a husband within his marriage. Khaleefa states that caring for his Egyptian family is his moral and religious obligation. Although Islamic culture mandates an enduring obligation to aging parents, it gives equal importance to his wife and children.

    Because Khaleefa apparently tolerates the use of drugs and alcohol by his brother, he appears to be inconsistent in his approach to his religious and cultural duties, which makes the case complicated.

    Michelle has been married before. She may be fearful that they will not reach their expressed goals if they wait until Khaleefa's family becomes more self-sufficient. Yet, we must consider American culture,

which values the present and the attainment of material wealth as a sign of personal success. These ideals may contribute to Michelle's impatience with their progress toward mutual goals.

11. Are the respective positions taken by Michelle and Khaleefa reasonable?

    The couple dated for 6 months and has been married for 1 year. Young couples often wait several years before buying a house and considering children, yet Michelle is impatient and feels as if they are not reaching their goals. Michelle seems despondent and hopeless about Khaleefa's unwillingness to change, but her response may be premature. In many ways, Khaleefa seems unresponsive and unconcerned, but he has accompanied Michelle to counseling, which indicates that he does care. His emotional style, however, is distant, and he shows a stoic refusal to compromise. This may be a reflection of his culture.

12. Are their respective actions and beliefs consistent? What, if anything, does this suggest? (For example, how should one interpret the inconsistency in Khaleefa's approach to culture and religion?)

    There are inconsistencies in Michelle and Khaleefa's actions and beliefs. Khaleefa speaks of his familial obligations, bound in culture and religion, while he tolerates his brother's drug and alcohol use, which contradicts a strong religious behavioral mandate. Michelle is also inconsistent. She is attracted to Khaleefa because of his close family ties and devotion, but she is critical when she finds that this same devotion prevents the couple from meeting their expressed goals.

13. What beliefs do the couple hold about the processes required to meet their goals?

    Khaleefa and Michelle have not defined a process that will help them attain their goals. Although they appear to have enough money to meet their basic needs, they waste money on lavish dinners and expensive weekends. While they each express their desire to reach their goals, they make no concessions in their lifestyle to facilitate the process.

14. Is Khaleefa's behavior the result of his devotion to his family, or his culture or religion, or his personal needs?

Khaleefa has the characteristics of the "family hero." In this role, he helps the family in order to gain praise and recognition out of a need for acceptance and love. Although his devotion may be rooted in culture and religion, the discrepancy in his acceptance of religious mandates suggests a codependent aspect to his behavior.

15. What is the relation between culture, religion, and behavior?

There is a close association between culture, religion, and behavior. Religion provides admonitions and specific prescriptions for behavior. When actions are not particularly illuminated by religion, individuals may behave out of generally accepted custom. All of our choices for behavior are framed by our own personal contexts, which include at the least biology or genetics, family dynamics, and personal psychology.

Culture is essential to understanding human behavior. However, human behavior is complex and is not driven by a single dimension. We may see Khaleefa's behavior as culture-bound, but a further examination reveals behavior that may be family-based or personally idiosyncratic. Therefore, we need to seek an understanding of each dimension and then integrate them into a coherent whole.

Although culture and religion should always be considered or accounted for, it is also useful to see the person and her or his behavior as unique. One significant difficulty encountered in this case is the social worker's inability to simultaneously negotiate two equally valuable domains: culture or religion and personal psychology.

Although culture and religion can contribute heavily to an individual's behavior, it cannot offer a complete explanation. Emma seems stuck with a conundrum: "What if the problem is due to culture, and what if it's not?"

16. If Emma believes that Khaleefa's culture and religion are at the heart of his reluctance to compromise, will this interfere with her ability to move the case forward?

Social workers are taught to respect culture and religion, but this does not relieve us of our obligation to understand its impact on behavior and the system as a whole. It is easy to get stuck by focusing on culture and religion alone. Emma may not believe that she has the right to be critical of Khaleefa's behavior.

17. What else impedes experienced clinicians? Burnout? Complacency? Boredom?

All of the above and more. Experienced clinicians have different problems than newly educated social workers. Often, they take things for granted and can get lost in the case.

18. How are goals and objectives managed in these counseling sessions?

In this case, the goals and objectives appear too global, for instance, improving the couple's communication. These are not as effective as goals and objectives that are clearly defined and readily measurable.

19. What theoretical perspectives contribute to Emma's methods?

Her theoretical perspective is not apparent. If she were using a brief model, the case may have moved along faster, with more clearly defined outcomes and tasks.

20. Does this couple have other characteristics that contribute to Emma's inability to assist them in bringing about changes in their relationship?

Khaleefa and Michelle appear unable to compromise. Although they disagree about some fundamental issues, they also go through periods where they ignore these differences and enjoy themselves on expensive dates. These periods undermine progress and cloud the issues.

21. What are Emma's clues that something is not working in her therapy with this couple?

The couple has been coming to therapy for six sessions with little or no apparent progress. Like the couple, Emma appears to feel "stuck," having little sense of hope for change and few ideas about how to proceed. In particular, she appears to have accepted several of the stark, dichotomous choices presented by Michelle and Khaleefa. Wishing to respect cultural and religious differences, she has been stymied by the partners' conflicting claims. In addition, there is some evidence that Emma's relationship with Khaleefa may arouse her own gender-related tensions, leaving her uncertain and confused.

22. If change seems unlikely, what is the therapist's responsibility?

The social worker has an ethical obligation to provide treatment in the most efficient and cost-effective manner. The therapist has a responsibility to inform the clients of the likely outcomes to the treatment. If she is stuck, she should tell them.

After a few sessions with no discernible progress, the therapist and the clients should undertake an evaluation of progress, a recommitment to or reconstruction of goals. In fact, admitting to being stuck may help the clients and the therapist to renew their goals and get the therapy moving again.

23. What does it mean for a social worker to be culturally competent?

At the very least, the social worker should understand general information about various dimensions of culture and religion. This might include, but is not limited to, issues of gender, family hierarchy, responsibility to other family members, affective styles including nonverbal communication, and views about the helping process. Religion also dictates certain codes of behavior. The social worker should be familiar with the possibilities or proscriptions for behavior associated with each cultural or religious identity.

Action

24. Should Emma close the case? If not, what treatment alternatives are available to her?

Emma has several choices. She may close the case. She may refer the couple to another therapist. Or, she may reevaluate progress and reset goals with a focus on a more structured therapeutic process. A renewed process should include time limits and specific measurable objectives.

Emma needs to take the initiative to discuss these decisions for proceeding with her clients. Together with the clients, she can consider if these goals remain feasible and within Emma's capacity to help the couple reach them.

The couple's new goals should be elicited and operationalized into identifiable behavioral tasks. Task-oriented, behavioral activities may be the best way to move forward. The couple needs to identify what compromises are possible, and a plan of work needs to be developed. To continue the therapy unchanged should not be an option.

25. Could you work with this couple? Where might you get stuck?

Many experienced social workers get stuck, but something that "sticks" one person may not be an issue for another. Understanding our own roadblocks is an important exercise for practicing social workers, whether experienced or newly trained.

26. In marital therapy, with couples in conflict, where should the therapist stand?

Each case offers unique circumstances. For instance, in a case of domestic violence the social worker cannot stand neutral, and it must be made clear that violence is unacceptable. Social workers are not value neutral. We have to account for issues of gender, race, and class that preempt a neutral stance.

Despite our understanding of the value issues of race, gender, and class, we still have to form a therapeutic alliance that works for both parties if progress is to be made. Balance is key. Even if that balance is tipped in one direction, by domestic violence, for example, it needs to be offset by supportiveness, acceptance, and validation on both sides.

27. How do therapeutic alliances with each individual influence change?

In therapy, we often shift our alliances back and forth. In family counseling, we are often using ourselves as a means to shore up a weak member or compensate for a smaller voice. The therapist must be acutely aware of these shifting alliances and make adjustments accordingly.

28. How can you use these relationships to promote change?

The therapist, through use of self, maneuvers the client in one way or another, thus fostering change by either providing an in vivo model for behavior, or more directly by simply prescribing behavior. If the therapeutic relationship is intact, clients can respond in positive ways.

Teaching Suggestions

An instructor may begin by asking students to identify facts about the three main characters and each of their subjective perspectives about the other participants. Starting with possible discrepancies in their perspectives, explore the basic issues in the case. These include effects of culture and religion, culturally based marital conflict, ambivalence regarding individual and family expectations, family formation (especially for blended families), and gender differences. If necessary, raise questions about Emma's role to help students focus on her response and contribution to the marital impasse. Lead students to identify evidence that social workers can use to recognize when they are stuck, and then consider ways to move forward.

If the class discussion mirrors the marital and therapeutic impasse, use the parallel process to deepen students' exploration of the case. Specifically, encourage students to reflect on the experience of "stuckness," identifying both internal and external evidence for this situation. Then, use the process focus to develop plans for dealing with the impasse.

Additional Notes

08.

What's a Supervisor to Do?

Sharon Weaver Pittman and Luis A. Perez

It was a mid-March afternoon and a snowstorm had been blanketing Denver all day. Karen Peterson was drinking a cup of coffee in the kitchen of the Victim Recovery Center (VRC) before seeing her next client. Don Jacobsen, the agency director, came into the kitchen, closing the door behind him.

"Did you know that Anna told her field seminar last week that she had been able to help one of our clients, as she put it," Don made the quotation marks gesture with his fingers, "'invite Jesus into her heart'?"

Karen's mind raced. She knew that Don, new to the agency just two years ago, had strong reservations about conservative Christian students from nearby Columbus University. He had told her shortly after he arrived and learned about the relationship between the agency and the university that he did not want students using their role with VRC clients to proselytize. Over the past two years, he had learned to trust her as a supervisor and to rely on her students as capable young professionals.

Now she felt the anger grow in her. "How could Anna do this?" she thought. To Don, she said, "She did *what*? How did you hear about this?"

"Oh, I had lunch today with Professor Cantera. The subject of Anna and her placement with us came up," he replied.

Karen thought to herself, "It sounds like dealing with Anna may be just the beginning." She heard Don talking.

"I'll expect you to let me know how you've handled this after you've talked with Anna."

Supervising Students at the Victim Recovery Center

Supervising students had been one of the professional roles that Karen enjoyed most since being hired as the clinical director at the VRC, a federally funded, nonprofit agency located in a suburban neighborhood not far from the heart of Denver. The agency served adults and children who had been victimized by violence. Much of their work was with the victims of family violence, but VRC also served victims of crime in the larger community. The agency provided legal, medical, and social work services. Karen enjoyed helping students gain new skills in crisis intervention and ongoing counseling services with clients. She knew that she was well-respected by the faculty at Columbus University because they frequently invited her to be a guest lecturer in their classes. She had been supervising students from the Columbus social work program for more than 10 years, long before Don Jacobsen arrived as the agency director.

Columbus is a private Christian university that draws a diverse student body from all over the Midwest and the western United States. Many students seek it out because it is known for its small classes and Christian environment. Students come from diverse backgrounds and faith communities, but there is a significant minority who come from very conservative Christian backgrounds. These conservative students concerned Don the most, because he believed that they might use their professional roles for proselytizing. Over the years, Karen had worked with many students from Columbus, some conservative and some not, some religious and some not. Several had been so successful that VRC had hired them upon graduation.

Karen was Episcopalian herself and a leader in her congregation. She had often thought about how important personal faith could be in sustaining a social worker's commitment to service; it had certainly been a driving force in her own life. She even considered that she felt "called" to the hard task of providing social work services to victims of crime and abuse, although she had never said that to anyone else. When she had come through her MSW program, she was taught that whatever one's personal faith, it had no place in the professional relationship with a client. Nothing in Karen's own professional education had prepared her to think about or address religion and spirituality in the lives of clients, much less to consider how she might use her own faith and religiosity in her practice with them.

For the past 10 years, the program at Columbus had reinforced Karen's own training by emphasizing that one's professional practice and personal faith should be kept separate. Although Karen knew that most of the faculty were Christians, she knew of no talk of faith or religion in the classroom; such topics had never even been mentioned in field supervisory meetings. Clearly, the proselytizing that concerned Don was out of the question. It was considered unacceptable not only by agency, but also by the social work faculty at Columbus.

However, over a year ago changes had begun to take place at Columbus. In a field supervisors' meeting, Professor Cantera, the director of field education, had told the field supervisors that social work programs were beginning to include content on religion and spirituality in their courses as an important dimension of human experience. Columbus was adding content on religion and faith development in its coursework sequence, human behavior and the social environment. A couple of faculty members had been hired who had written articles on religion and spirituality in social work practice.

Karen had talked with field supervisors for Columbus from other agencies, and she knew she was not alone in feeling a little concerned about this shift in focus. She worried that the boundary between professional practice and personal faith might not be so well defined. Yet, she also knew most of the faculty well. Last fall, during another field supervisors' meeting with Darla Cantera, one of the other supervisors specifically asked what the faculty taught students about the role of prayer in social work practice. Darla replied that she taught her students that social workers should not make it a practice to pray with clients. That was the role of clergy, not social workers. "So," Karen had thought at the time, "we agree on that."

Preparing to Talk with Anna

After seeing her next client, Karen had time to think about the conversation between her director and Darla Cantera. Even though she was alone in her office, Karen's face flushed with anger and embarrassment as she imagined the scene in her mind. Why was Darla talking to Don instead of to her about her concerns with Anna? And how much trust had Don lost in her?

Karen began to review in her mind the students she had recently supervised. "There was Maggie, Ebony, Dana, and Felipe. I've helped a lot of students through some tough learning experiences," Karen comforted herself.

She remembered the first time Darla Cantera had talked to her about this field student. "Anna is a person with a deep faith that really motivates her desire to serve others." Darla had added, "And she has made significant progress in understanding and affirming the values and principles of professional social work."

At the time, Karen had been astute enough to wonder to herself, "Progress from where? What issues does this student have?" She had asked Darla to explain.

Darla had gone on to say that Anna is a member of a very conservative, Christian nondenominational congregation well known in the community for its political stands against abortion and against gay and lesbian lifestyles. Anna had initially expressed to her professors that she did not think social workers should have to make referrals for abortions for clients who asked for them or to talk with sexually-active teenagers about birth control. Over the semesters in her graduate program, however, Anna had learned the meaning of client self-determination as a cardinal social work value, even when the social worker disagreed with the client's life choices.

Karen reflected back to her placement interview with Anna. "Anna, how do you handle your strong commitment to Christian faith in your work with clients?" she had asked. She did not usually ask questions about personal values, but her conversation with Professor Cantera had alerted her that she needed to discuss this student's values as they related to her practice.

After a pause during which she seemed to be thinking, Anna had confidently affirmed, "All clients have the right to self-determination!"

At the time, Karen remembered smiling to herself at the textbook answer, and thinking, "We'll have a lot to talk about."

Anna had blossomed professionally during the fall semester. She had changed from a shy, nervous young woman to a confident young professional who appeared energized by the work she was doing at VRC. One day toward the end of her first semester, she told Karen, "I referred a client considering an abortion to Planned Parenthood, and I think she will be going."

Anna was somber, and Karen remembered saying, "I know that must have been hard for you; this job can be really tough." At the same time, Karen had silently congratulated herself as a supervisor. She had helped Anna learn to handle this very difficult value conflict. Anna had told her how vehemently opposed she was to abortion as a choice for ending an unwanted pregnancy. Yet she had learned to separate her own choices from the right of clients to decide for themselves. In fact, Anna had herself made the connection to her own religious values. She had said to Karen that Christians also believe in self-determination, although they often call it "free will."

Anna had left that supervision session saying to Karen, "I praise God for letting me work at VRC. I have learned so much here." During the semester evaluation that followed a couple of weeks later, Karen noted the growth she had seen in Anna's ability to value clients' experiences and decisions.

During the first weeks of her second semester, Anna's enthusiasm had remained high, and her performance made Karen proud. Not only was she bright and competent, but she also did the agency's often-dreaded paperwork efficiently and effectively. Karen had been ready to count her as one of the best students she had ever supervised.

So what had happened? Had Anna used her role as a social worker to convince a client in the middle of a life crisis to become a Christian? Clearly, Karen needed to hear from Anna. Karen picked up the phone and dialed the student's office. When Anna answered, Karen said, "I need to talk with you, but I've got a client in a minute. Let's get together in my office at 4:00."

Anna replied, "Okay, I'll be there." Karen knew Ann wanted to know what the meeting was going to be about, but Karen did not want to say any more until they could talk it through.

Anna's Story

At 4:00, when Karen returned to her office after walking her client back to the waiting room, Anna was sitting in the chair beside her desk. She looked puzzled and a little anxious. Karen plowed in without the usual pleasantries with which their supervisory sessions usually began. She was anxious herself.

"Don stopped me this afternoon and told me that he had lunch with Professor Cantera today. It seems that Professor Cantera told him that during your field seminar, you shared that you had led one of your clients to become a Christian." Karen tried not to sound accusatory. "Tell me what happened, Anna."

Anna looked confused. "I don't think I did any leading. I was just facilitating my client's right to self-determination when she brought up her desire to become a Christian," she said.

Karen tried to hide her impatience with the jargon. "What did your client say, and what did you say, and how did you end up talking about Christianity?"

Anna paused. "Okay, let me start at the beginning. This is my client Debbie Smith. You and I have talked about her before. You remember that Debbie's brother sexually abused her when she was a little girl until she was almost 16. She tried to tell her mother, but her mother never believed her. All those years of hurt and rejection have made her self-destructive and angry and bitter. But she had finally been making real progress in getting her life on track."

Anna's voice became a bit more confident, "We had talked many times before, but this time was different. She was crying, and she said that she just wanted peace, and she asked me how I found peace. She told me how much she had grown to look up to me and that she had noticed something special in my life."

Anna went on. "I really just tried to honestly answer the questions she was asking. And I tried to tell her that it wasn't important what I thought or did. I could only help her explore what she wanted. Finally she said, 'What I want is for you to tell me how you handle it when things get hard.' That's when I told her I found peace in my relationship with Jesus."

Without pausing, Anna continued, "Debbie said that she wanted the peace that could come from a relationship with God. Then she asked me to pray with her, so I did."

Karen saw Anna's confidence fade as she realized that Karen did not share her perception of the situation. With a defensive edge in her voice, Anna said quietly, "I didn't bring the issue of faith up. My client did. She was the one who asked about it. Isn't faith in God an alternative clients like Debbie have a right to know about? How is it that different from abortion being an alternative that needs to be given to a woman who wants to end her pregnancy?"

08.teaching note
What's a Supervisor to Do?
Sharon Weaver Pittman and Luis A. Perez

Case Synopsis

As a seasoned supervisor, Karen had enjoyed working with students from Columbus University. Motivated by a sense of religious calling to serve victims of violence, she had kept a boundary between her personal faith and her work with clients, and she taught her students the importance of maintaining this boundary. Anna, a conservative Christian student, had been doing well as she entered her second semester of field instruction. However, Karen heard that Anna had led a client to become a Christian and had prayed with her about that decision. Anna did not believe that she had been evangelizing, but instead thought that she had been respecting her client's choice to explore spiritual options.

Learning Outcomes Related to Religion and Spirituality

The case discussion will facilitate the work of students as they

1. Identify the values and ethics pertinent to sharing one's own faith and beliefs with clients.

2. Define the significance of practice context and agency expectations for deciding what is appropriate in the integration of spirituality and practice.

3. Understand the complexity of the supervisor's

roles and responsibilities in helping students learn to handle value dilemmas.

Other Learning Outcomes for Which This Case Can Be Used

The case discussion will facilitate the work of students as they

4. Understand how the profession of social work changes its knowledge and practice principles over time, such as the recent increase in the profession's consideration of spirituality and religion as dimensions of human experience.

5. Explore organizational issues involved in defining practice boundaries.

Courses and Levels for Which the Case Is Intended

This case may be used for BSW or MSW student training. It could make a significant contribution to the delivery of content on values and ethics, professional use of self, assessment, critical thinking, organizational governance, crisis intervention, and supervision skills.

Discussion Questions Related to Religion and Spirituality
Establishing the Facts

1. What do we know about the situation leading

up to this supervision session?

The agency director has made it clear that social work practice in this agency is not to include "proselytizing"; VRC is an agency supported by public funds. Karen is a Christian motivated by her own faith to serve this client population, but she has been taught, and reinforces for the students she supervises, the importance of a strong boundary between personal faith and professional practice. Columbus University's social work program has recently been integrating content on religion and faith into its theoretical courses, but Karen is not certain about what this content involves. Anna, Karen's supervisee, is a conservative Christian who has struggled with the expectation of her faculty and the agency that she offer her clients the alternatives of abortion and birth control outside of marriage because she has personal objections to these practices. She has learned to equate these choices not only with the social work value of self-determination, but also with the Christian value of free will, and therefore has been successful up to this point in her field internship. In the past week, she has shared her own faith and prayed with a client at the client's invitation, believing that these actions were congruent with the social work value of self-determination.

2. Who are the persons with whom Karen needs to speak concerning Anna's actions? What are the issues Karen needs to explore with them? Who else might Karen consider involving?

The student herself, the agency director, the director of field education from the university.

3. What other concerns does Karen have?

She wonders why the director of field education was talking about her student with the director of her agency instead of her. She is concerned about issues of confidentiality and about the changes that have taken place in the education of students at the university. Finally, she is also concerned that she has lost the trust of her agency director.

4. What do we know about the needs of a person in crisis?

The vulnerability of clients in crisis suggests that spiritual or religious interventions should be used with great care and only from the client's orientation. Sug-

gesting a particular "way" to peace may be problematic when a person is in crisis. Referral to a spiritual advisor or to the clergy within the client's tradition may be a more careful alternative when a client seeks a spiritual intervention while in crisis.

Analysis

5. What do Anna and Karen mean when they talk about self-determination? What does Anna mean by the term "free will?" What is the relationship between professional values and ethics and religious values and ethics?

For both Anna and Karen, self-determination appears to mean that clients need to be made aware of all the choices that are available to them, and they need to have their freedom to make life choices protected in the social work relationship. "Free will" is a theological concept that seems to mean to Anna that God gives humans the freedom to make choices, even to choose wrongly. Inevitably as professionals, we look for ways that our personal values and beliefs fit or conflict with our professional values and ethics. In this case, the principle of free will appears to reinforce the belief that clients have the right, as well as the ability, to make their own choices.

6. What factors appeared to influence Anna's decision to share her own faith and pray with her client?

The client was in distress and asked Anna to share her own experiences with her and to pray with her. For Anna, the fact that the client requested this sharing seems to have meant that Anna was not forcing her experiences on her client. Anna also believed that her life experience would be helpful.

7. What were the issues in this setting that raise questions about the appropriateness of Anna's actions?

The client communicated her admiration for Anna. Anna's sharing of her own experience carried the additional weight, whether or not Anna realized it, of the client's desire to be like her. The Christian faith was not just another life choice she was making available to her client. Because it was her own faith, the client may have experienced Anna's sharing as carrying authority and perhaps even pressure to adopt that faith.

8. What social work values are involved for Karen's supervision of Anna?

    Self-determination is a value we protect with our clients, but not necessarily with other professionals and student professionals. Although Anna does not have the "right" to share her faith with her clients, she does seem to have shared her faith in what she believes was a way that protected her client's self-determination. The non-profit setting of this agency may play an important role in determining appropriate boundaries. Many social workers operate in faith-based settings, where clients are encouraged to request prayer interventions. From Anna's perspective she was simply responding to the client's request and speaking honestly from her own experience. Particularly significant for Karen is the possible breach of the client's confidentiality and certainly of protocol in the discussion of her student's practice by her agency director and the professor from the university.

9. Do you think that the response of Karen, Don, and Professor Cantera to Anna would have been different if what Anna had shared in response to Debbie's questions had been her practice of meditation, her use of a vision quest, or her realization of her own infinite value? How might the response differ? Why?

    When it comes to explicitly religious issues, many social workers perceive a strong boundary between personal beliefs and values and what is appropriate to share or engage in with clients. However, social workers may be less likely to identify the sharing of more generalized "spirituality" in the same way. They may also be less aware of the influence of their political and ideological beliefs (including their perceptions of social work values) on their interventions with clients.

10. In what ways might similarities and differences between Karen and Anna's personal beliefs contribute to the professional issues they face?

    Sometimes persons within similar religious traditions may be less trusting and tolerant of one another than they are of persons from radically differing religious traditions. For example, liberal and conservative Christians may be far less trusting of one another than

they would be of someone from a different religious tradition or no religion at all. It might help Karen and Anna to explore how their similarities and differences have an impact on the supervisory relationship.

11. Would the ethics of this situation be different if this agency had an explicitly religious identity and mission?

    Issues would still be complex, but explicitly religious auspices and mission could potentially change the nature of the expectations that clients would bring with them about the helping process. Clients might even expect religious assistance. Social workers would still need to engage in a careful and respectful process of assessment and exploration of the clients' needs and desires so that the social workers could help them without exploiting the relationship.

Action

12. If you were the supervisor, what would you say to Anna next?

13. Would your response be different if Anna had not been a Christian and had recommended a spiritual practice such as meditation?

14. In what ways do you think Karen needs to respond to the agency director's expectation for a report?

15. What changes, if any, need to be made in the formal and informal policies of the agency?

16. If you were Karen, would you contact Professor Cantera? If so, what would you say to her? What would be the goal of your conversation with her?

17. How do you think Karen's supervision should change as a result of this experience?

Teaching Suggestions

Begin with a question about what Karen's greatest concerns are at this point. Help students to trace Karen's own development as a social worker and a supervisor, including her own sense of calling and her concern to protect vulnerable clients, as well as the complex concept of client self-determination as it relates to a social worker's own life choices. To explore these dynamics more deeply, lead the class to consider the variables that influence Karen's supervision of Anna and to consider how she will chart a course between her director's expectations and this student's understanding of client self-determination.

Additional Notes

09.

To Leave or Not to Leave: That Is the Question

Erlene Grise-Owens

Anger and disbelief churned inside John "Nick" Nichols as he digested the news on the front page of the morning paper. His agency's Executive Director, Reverend Carl Matthews, had fired an employee because she was lesbian.

Nick, the Director of Family-Based Services, had worked at Louisiana Christian Homes for Children (LCHC) since 1990. LCHC's main headquarters were located in Shreveport, Louisiana and the agency was well respected by the social work community in the state. Public child-welfare workers as well as church leaders referred families in crisis to the agency, and state agencies relied on the agency to provide crisis and residential care for children who were removed from their homes due to abuse and neglect. The staff was frequently involved in agency coalitions that advocated for the needs of children and families to the state government, and the staff were also often involved in professional leadership in child-welfare conferences. Nick had found the work meaningful and fulfilling. He was proud of the agency and its work.

A little more than a year ago, however, Nick sensed a shift in the agency that seemed to parallel a trend toward political and theological conservatism in the denomination that supported the agency. The board had hired a new Executive Director, Reverend Carl Matthews, who was not known to the staff before he was hired. Some of the staff did not trust him and believed that he had been hired more for his conservative theology than for his knowledge of family and children's social services. The news in the morning paper seemed to confirm Nick's fears that the needs of children would be less important than church politics. Nick wondered what he would do; after all, the staff would be looking to him for leadership.

A Calling

Nick grew up in the Christian church. He had been born in a Christian hospital in Louisiana. Heavily involved throughout his youth, Nick found all his peers and primary role models in the church. After high school, Nick attended a Christian college and then a seminary, where he met and married his wife. Twenty-two years ago, Nick had entered social work because he saw the profession as an ideal way to live out his religious beliefs and principles. In Christian terms, Nick felt "called" to social work. His personal life and professional career had been formed, nurtured, and sustained by his faith and the denomination that had nurtured him.

While obtaining his MSW, Nick had worked as a houseparent at LCHC, and had fallen in love with the children in the program. Furthermore, the mission and purpose of the agency—"to provide a safe haven and loving home for hurting children"—resonated with Nick's calling. After graduate school, Nick worked in mental health agencies as a therapist and then as an administrator. But child welfare was Nick's passion, and he had been thrilled when, more than a decade ago, the opportunity came to return to LCHC as the Director of Family-Based Services.

Nick enjoyed his work. He was proud of the investment he had made in building the agency and making many positive contributions. The agency enjoyed a positive reputation both locally and statewide, and it was one of only two agencies in Louisiana accredited by the national child-welfare accreditation organization. When Nick had been seeking employment, other professionals in the field had recommended the agency as one of the best. The schools of social work of two local universities valued the agency for the opportunities it presented for students' field education. Furthermore, the benefits package of the agency was exceptional for a child-welfare agency, including four weeks vacation, several holidays off, and the best insurance benefits and retirement plan of any child-welfare agency in the state. Nick planned to retire from the agency in about 10 more years and looked forward to the opportunity to have time for his passions of travel and golf, as well as some work as an international missions volunteer.

Over the years, LCHC's services had grown and changed as it responded to new needs and opportunities. At several sites throughout the state, the agency currently provided an array of services including residential care, foster care, adoptions, family counseling, and in-home family services.

When it first began more than a century before, the agency's funding came exclusively from supporting churches, and its faith-based identity had been clear. Over the years, the funding sources changed, and now the agency received over 75% of its revenue from public sources (i.e., the agency received per diems for clients in its care, most of whom were in the custody of the state, and therefore the Department of Social Services was the primary funding resource for the agency's services). Even though the agency was now incorporated separately, it was still identified with its denomination. The LCHC Board was appointed by the state denominational Board, with considerable input from the LCHC Executive Director. The Executive Director gave a list of recommendations to the state Board, which then chose from that list those who would serve on the LCHC Board. Although only 25% of its annual budget came from the denomination (i.e., the denomination's congregations and individuals), that portion was vital to the agency's operation. The Christian identity and mission of the agency was an issue that it continued to grapple with over the years, particularly the expression of this identity through staffing and programming.

Matthews had told Nick that he did not pretend to be a social worker. Instead, what he brought to the agency was his ability to relate to congregations, who provided financial support for the agency. Congregations could also provide volunteers, and perhaps communities of support for families and children at risk of disruption, or who had already been damaged by life circumstances. Nick agreed in part with Matthews's perception of the role of congregations in the work of the agency. He knew that many of the families they served needed community support and mentors, resources that the professional staff could only provide in limited ways. Could the agency both provide highly professional services to troubled children and families and also work with congregations who could be communities for these families? It made sense theoretically, but Nick wondered if some of the conservative congregations in their denomination would really be able to understand the situations of the families in the agency's programs.

The previous Executive Director had been a social worker and, from Nick's perspective, had led the agency with both social work expertise and religious values. Since the appointment of Carl Matthews as Executive Director, Nick had worried about the direction of the agency. Matthews had made several administrative decisions that troubled Nick, for example, appointing people without social work credentials or experience to key positions in the agency. Because he was not a social worker himself and because most of his experience was with congregational ministry, Reverend Matthews seemed to have a limited understanding of social services in general and child welfare in particular.

Nick believed that the previous Executive Director of the agency had valued its independence. Similar to trends in many faith-based organizations, the previous director had sought to put distance between the professional services of the agency and the denomination that had historically supported it.

He had focused on hiring professionally competent staff members and had paid less attention to denominational and congregational ties. Although they continued to talk about the agency being a Christian agency, many staff members did not belong to any of the denomination's congregations—or any congregation for that matter. Religious beliefs and values had not been considered in the hiring process.

Carl Matthews preferred the reverse strategy. He believed that the denominational ties were vital to the future of the agency and had sought to bring LCHC even closer to the denomination. First, he believed that the agency should strengthen its identity as a Christian organization. Second, in a time of shrinking government support for social services, Matthews believed that the agency's future would be brighter if their work was clearly positioned as the ministry of the church. Consequently, he acted in ways that would actually give the denomination more involvement with the agency. Moreover, in his private and public statements, Matthews conveyed a clear and unquestioning alignment with the conservative trend of the denomination. This position particularly troubled Nick. Although he was frankly more comfortable with downplaying the religious identity of the agency and emphasizing professional standards and services, Nick had some appreciation of the rights of a faith-based agency to define its mission. However, he did not like the way the more conservative elements of the denomination were interpreting what it meant to be a Christian agency. There was a lot of talk about "family values" and the importance of the nuclear family, a focus that seemed ironic to Nick because most of the children they served were in foster or residential care.

Despite the shifting priorities in the last year, Nick had continued to believe that he had an important role to fill in the agency. Carl Matthews had listened to his advice on several policy decisions, and he believed that he was having some positive influence. Perhaps he could be the voice for professional social work while Matthews dealt with the denomination and its congregations. Although it made Nick nervous, the plan seemed to make sense in some ways. He could see how these changes might increase the financial resilience of the agency and perhaps enhance the quality of services.

Whatever happened, Nick had commented to his spouse and friends that he planned to "wait this out" because he did not think that the agency's conservative shift would last too long. As Nick said to several confidantes about Matthews, "I was here before he came, and I'll be here after he's gone."

A Firing

Returning the night before from a relaxing summer vacation with his family, Nick had expected to face the usual onslaught of piled papers, multiple messages, and postponed situations—all needing "immediate" attention. Before he even left for the office that Monday morning, however, the newspaper sitting on the kitchen table caught his attention: "Lesbian Therapist Fired at Children's Home." With disbelief, he skimmed the article—it was about LCHC. Nick gulped down his coffee and headed for the office, wondering what would await him there. So much for relaxing vacations!

Joy, a supervisee, came into Nick's office as soon as he arrived, closed the door, and told him what he had already read in the morning newspaper: an employee in another department had been fired on Friday because she was a lesbian. Joy was furious and frightened: "How can they do this? If they can fire someone for being a lesbian, who will be next? An employee who has a drink after work? An employee who had an abortion? Anybody could be fired for anything they deem 'sinful'? Any of us could be next!"

Although Nick knew Joy to be a reliable source of information, he was sure that she had somehow misunderstood. There had to be more to it. "Perhaps a disgruntled employee is spreading the rumor that she had been fired to take the heat off herself," Nick thought. Quickly, Nick called other staff members, including his supervisor, to check the veracity of Joy's report. Each time, Nick was told that, indeed, the employee had been fired because she was a lesbian. There was no other reason.

Over the next few days, Nick continued to learn more about the situation. He learned that the fired employee, Maria, had been working with the agency for only a few months. She worked in another area of the agency, as a therapist in a group home for male adolescents. Being in a different department in the large agency, Nick had only met Maria briefly at her orientation when he presented some information about the agency. Nick continued to ask questions. "Surely there were other issues," he thought. But staff members familiar with her work said that she had excellent rapport with her clients and seemed very committed to them. Maria had her master's degree in art therapy and had previous experience working in child welfare.

Nick learned more. He learned that Maria was in a long-term relationship with a partner. She had shared information about her sexual orientation with her direct supervisor when she had been hired. Because of the agency's denominational affiliation, the agency had some unwritten policies regarding personal conduct. For example, if the staff consumed alcohol or engaged in sexual relations outside of marriage—whether homosexual or heterosexual—their actions could be considered unethical and grounds for discipline or dismissal. Because of these policies, Maria's direct supervisor had advised her to follow a "don't ask, don't tell" policy. Maria agreed to keep her sexual orientation confidential because she wanted to do the work of the agency.

In her personal life, however, Maria chose to live openly. Another employee, a houseparent in a cottage, had seen Maria walking with her partner in a community gay pride march in downtown Shreveport. The employee observed that Maria and her partner were holding hands, and he reported this information to his supervisor and then to Carl Matthews. When confronted, Maria had acknowledged her sexual orientation, and Matthews had decided she should be terminated immediately. Her direct supervisor told Nick that he had argued that Maria was an outstanding clinician and that losing her would be very hard for the children she worked with, many of whom had suffered multiple losses when removed from their homes and put into the child-welfare system. The clinical supervisor had said Maria's job performance had been stellar, and discrimination based on any reason, including sexual orientation or behavior, was wrong. Matthews had said, "I appreciate her good work, but I have a responsibility to uphold standards of behavior that our church believes to be right. And I have to say, I agree with the church on this. These children are in our care." After the

firing, Matthews wrote and disseminated a policy statement that read "a homosexual lifestyle is not congruent with the agency's values."

Later in the week, Nick learned that Maria was at the agency cleaning out her desk. He felt compelled to go see her to express his disappointment and dismay about the actions taken against her. Nick introduced himself to Maria, who was quite cordial, under the circumstances. They talked briefly about the situation, and Maria confirmed what Nick had already learned from the staff. Nick offered his support and encouraged Maria to follow the grievance process outlined in the agency handbook. Nick was particularly familiar with this process since he had chaired the committee that wrote the policy.

Maria stated that she did not know exactly what she would do because she had been completely blindsided by the situation. She felt that because her supervisor had known her orientation and had hired her anyway, she had done what she needed to do to be honest. Nick essentially told her that he felt she had been wronged by the agency, particularly because she had been forthcoming about her sexual orientation when she was hired. Even more, Nick personally believed that this kind of discrimination was not only in violation of his social work values but also his Christian beliefs.

A Dilemma

After confirming the facts of the situation and talking with Maria, Nick only felt worse. Should he have encouraged her to take grievance action? Personally, Nick thought Matthews's firing of Maria was repugnant and morally violated what it meant to be a Christian agency. Professionally, Nick believed that this action would cause irreparable damage to the agency's reputation in the social service community and in the community at large. The media was already broadcasting the story. He believed the Executive Director's decision was a major mistake on several levels.

In the days that followed, there were strong reactions from social workers and others. The social work faculty at St. Regis University, a private, faith-based university in Shreveport, led a campaign, along with the public University of Shreveport, condemning the actions of the agency in a written letter to the media. St. Regis discontinued the placement of social work students in field work at LCHC and the state university did the same. The local chapter of the National Association of Social Workers (NASW) began to lobby at the state level for state contracts with the agency to be withheld, and for children to be placed elsewhere, if the agency continued in its discriminatory personnel policies. Matthews simply dug in deeper in his adamant statements that the agency would support "family values" and its right to protect children from gay men and lesbians. Within a few days, the American Civil Liberties Union (ACLU) released a public statement condemning the actions taken at LCHC.

Instead of being an employee in a highly respected agency, Nick suddenly found himself working for an agency that was being boycotted by his profession. There was no ducking the issue either. The local newspapers were publishing front-page stories, and the incident was starting to gain national attention.

Trusted professional colleagues and personal friends differed in their advice, which was given quite freely. Some people advised, "You must leave immediately. Make a statement that this is wrong!" Betty, a trusted colleague from another agency said, "Nick, you should leave! Staying will only give the message that you condone the agency's decision." Following the same rationale, other colleagues agreed with Betty that Nick should cut all ties immediately

Others advised, " You should stay and try to work to change this policy." Kathy, another colleague outside the agency, said, " Nick, you should stay and use the power you have as a long-term employee, who is respected in the agency, to bring about change." Likewise, others said that Nick should not let the negative forces "win," but should stay and fight. One colleague asserted, "You have invested too much in this agency to just walk away from it. Stay, and keep what is yours."

Representatives of other faith-based agencies in the community had a mixed reaction. A few of them agreed with Matthews on all levels, some agreed with Nick, and others found themselves conflicted.

Nick's friend Roger said, "I disagree with what Matthews did, and I disagree with his interpretation of the Bible, but I think faith-based agencies must have the religious freedom to define their own mission and to employ people who can conscientiously work within it." Another friend said, "My agency is dealing with some of these same issues, and I think it's possible to be conservative and have ethical policies at the same time—you don't think being liberal makes you automatically ethical, do you?"

People in Nick's faith community were equally divided in their advice. Although his wife and most of his family members struggled with him in his decision, a few members of Nick's immediate and extended family were bewildered by his dilemma because they agreed with the decision made to fire Maria. The confused reactions of these family members did not surprise Nick, because he had become accustomed to family members seeing some of his social work values as "strange." These reactions were troubling, however. If his family felt this way, then so did many others in the congregations that identified the agency as "theirs" and supported it. How realistic was it to believe that change could take place? Was Reverend Matthews the problem or was it broader and deeper than that? Are there ways a conservative denominational agency might handle these issues in an ethically serious way? But even if there were, Nick wondered if he could be associated with it.

Nick considered the situation from the personal perspective by praying about it, and from the professional perspective by considering the possibilities for change. He debated the ethics of staying versus leaving and the complexities of creating and maintaining an authentic faith-based agency. He was faced with his own version of Hamlet's question: "To stay or not to stay, that is the question, whether 'tis nobler to. . ." But Nick was not sure what was noble, or just, or right. Were these ideals, like beauty, in the eye of the beholder? And how could he balance these ideals with pragmatic questions such as, "What is realistic?" and "What can I do to make it better?"

To Leave or Not to Leave: That Is the Question
Erlene Grise-Owens

Case Synopsis

The Executive Director of Louisiana Christian Homes for Children (LCHC) fired an employee when he learned that she was a lesbian. Nick Nichols, the Director of Family-Based Services, had been with the agency for a decade and loved his work. When he learned about this situation, Nick was appalled. He found himself facing the difficult decision of whether to stay in the agency where he had invested 10 years of his career or leave in protest. He had to think again about what it meant to maintain his own ethical standards in a complex situation where many competing sets of values were in conflict.

Learning Outcomes Related to Religion and Spirituality

Case discussion will facilitate the work of students as they

1. Identify ways that religion can be both a positive and a negative force in social work practice.

2. Describe how religious and spiritual values can be both congruent and in conflict with social work values and ethics.

3. Appreciate the complexity of the relationship between personal beliefs and professional practice and how they affect service to clients.

4. Consider whether and how best to work for organizational and societal change consistent with one's religious and spiritual values.

Other Learning Outcomes for Which This Case Could Be Used

Case discussion will facilitate the work of students as they

1. Appreciate the complexity of ethical dilemmas, not as simply either/or situations, but rather as multifaceted issues.

2. Understand the importance of critical thinking and reflective practice in social work.

3. Appreciate the systemic nature of both oppression and social justice.

4. Increase awareness regarding discrimination in general and heterosexism in particular.

Courses and Levels for Which the Case Is Intended

This case study may be used at any level of social work study, including continuing education workshops, although the instructor should choose questions and lines of discussion appropriate for the student level. For instance, the case can be used at a BSW level for an introductory discussion to enliven ethical situations. The case can be used at an advanced level to provoke a complex, multifaceted discussion about ethical issues. It can be used in covering content on discrimination and heterosexism, child welfare, critical thinking and reflective practice, values and ethics, spiritual and religious diversity, organizational governance, mission, and funding, and the relationship between religion and social work practice.

Discussion Questions Related to Religion and Spirituality

Some possible responses are given for the Analysis and Action questions. However, it is expected that these responses will be developed much further through the class discussion process and the input of the instructor.

Establishing the Facts

1. What do we know about Nick's personal religion? How is his religion related to his decision to be a social worker?

2. Who are the primary "players" in this scenario? Who are some larger systems players that could impact the situation?

3. What do we know about the changes within the agency over the years of its existence?

Analysis

4. Both Nick and the Executive Director, Carl Matthews, are approaching this issue from a "Christian" perspective. What are some of the differences and commonalties in their definitions of their Christian perspective?

   Both Nick and the Executive Director view their Christian perspective as paramount in making decisions. Both Nick and the Executive Director view their employment as a way to live out their Christian commitments. Further, both view the agency as an extension of their own personal commitment of faith. However, Nick and the Executive Director differ in their interpretations of the Biblical messages regarding homosexuality: The Executive Director views homosexual behavior as sinful, and Nick disagrees with this interpretation. The Executive Director believes he has a

moral responsibility to express his beliefs and those of the supporting denomination as agency policy (e.g., hiring and firing based on religious beliefs and behavior). Nick believes religious requirements and behavioral standards can be discriminatory and not in keeping with his faith.

5. What are arguments for an employment policy that allows the agency to fire an employee based on sexual orientation? What are the arguments against this policy?

   The primary argument for allowing the agency to fire an employee based on sexual orientation is that the agency is a private, faith-based agency and can therefore operate out of the denominational beliefs of its supporting churches. Also, Louisiana is an "at will" state, which means that agencies can fire employees "at will"(i.e., without any particular reason or cause). The primary argument against this policy is that the agency is primarily supported by public funds, which means that it has a public accountability. Also, this situation raises the issue of whether any agency, private or public, should be allowed to discriminate in hiring.

6. What are the personal values influencing Nick's response to this situation? What are the applicable social work values? Do any of these personal and professional values conflict? If so, how would you resolve that conflict? If not, explain your rationale.

   Nick's personal values include meaningful work, personal travel, a certain lifestyle (e.g., having a stable and adequate income and being able to retire at an age early enough to enjoy it), and a commitment to the social work profession as a means of living out one's sense of personal calling. He sees his social work values and religious values as complementing each other. Social work values include social justice, service to clients, and nondiscrimination. Although these social work values are also values held by Nick, they could conflict in several ways with his personal values. For example, the value of a certain income might conflict with a choice to quit the job in protest. Discuss the personal and professional costs and how to resolve those.

7. Using the National Association of Social Workers (NASW) Code of Ethics, identify the ratio-

nale that could be used to argue that Nick should stay at the agency. Identify the rationale in the Code that could be used to argue that Nick should leave.

The purpose of this question is to encourage students to link their professional decisions with the Code of Ethics and to increase their understanding of the Code's complexity. For instance, the Code states that social workers should not be employed in agencies that discriminate—possible rationale that Nick should leave the agency. At the same time, the Code states that social workers should work in systems to eliminate discrimination—possible rationale that Nick should stay and work for change (e.g., see Code of Ethics, 3.09, Commitment to Employers). The Code of Ethics also recognizes that its principles can sometimes come into tension or conflict with one another in practice situations and judgments have to be made to prioritize principles in such situations. It could also be argued that religious freedom is another value or ethical principle that is involved in this case, and that Nick and Carl Matthews may both be trying to honor that value in their own ways. The Code says, for example, "the NASW Code of Ethics does not specify which values, principles, and standards are most important and ought to outweigh others in instances when they conflict. Reasonable differences of opinion can and do exist among social workers with respect to the ways in which values, ethical principles, and ethical standards should be rank ordered when they conflict. Ethical decision making in a given social situation must apply the informed judgment of the individual social worker. . ." The Code continues, "Social workers also should be aware of the impact on ethical decision making of their clients' and their own personal values and cultural and religious beliefs and practices. They should be aware of any conflicts between personal and professional values and deal with them responsibly." (Code of Ethics, Preamble)

8. How might Nick's decision be impacted if he was a gay man? What if he had only begun his employment recently, or if he was within a few years of retirement from the agency? What if the agency was located in a rural area with limited employment opportunities and for compelling personal reasons he needed to stay in the area? Discuss the costs and benefits of each scenario, both personally and professionally.

This question follows up on the discussion from question 6. Its primary purpose is to provoke a greater understanding of the complexity of costs and benefits in ethical decisions, helping students challenge standard, uncritical responses in decision making.

9. How does the organizational structure of the agency impact this situation? What about organizational auspices? Policy?

The power of one person, the Executive Director, in setting policy is evident in this situation. Furthermore, the Executive Director has influenced the path of the agency by making moves to enhance the connection between the agency and the conservative denominational auspices. Additionally, the Board of Directors also has significant power in setting policy. The unwritten "don't ask, don't tell" policy had significant implications in this situation. The implementation of a new policy regarding sexual orientation in response to these events has significant ramifications at several levels. Other policy issues related to this matter include the policies of the state Department of Social Services (i.e., this presents a question about the legality of the state contracting with an agency that discriminates based on sexual orientation).

10. What impact does the fact that the agency's primary funding source (over 75%) is the state Department of Social Services have on this situation? Does the funding matter? How do issues of separation of church and state play out in this scenario?

Here it is important to know that since this incident, the American Civil Liberties Union (ACLU) has brought a federal lawsuit against the agency and the state Department of Social Services. The basis of their lawsuit is that the funding does indeed matter. The ACLU contends that a private, faith-based agency cannot have discriminatory practices when they are primarily supported with public funds—even if the agency argues that these practices are based on religious principles. Further, the ACLU argues that a public entity (i.e., the state) should not contract with private agencies with discriminatory practices. Also, this question can lead to an interesting discussion on the broader topic of faith-based social services supported by government funding.

Action

11. What decisions must Nick make soon? What are the longer-term decisions? What will help Nick decide which is which?

    An important point for this discussion is that this ethical situation, like many others, is not an either/or decision. That is, Nick could decide to stay for a period of time in order to see if he could make changes within the agency or until he has another job, thus deciding both to stay and to leave. The decisions that Nick must make soon involve his immediate response to this firing (e.g., What should he say to the other staff? Should he ask for a meeting with the Executive Director?). Longer-term decisions involve whether he should contact NASW, the media, the ACLU? If he decides to leave, should he continue to be involved in the issue? Slowing down the process of decision making, discussing his choices with trusted advisors, and remaining focused on his principles will help in the decision process. Also, simply asking questions like, "Do I have to decide about this at this moment? What information do I need to make this decision?" will help Nick decide what is most pressing and will help prevent premature reactions.

12. How might you respond to this issue if the agency fired someone, based on religious reasons, because she was divorced or cohabiting with a male? What if she was fired because she was seen drinking alcohol in a restaurant, she was black, she was Muslim, or she had an abortion? Would your response be different or much the same?

    This question should be used to help students think critically and recognize biases.

13. If Nick decides to stay, what actions should he take? What might be some of the costs and benefits of these actions? If he decides to leave, what additional actions should he take? What might be some of the costs and benefits of these actions?

    If Nick decides to stay, he could meet with the Executive Director and other administrative staff and work to change the policy. As an informed social worker, Nick could share with appropriate agency personnel NASW's position on this issue and probable reactions of the social service community. Nick could consult with NASW about possible actions to address this issue of discrimination. He could speak out in various forums in the agency against the policy and offer constructive alternatives. Nick could also organize agency personnel to protest the action. Any of these actions have the benefit of pursuing justice and correcting oppressive policies and actions. The costs might include being ostracized within the agency, being misunderstood by colleagues who believe he should leave, and continuing to deal with the stress of an unfriendly environment. Also, Nick could contact the Board of Directors and communicate his dismay with the Executive Director's decision. He could contact the media, the ACLU, or other sources to provide information about the events at the agency and to promote the correction of the action. If Nick was discovered taking any of these actions while an employee, he could be fired.

    If Nick decides to leave, he could make the same contacts, but the costs would be different (i.e., he would not risk being fired, though he might risk the agency's retribution in other ways, such as refusing to provide a job reference). Nick could attempt to bring public attention to his action of leaving as a protest, which could bring personal and professional gratification. If Nick left the agency, he would lose his source of income (unless he had an immediate job), and he would lose the exceptional benefits package. He would also risk not being able to find a job that provided him meaningful employment.

14. Identify the micro, mezzo, and macro issues in this scenario. How do these levels influence and relate to each other? What are some rights and responsibilities associated with each of these levels (e.g., the rights of the clients in this situation)? What are some actions that could be taken at each of these levels?

    Micro issues include the individual impact on Maria, Nick, other affected employees, and Maria's clients. Mezzo issues include the impact of this policy on the staff and the clients as groups and the use of group power to influence decisions. Macro issues include the impact of organizational and state policies. Each of these levels systemically influences the others. For instance, the organization's policies determine the firing of an individual employee, which in turn affects the clients' experiences. Maria, Nick, and the other employees have the right to fair employment policies. Clients have the right to uninterrupted and competent service, and the right to a spectrum of role models. The individual employees and the agency have a responsibility to provide the best service possible to clients. At each of these levels, the best service to clients should be a primary determining factor, and the clients' voices should be heard.

Teaching Suggestions

The instructor may divide the class into two sections to present rationales for the different aspects of any of the above questions.

Additional Notes

The instructor may divide the class into small groups to emphasize varying viewpoints and increase their understanding of these viewpoints. Assign each group the identity of one of the key players, both micro and macro (i.e., Nick, Carl Matthews, Maria, Maria's supervisor, Maria's clients, LCHC's Board, and the Director of the state Department of Social Services). Ask the groups to assume the role of their assigned identities. In a role-play format, have the class discuss the different perspectives. Ask the students to talk about the beliefs, thoughts, and feelings surrounding their perspectives and to defend their positions in this case.

10.

Do We Have to Go Now? Challenges in Foster Care and Adoption

Elisabeth Kenny

September 2

"Sometimes it all works out," thought Sarah Roberts, as she planned her September visits to the foster and adopting families she served. After 14 years as a worker in her state's Family and Children's Bureau, she had handled all kinds of problems and situations with foster and adoptive parents–problems with children's behavior, problems with foster parents' lack of understanding or skills for handling children, and serious breaches of the licensing code governing the care of children. She felt she had learned to deal with any situation and to find the best solutions for the safety of the children who were placed by the courts in the guardianship of her agency. Now she faced a wonderful situation, a reward for all the educating and problem solving she had done. Nine African American families had accepted children to foster or adopt, and the children were all stable and adjusting—an ideal caseload. Yet she also knew the precarious nature of the period when adoptive families are forming and getting to know one another: the children testing their parents' commitment, and the parents learning how to love and nurture children who may have been damaged in their earliest days. She had high hopes for these families—and some apprehension and concern as well.

The Beginning—January 6

In the tiny community of Prairie Grove in the northeastern corner of Montgomery County, many children had recently found homes through Sarah's agency. Most of the people in Prairie Grove lived in stable families, occupying the same community since childhood. Many had already raised children, and many were related to one another, working in the same factories and agricultural businesses, and attending the same small church. Their minister, Rev. Elijah Parker and his wife, Mary Parker, had come to the conclusion that they personally were led by God to be foster parents. When they called to talk about their intention, Sarah recalled that she had heard of this couple and their congregation— New Salem Independent Missionary Christian Church. The couple had been active for years, working to improve services for the children in their local school. Sarah had been impressed with them and their group at a community advocacy meeting several months before. She already knew them to be committed to their cause, and that was a wonderful attribute in a foster or an adoptive family. The couple told Sarah that the information circulated by the Independent Missionary Christian Synod about "Our Children Sunday" had stuck in their minds. This exhortation for each congregation to consider supporting a family from among its midst in fostering or adopting a child in need had "worked powerfully" on him, said Rev. Parker. "My wife and I have prayed over this matter for a long time, Ms. Roberts, and we feel called to open our home and our family to a child who needs us."

This was a typical statement for Rev. Parker—he firmly believed in divine guidance in everything he did. His strong religious faith made him a powerful preacher and a guide for his congregation in helping to discern the right path. Mary was no less strong in her beliefs, and she stated that prayer, discussion, and searching of the Scriptures, which she and her husband pursued in determining the course of their lives, had of late turned their minds toward parenting children who needed stability and love in a Christian home. Mary Parker spoke of another strong belief which helped form their intention to foster a child: "As African Americans, we need to take care of our own...how can we ask others to care for our children?"

When they contacted the child-welfare office and spoke with Sarah, she immediately sensed their commitment and their strong feelings. She was experienced with new foster parents and appreciated how much their commitment and their strength would sustain them. She still tried to tell them of the pitfalls ahead—children coming into foster care often have health, learning, and behavior problems. They may have habits that are difficult to live with, and they very often regress in behavior, bedwetting or becoming passive and noncommunicative from the injuries they have experienced and the strangeness of foster parents' expectations. It seemed to Sarah that the Parkers had done their homework about foster parenting and were aware of these difficulties.

"We've read the pamphlet from Family and Children's Services, Ms. Roberts." said Rev. Parker. "We've talked to foster and adoptive parents in our partner church across the state. We know it'll mean three months of classes and a home study. Oh, yes—physical exams, get the water well tested, fire inspections, background checks. We know too that these children are often real troublemakers at home and school, but we know it is because of how they've been treated...and our two boys were no angels!"

Sarah was pleased that the Parkers had taken the initiative. "There's more you have to consider, though. You will lose your privacy to some degree, you know, because we will be talking with you to get to know you well, to be able to place and to supervise the children with you. We want the children

who come to you to fit with your way of life and for all of you to succeed as a family. But it does mean a lot of intrusion."

"Miss Sarah, we know that," Mary Parker told her. "We understand you all have to be sure we can care for children. And as a minister's wife, I am certainly used to being in the public eye!" she finished with a smile.

Preparing—February through May

The Parkers knew that it would take months of training before they would have a child in their home. However, they were very committed to the idea of foster parenting, so Sarah began the application process. When Rev. Parker shared his vision with the New Salem congregation, he received an enthusiastic response. After much discussion and prayer, several other couples declared their intention to join the Parkers. Sarah's foster parents' training class for that spring consisted of 15 members of Rev. Parker's congregation, seven couples and one single parent. Sarah told them, "I have never seen such a dedicated group of beginning foster parents—you really must feel you have a vocation for caring for children!"

As the classes continued, Sarah tested them on issues which often discouraged foster parents, bad language, stealing, lying, sexual acting out, and other behaviors which often occur in children who have been neglected, physically assaulted, subjected to foul language, and infected with lawless adult behavior experienced throughout their formative years. Often, this behavior shocks foster parents from strongly religious backgrounds because of its contrast to what they expect of children in their community. But the class was not daunted by descriptions of the possible problems ahead, and instead seemed more determined than ever to learn how to help and nurture these children. Sarah admired the spirit of solidarity among these parents. She thought to herself, "they are going to be able to support one another; what a strength!" She viewed the stability and the empathy that the children would experience in these homes as probably the most healing environment possible for traumatized children.

Sarah herself was not a church member. Sometimes she found herself uncomfortable with Rev.

Parker's outspoken trust in his Lord and his constant references to what the Lord required of him. She had in the past encountered the judgmental attitudes of some "religious" people who felt they knew the right path and discounted, or even condemned, those on another path. These past experiences were one reason she had tried to make the realities of fostering or adopting children clear to the people of New Salem Church and to prompt them to develop strategies for dealing with problems they had not faced before, even those who had raised children previously. She was so pleased when they supported one another as they found solutions to problems, and when they expressed real empathy for the children who had experienced traumatic home and family life.

During one class they "brainstormed" how they might deal with children who used unacceptable language in school and at home. "Miss Sarah," one grandmotherly foster parent told her, "I have never allowed the kind of four-letter words you just described to be used in my home. I know, though, that if that is all these babies have ever heard around them, that is how they'll talk. I can understand why, but how can I change it? Because I *must* change it!"

"Maybe we can do like we did when my Cedric came back from visiting his cousins in Detroit," said her sister-in-law, Anna Baker. "Remember? He had learned so many of those big-city words that we were embarrassed for him to go into public. We told him the words he should not use, made up some silly words to use instead, and put a nickel in a jar each time he used a 'non-curse' made up word. He treated it like a game, and we rewarded him for using the 'non-curse' word. And we didn't tell him he was bad for picking up that city talk."

Sarah was delighted when the group continued to discuss other ways they might work on bad language in children, as well as other problems they might encounter, without stigmatizing the children for the unacceptable behavior they might bring with them.

The Children Come Home—June, July, and August

The initial placements into the New Salem homes went well. Sarah was secretly glad that the individual children and sibling groups chosen for the newly-certified foster homes were younger children. Teaching preschoolers how to use a toothbrush, how to eat with spoons and forks instead of hands, and how to overcome bedwetting and other regressive behaviors seems natural for children of 3, 4, and even 5 or 6. Teaching 10 year olds not to do these things would have been much harder.

As Sarah checked her stack of forms, before her monthly visit to the Parkers' home, she felt pleased with the way their placement was going. The Parkers had eagerly welcomed a sibling group of three, boys 6 and 7, and their 3-year-old sister. Removed from their birth home because of severe neglect by their substance-abusing mother, they had lived in different homes until all three could be reunited in a single foster home. Now James, Paul, and Miriam were free for adoption, and because their foster family did not wish to adopt, a gradual transition over weeks of visits and overnights had taken place, until they were finally placed with the Parkers during the summer vacation.

The children had all at first overeaten, sometimes to the point of making themselves sick, in the Parkers' home. The Parkers knew that this was not unusual for children who have experienced hunger on a regular basis and who have led a chaotic existence, not knowing whether or when they would be fed again. James, the eldest, was a little parent to his siblings, worrying over them and telling the foster parents how to feed his little sister.

"Another thing we learned in Fostering Class!" the Parkers told Sarah, "a 'parentified child'!"

They related how they had called the first foster parents to discover how they had handled these situations. When the children first visited the Parkers, they had met with the Jenkins, the foster parents with whom the children had lived for a year, and they had talked about the children's habits and preferences. Wilbur and Elizabeth Jenkins had urged them to call any time they had questions.

Miriam's dependence on her brothers, and her unwillingness to learn to "do" for herself, to put on her shoes and dress herself, to give up the bottle, and to sleep in her own bed were readily accepted by the Parkers. And the couple welcomed and understood Paul, the "typical" middle child, with his sudden rages and aggressive behavior, his dependence upon and strong competition with James.

"That's how our grown sons were, too, Ms. Roberts. Very competitive. We called them Cain and Abel, between my wife and me," Rev. Parker explained with a smile.

"The first four months have gone pretty well," thought Sarah. The Parkers and their cohort of new foster parents had coped well initially, had shared with one another how they were handling their new situation, and now had enrolled their children in school for the beginning of the school year, approaching the teachers and administrators in a spirit of helpfulness and cooperation in educating their children.

A Problem—September

Sarah's first clue that there was a problem came when she drove up to the Parker home next to the church. Instead of three little people playing on the swing set, as was the usual sight at 4:30 on a September afternoon, Sarah saw James and Miriam sitting silently on the swing. They rushed up to her, and hugged her legs.

"Where's Paul?" she asked.

"Inside," James said in a frightened voice.

Miriam whispered, "Do we have to go now?"

Sarah gave each child a pad and crayons she had brought for them, and set them to coloring at the picnic table, a little calmer now, before she rang the doorbell. She was met by Elijah Parker, who looked more solemn than she had ever seen him. Mary Parker was behind him, appearing serious and annoyed. "We have to talk, Ms. Roberts," said Rev. Parker.

Mary Parker began. "Miss Sarah, I think we've done a good job helping these little ones with their fears. We understand their anxiety about being fed and cared for—we expected it, and when Miriam got bellyaches after eating more than she needed at every meal, and the boys put food 'for later' under their beds, we coped. We told them a bedtime story about the joy we felt when they came to us, about how this was their 'forever home' and that there would always be love and hugs for them from us. The story told them about the things they would have—food every day, a teddy bear for Miriam, clean clothes and bunk beds to sleep in for the boys. They love the story and ask for it every night. They began to relax, and accept that they would not be sepa-

rated, nor would they leave their home. Elizabeth Jenkins told me they had crackers and juice boxes available all the time on a special shelf in the kitchen, so the children would always know they could get food. We thought that was such a good idea that we have done that, too."

Rev. Parker continued in a serious tone. "We've got no more bellyaches, no pockets full of cookies. We thought the food hidden under the bed was all over, Ms. Roberts. The boys are learning right from wrong in Sunday School. What would make Paul steal? And keep on stealing, even after we tell him he should not?"

"Stealing?" Sarah asked in a surprised voice.

Rev. Parker began describing the day's events. "We are still finding food under his mattress, behind the headboard, in a sack under the bed."

Mary Parker exclaimed, "Not even food that keeps easy like bread or crackers, but bananas and half a can of Vienna sausages! I smelled it and had to check under his bed. It was really awful."

Mrs. Parker explained that she felt Paul might still be reacting to his early years of deprivation, and that her husband was being too strict, "I think Paul needs more time, maybe, than the others, to settle down and believe that he is here to stay. Just because Miriam and James have settled down doesn't mean he has, too. He's a different child, much more intense than his brother."

But then Mary Parker asked, "You know, the children were in a good foster home with the Jenkins before they came here. For over a year they have had regular meals, all they wanted, and good nurturing care. How long does it take before they get over it?"

Elijah Parker said, "No, Mary, I believe he has been with us long enough that he has learned better. Ms. Roberts, she has just told you some of the things we have done to help the children get over the terrible deprivation they experienced when they were just babies. I think all we have done has worked. Look at James! Look at Miriam! And besides, these children have been learning right from wrong. They are in Sunday School and my wife and I pray and talk with them daily. Yes, I know children are not perfect in understanding and in being responsible for choosing to do right, but he is a bright boy—his understanding is so good about other things, that I am sure, very sure, that Paul is choosing to do wrong, to take food and hide it. He is choosing to steal!"

Sarah could see how seriously the Parkers viewed the incident. Paul was in his room, and all three children had been told that Paul had stolen.

"How do you want to handle it?" Sarah asked the Parkers, to give herself time to think, and also to assess more deeply the parents' feelings.

"Well, Ms. Roberts," Rev. Parker said. "I remember from our Fostering Class that we don't use physical correction with the children. You told us that spanking a child who has already been physically abused just makes the problem worse. Interferes with the parent-child bond we're trying to form, and only teaches children to use force themselves. I understand all that. But here is a case where I think a serious talk and a spanking would help Paul learn just how bad stealing is. When we were raising our boys, we did not correct them physically very often. But for offenses like this, for something Paul knows is wrong, a spanking will help teach him. Now, I haven't laid a hand on him yet. But I think I should, to discipline him about stealing. You know, Scripture tells us 'He who spares his rod hates his son but he who loves him takes care to chastise him,' and I think this is a mighty serious matter."

Sarah wondered if this placement might be in jeopardy. If the Parkers used physical discipline, they would contravene the licensing regulations which govern foster and adoptive homes, and a corrective action by the agency would result. This could affect the final decision on completing the adoption. On the other hand, if they were not empowered to deal with a matter they viewed as very serious, how could they continue to bond with and parent Paul and his brother and sister?

10.teaching note

Do We Have to Go Now? Challenges in Foster Care and Adoption

Elisabeth Kenny

Case Synopsis

As an employee of the state Family and Children's Bureau, Sarah had always upheld standards for foster parents that supported humane and psychologically sound treatment for children. But when she visited three children recently placed in an African American, faith-based New Salem community, she found the adoptive parents, the Parkers, reluctant to abandon cultural discipline practices that contravened her agency's standards. Sarah believed that the main cultural factor behind these disciplinary measures was the Parkers' deeply held religious beliefs, which also accounted for the for the strength and stability of the Parker home. Sarah did not want to shift the children to another home because the move would have destroyed the trust that Miriam, James, and Paul were developing toward the Parkers.

Learning Outcomes Related to Religion and Spirituality

The case discussion will facilitate the work of students as they

1. Identify the potential conflicts between social work practice and the beliefs of diverse populations, especially religious communities.

2. Identify the strengths of a faith-based community that can be used in interventions chosen for clients.

3. Identify the choices of action that often result from the spiritual or cultural values of a population.

Learning Outcomes for Which This Case Can Be Used

The case discussion will facilitate the work of students as they

4. Identify possible cultural sources of conflict between social workers and clients.

5. Identify agency policy and conflict with the community, whether it be a client community, as in this case, or the larger community. Is child-welfare work especially prone to lack of community understanding?

6. Connect actual social work situations with the values and ethics of the profession (in this example, respect for cultural diversity and the right of self-determination of clients).

Courses and Levels for Which the Case Is Intended

This case may be used at either the BSW or MSW level. It may be useful in discussions on values and ethics, foster care and adoption, parenting, childhood development, spirituality, organizational policy, congregations, and faith-based organizations.

Discussion Questions Related to Religion and Spirituality

Establishing the Facts

1. What do you know about Sarah's personal religious beliefs? Are her spiritual values different from those of the New Salem community?

    Sarah subscribes to no set religious belief and does have some distrust of "religious" individuals who condemn others' choices. Yet she recognizes the strength and internal support which the religious community of New Salem possesses, and the stability the faith of the community will give the children placed in these homes.

    Sarah believes the use of physical correction is harmful to children who have experienced abuse and neglect, whereas the New Salem Church community believes that Scripture admonishes them to use physical correction.

2. What do you know about the Parkers' personal beliefs about children and discipline?

    See section "A Problem – September."

Analysis

3. What conflicts do you see here?

    Conflict between Sarah's standards and the Parkers' and the community's belief that physical discipline is sanctioned by Scripture, the revered basis of their religious belief.

4. What is Sarah's dilemma?

    Sarah's dilemma is the conflict between her responsibility to uphold the regulations that ensure the children's safety and appropriate care in foster and adoptive homes, and her need to support this very strong family in finding ways to discipline and to understand the children who have come to them. Unless Sarah can find a way to help the Parkers correct their children with measures compatible with both their beliefs and the agency's standards, these parents may feel they cannot take on the job of raising the children within their value system. On the other hand, they are faced with a common situation for foster and adoptive parents: their home, with all the love, attention, and religious values it offers Paul, James, and Miriam, will not provide a quick remedy for the children's earlier trauma.

5. What do you see as "the best interests of the child" in this case?

    Children are badly served when foster or adoptive placements break down, and children are forced to move, once again leaving a home and a family in which they have begun to get comfortable. Additionally, the children often feel that they were at fault to some degree. The long-term effects of multiple moves are well documented as leading to instability in the child's psychological and emotional development. The "best interests of the child" in this case might be to support the permanence of the placement by helping the adoptive family find ways to teach their values while insuring the children's safety from discipline which might be traumatic in light of previous abuse or neglect. No home is perfect, and to wait for a "perfect" adoptive home would entail keeping children waiting for years. On the other hand, the Parkers clearly wish to violate their agreement to avoid physical correction. The policy that foster parents refrain from using physical correction has been established for the best interests of the child.

6. What qualities and strengths do the Parkers and the New Salem community possess which can be brought to bear on the healing process which the children must go through?

    A strong religious belief gives this church community close identification with other church members. They have the stability of knowing their beliefs are shared by their community. Their religious beliefs give them positive standards which can help them provide structure and values to the children in their homes. The closeness of their community will aid them in becoming the proverbial village that it takes to raise a child.

Action

7. What must Sarah do? What decisions must she make?

    She must help the Parkers and the other New Salem parents find ways to teach their children according to their beliefs and yet not contravene the agency regulations for humane treatment of children. She must advocate for understanding of the long-term effects of past abuse and neglect on the children and remind the parents that recovery may take a very long time. She must, ultimately, decide on the placement of the children.

8. How might Sarah help the Parkers and the other New Salem families to express their strong values without compromising licensing standards with regard to discipline?

Rev. Parker mentioned his discussion of fostering with foster and adoptive parents in New Salem's "sister church" across the state. Experienced adoptive families from that congregation might be sought out to share with the New Salem families how they handled discipline and how they coped with similar situations. Other experienced African American foster and adoptive families might be found in Sarah's case list to provide the same guidance. These families might form the nucleus of a support group for the parents of the New Salem congregation, where questions of discipline such as the one faced by the Parkers might be opened to all. A culturally sensitive therapist could consult to help them resolve this issue. A number of texts on parenting address education in values comparable to the values of the New Salem families. Other culturally sensitive sources might be books such as the following:

Comer, J. P., & Poussaint, A. F. (1992). *Raising black children.* New York: Plume Books.

Rycus, J. S., & Hughes, R. C. (1998). *Field guide to child welfare: Placement and permanence* (vol. 4). Washington, DC: Child Welfare League of America Press.

Fahlberg, V. I. (1991). *A child's journey through placement.* Indianapolis, IN: Perspective Press.

9. How might Sarah be proactive in her social work practice with the other parents to avoid similar problems?

Similar problems with "stealing" or "lying" and other behaviors are bound to surface in the New Salem foster and adoptive families. Sarah would be wise to put into place some techniques to support the parents through these coming crises. Once the Parkers have come to terms with Paul's behavior without jeopardizing their adoptive status, they are in a position to mentor other parents. Rev. Parker's position as a natural source of advice and leadership for his congregation makes certain the couple's inclusion in efforts to help other parents struggling with similar problems. Sarah may also make available some educational sources in training sessions for the whole parent group. A support group for these parents might be a way to present helpful material and also elicit input from other parents of the group who are handling similar situations.

Teaching Suggestions

The instructor may begin with questions to set the context for this worker's dilemma. Help students recognize the strengths and limitations of using congregations as a resource in social work. Lead students to understand how agency policy and legal issues function in this kind of a dilemma. Encourage students to consider proactive and preventive measures to address potential problems in parenting. To explore these issues more deeply, students may be divided into small groups to design culturally and religiously sensitive programs of education or support for foster parents.

Additional Notes

11.

Helping the Homeless: Our Way or the Highway
Beryl Hugen and Pam Doty-Nation

On a hot afternoon in June 1999, John Ashland received a call from Sherry Palmer. John was the director of Love Your Neighbor, a small, faith-based Christian agency in rural Dolton, Kentucky. Sherry had been asked to leave the local homeless shelter where she was living, and she wanted help finding permanent housing. Although her request initially appeared to be a simple one, it would eventually force John into a major confrontation with his friend Fred Lammers, the director of the homeless shelter.

Love Your Neighbor

Love Your Neighbor was an ecumenical, nonprofit agency whose primary mission was to serve Dolton by providing opportunities for church members to assist their community. The goal was to connect church people to their neighbors in need. Volunteers had the option of sharing their faith with clients, but this aspect had to be secondary to meeting the specific need for which they had agreed to provide assistance. These needs typically included transportation, medical assistance, legal services, lawn mowing, and house painting. Volunteers rarely provided money.

Love Your Neighbor had been open for only 6 months when Sherry had sought help. Hired to get this new nonprofit agency started, John had moved to Dolton 9 months earlier. For the past 20 years he had worked in churches and faith-based organizations in Tennessee and northern Georgia. He had

also recently completed his BSW social work degree, and he felt well equipped to assist Sherry with her problem.

Good News Mission Shelter

The Good News Mission Shelter served about 35 residents, both men and women who were a mixture of transients, indigents, and others with short-term shelter needs. Located in an old downtown hotel, it had been founded 15 years before by Don Wilson, who had converted to Christianity while serving time in prison for robbery. Upon his release, he started the program as an evangelistic ministry to the homeless. Fred Lammers, his stepson, had directed the program for the last 5 years and lived with his wife and two children in the basement of the hotel.

The program consisted of providing shelter, meals, and a Bible-study support group. Residents were required to leave the mission during the day to seek employment. Length of stay at the shelter was flexible as long as clients were making progress—seeking and finding work and saving money for an apartment. Both job hunting and involvement in the Bible-study support group were mandatory program requirements, with noncompliance resulting in dismissal from the program. The agency accepted no public funding, was supported by local churches, and was the only homeless shelter in the county.

Sherry

Sherry recently had moved back into the community. She had lived in Dolton several times previously and she considered it home more than any other place she could remember. Upon returning to the community, she had sought assistance from the Good News Mission Shelter.

Sherry, a 47-year-old single woman, had been unsettled for much of her adult life. She had been highly mobile, often to the point of being transient. Although she had experienced some difficulty controlling her temper and getting along with others in the past, she now recognized that she needed assistance to escape from her perpetual hand-to-mouth existence.

She also had become more realistic about her troubles maintaining regular employment, and was willing to take responsibility for her past and to be more tolerant of the terms with which help was offered. Sherry knew that she would have to "make her own breaks" if her life was going to improve. She was a hard worker and usually did not have too much difficulty finding employment.

Sherry quickly got a job at a supermarket that had just opened in town. She hoped to remain there and "get herself together." Because of her positive work performance and management experience, she was offered a position as an assistant manager for the evening shift, the only position in the store that paid more than minimum wage. Sherry liked her job and realized that it represented a rare opportunity for her to earn a livable income in this rural community.

Sherry's Problem

Sherry had been staying at the shelter for several weeks before she had found employment. Fred, the shelter director, was very supportive of her job search and was delighted with her new position—until he learned it was an evening job. Because the shelter's policy required that all residents attend the Bible-study support group each evening, Fred told Sherry she would have to change her work schedule to the day shift immediately or be terminated from the program. For Fred, involvement in the study was a nonnegotiable requirement.

Feeling frustrated and alone, Sherry contacted John at Love Your Neighbor on the recommendation of a fellow store employee. Over the course of the next week, John met with Sherry several times to talk about being forced from the shelter and in need of affordable housing.

Without the higher pay and the no-cost housing, Sherry did not know how she would ever save enough to pay deposits on an apartment and utilities. She was angry and discouraged, and it seemed that the world was collapsing on her. Fred's inflexibility regarding attendance at the Bible-study group was the primary cause of her confusion—he had strongly encouraged her to find work, but now he was forcing her to quit the job or leave the shelter. She had been aware of the Bible-study support group requirement when she entered the shelter and, before obtaining her job, she had attended all the Bible-study meetings without objection.

"What else can I do?" Sherry asked John.

"Don't worry," John reassured her, " I think I can help resolve this misunderstanding."

John's Dilemma

After talking with Sherry, John confidently called Fred to work out a compromise.

"Fred, I know you are familiar with the situation regarding Sherry. Is there any way you might be able to find an alternative time for her Bible-study support group or to waive the requirement? She needs to continue her job so she can save enough money to move on."

"I doubt whether we can do this," Fred replied. "The Bible-study support group is central to our program's success. But let me talk with my step-dad Don, and I'll get back to you."

John had worked in faith-based organizations most of his life. Although he respected the policies and rules, he found it difficult to understand the shelter's rigid position. Personally, John had been raised in a very structured religious environment and had an appreciation for the shelter's evangelistic mission. But to make this particular class the priority, rather than meeting other important needs of people, seemed unreasonable and even contrary to the teachings of the Bible.

Determined to find a solution, John contacted Sherry's manager and asked if there was any possibility that Sherry could move to another shift. But the manager needed Sherry on the second shift, stating that he understood her dilemma but was unable to accommodate the request.

John called the landlords he knew and any churches that might be willing to help. But there were no funds to subsidize rent, no one willing to defer deposits, and no one to step forward to offer Sherry temporary shelter in their home. John was frustrated, and he even considered contacting a church pastor or two to put pressure on Fred to find a way to help Sherry. Yet he thought this approach might be too aggressive and meddlesome for this community. In his short tenure, John had worked hard at facilitating ecumenical cooperation in Dolton, which had not existed in the community for several years. Because Love Your Neighbor and the Good News Mission Shelter were both faith-based and largely supported by the same faith communities, he feared a more confrontational approach might jeopardize support for his program. This was support he had worked hard to obtain.

But with no income or family support, Sherry's situation was becoming desperate. John strongly shared her frustration and discouragement.

Two days later, Fred called John. "I talked to my step-dad, and there is just no way we can do this."

John was stunned, and it took him a moment to reply. "I don't understand—Why not?"

"I'm sorry, John, but you know who we are and how important our mission is."

John did not know how to respond, but he was certain this could not be the end of the story. He thanked Fred, and hung up.

11.teaching note

Helping the Homeless: Our Way or the Highway
Beryl Hugen and Pam Doty-Nation

Case Synopsis

Sherry Palmer, a resident of the only homeless shelter in the county, was excited about a promotion that would finally allow her to break from her perpetual hand-to-mouth existence. Unfortunately, this new position was for the evening shift, which conflicted with the faith-based shelter's mandatory Bible-study support group. Fred Lammer, the director of the shelter, told Sherry that unless she quit her job she would be forced out of the shelter.

Sherry turned to John Ashland, the new director of a local church volunteer organization. John was very sympathetic to Sherry's dilemma, and although he was a friend of Fred Lammer and a devout Christian, he did not agree with Fred's decision. Despite his best efforts, however, John quickly found that he would not be able to change Fred's policy-based decision unless he adopted a more confrontational approach, something he was loathe to do, as it would destroy the community support he had painstakingly created for his organization.

Learning Outcomes Related to Religion and Spirituality

The case discussion will facilitate the work of students as they

1. Identify how personal spiritual and religious values can influence professional decision making.

2. Recognize how spirituality and religion are important in clarifying personal-professional boundaries.

3. Understand how faith-based organizations differ widely in terms of mission, goals, and policies.

4. Learn the importance of working with and within the value system of a faith-based human service organization.

Other Learning Outcomes for Which This Case Can Be Used

The case discussion will facilitate the work of students as they

5. Learn the importance of building community coalitions and of working with multiple client systems.

6. Identify the importance of organizational policy in social work practice and think critically about policy issues.

7. Understand the unique policy issues related to rural social work practice.

Courses and Levels for Which the Case Is Intended

Written primarily for the BSW level, this case

can be useful in the following social work courses: Human Behavior and the Social Environment, Introduction to Social Work, Social Welfare Policy, Micro and Macro Practice Methods, Values and Ethics, Diversity, and Religion and Spirituality. The case could also be used in MSW Administrative or Policy (Macro) Concentrations.

Discussion Questions Related to Religion and Spirituality

Establishing the Facts

1. Who are all the stakeholders (those with vested interests) in the case?

2. Who is the client?

   In this case, Sherry is clearly the client, as she is the person seeking assistance. The mission of John's agency, Love Your Neighbor, is to serve the larger church community by providing volunteer opportunities for church members in the Dolton community. Therefore, Sherry's needs are important to Love Your Neighbor, but are not central to the organization's mission. John, as the director, is responsible for carrying out the agency's mission. For John, the volunteers from the church community are also clients.

   Professional social workers do have a responsibility to be advocates for social justice in their communities. The Good News Mission is the only shelter program in the county, but its mission limits accessibility to the whole community based on religious and spiritual criteria. By advocating for Sherry, John could challenge these policies, and by doing so, could help make shelter services more accessible for all of the homeless population in his county.

Analysis

3. What is the role of religion or spirituality in this case?

   This is a complex question and perhaps is best addressed by building on the class discussion about clients in this case (Question 2). The question can be explored from the perspective of each of the actors: the client, the social worker, the human service organizations, and the community.

4. What role does religion or spirituality play in shaping organizational policy?

   For the Good News Mission Shelter, its mission, client eligibility criteria, program services, along with its understanding of the process of client change, are all anchored in a religious or spiritual framework. For Love Your Neighbor, the role of spirituality in service delivery to clients is not central, in fact it is optional— volunteers can share their faith if they choose, but meeting the concrete service needs of clients is the primary goal. Love Your Neighbor also has a faith-based mission, but the spiritual needs of local church volunteers is central to its mission.

5. A follow-up question could be: How would the policies of these two agencies need to change if they accepted public monies by contracting with state or local governments to provide shelter (GNS) and family assistance (LYN) in Dolton?

   Today there is growing interest in faith-based organizations playing a larger role in the delivery of human services. Legislation, specifically the Charitable Choice provision in the 1996 Welfare Reform Act and the more recent Community Solutions Act of 2001, has given significant impetus to this movement.

6. How has the faith of the social worker affected the decision making in this case?

   In John's situation, his faith not only serves as a strong motivational factor in this work, but also in his problem-solving deliberations. His beliefs about the role of evangelism in human services differ significantly from those of Fred and his father-in-law, Don Wilson, and these beliefs clearly influenced his thoughts about pursuing a more confrontational challenge to the shelter's Bible-study policy. Similarly, the beliefs and faith commitment of Don Wilson, founder of the shelter, contribute to Bible-study attendance being a nonnegotiable program activity.

7. What is the role of faith in Sherry's problem solving?

8. How might John have responded if he had known more about Sherry's spirituality and religious life?

   Unfortunately, the case only indicates that Sherry had attended Bible study before starting her night job and did not object to the policy. Knowing more about Sherry's spiritual and religious beliefs would have helped John better understand Sherry's perspective on her dilemma.

The case also lends itself well to a discussion of the role of grassroots organizations and faith communities in addressing social problems. Some critics of public human service programs believe families, local neighborhood organizations, and normal person-to-person caring relationships are better able to address the moral and social problems in our communities today. The Love Your Neighbor program is an excellent example of this philosophy.

Action

9. What is John's dilemma? What is Sherry, Fred, or Don Wilson's dilemma?

10. What choices are involved in each actor's dilemma? What systems (person, family, group, organization, or community) are involved? What role (advocate, broker, facilitator, etc.) would each actor employ in implementing her or his

Additional Notes

decision choices? How would social work values and each actor's personal values impact their decision?

11. What decision would you make if you were John?

Discussion of each actor's dilemma along with the systems, roles, and values that are involved in each dilemma clearly illustrates the importance of the ecological perspective in social work practice. Grappling with John's dilemma also teaches students critical thinking skills.

Teaching Suggestions

An instructor could begin by asking students to define the clients. This questioning leads nicely into a discussion of the different constituencies involved in the case—providing an opportunity to explore the role of religion or spirituality in different systems in social work practice. Work group reports may help focus these discussions on specific actors and systems in the case. From here the instructor could facilitate the application of the insights from these discussions to the specific course objectives.

12.

I Will Not Be God's Entertainment

Michael E. Sherr and Terry A. Wolfer

In 4 years at Pitt County (NC) Mental Health Center, child and family psychiatric social worker Noah Andrews had seen all kinds of psychosocial problems, from prosaic family conflicts to severe individual psychoses. As a result, he found that few things really surprised him anymore, and he was starting to trust his professional instincts. But every once in while, someone came along who sparked his curiosity and challenged his professional skills.

Missing Charts

As usual, Noah made his Monday morning walk over to the medical records office to prepare for his 10:30 intake appointment. As part of his clinical responsibilities, Noah had intakes scheduled every Monday and Thursday. About an hour before the appointment Noah went to the medical records office to review Gregory Lange's chart and to put together the 24-page packet of forms required to open the record.

At the medical records office Noah went up to the counter to request Gregory's chart from Michelle, the receptionist.

Before Noah could speak, Michelle asked, "What chart do you need, Noah?"

"Record Number 68477."

As Michelle disappeared behind rows and rows of charts, Noah gathered together the necessary forms. Moments later, Michelle spoke from behind the counter, "Noah, that chart is at the Ridgeway Office. It won't be here until after 12:00."

"Michelle," he replied, "this is the third time this month that a chart ended up at the wrong office. My intake will be here in less than an hour. Do you at least have the screening form?"

"Sorry, Noah," Michelle shrugged, "it's in the chart."

Noah had been meaning to talk with the medical records supervisor about this issue, but had been unable to find the time since taking on 14 new cases from a colleague who was on maternity leave. However, Noah still felt confident he could handle the first session with Gregory. He had become accustomed to beginning assessments in the initial session without any information about his client.

Meeting Gregory

As he did before each session, Noah sat still momentarily staring at the picture of his grandfather on his desk. Over Noah's 4 years as a psychiatric social worker he had discovered that reflecting back to something his grandfather said to him as a young boy helped him focus and prepare for sessions. Noah remembered sitting next to his grandfather in synagogue. Rabbi Rosenfeld had just finished his sermon on caring for the suffering. Noah asked his grandfather, "Is that why you and Nana spend so much time volunteering at the Yeshiva Thrift Store?"

"Bubula, we do that because the Lord loves all of his creation."

Noah got up and made his way to the waiting room with his grandfather's words resonating in his mind. As he was approaching the waiting area, his eyes focused in on a young man standing in the doorway. His face was triangular with sunken cheeks and a gaping mouth, and bandanas completely covered his neck. The young man's left arm was stiff and bent so sharply at the elbow that his hand dangled limply from above his shoulder blades. His right hand appeared flexible and rested casually in his pocket. Noah tried to avoid staring at this figure, thinking to himself, "I am glad I don't work on the MR/DD [Mentally Retarded/Developmentally Disabled] unit."

Arriving at the front desk in the waiting area, Noah turned to the receptionist, Lucy. "Which one is Gregory Lange?"

"He's over there by the door." Lucy nodded toward the young man with the triangular face. "His mother is sitting in the third seat by the window; poor kid, he looks like he got hit by a truck."

Noah momentarily paused, staring in disbelief. "If I had the chart," Noah thought, "maybe I could have prepared myself to meet Gregory or to refer him to an MR/DD specialist." Taking a deep breath and attempting to mentally suppress his feelings, Noah walked over to greet Gregory.

"Hi, Gregory, my name's Noah. Are you ready to come on back?"

Gregory turned to Noah with his mouth wide open. He had a solid streak of drool hanging from his lips to one of the bandanas. He then made an awful moan and pushed Noah with his right hand toward mom's direction. Noah was startled by the force of Gregory's push and needed a moment to regain his composure.

"Good idea, let's go get your mom."

Mrs. Lange was already standing, with her hand outstretched. "Hi, nice to meet you. You must be Mr. Andrews?"

"Yes, you can call me by my first name, Noah." He started to turn, " Why don't we come on back to my office."

As Mrs. Lange started to gather her belongings, Gregory began poking his mother with his right hand on her shoulder. Mrs. Lange acknowledged Gregory without hesitation and took out a keyboard-type device, "Gregory wants to say something to you," she told Noah.

"Sure, is he going to write me something?"

"Oh no, he can speak with his voice machine."

Noah turned to Gregory in anticipation. As Mrs. Lange held the voice machine, Gregory slowly typed one letter at a time with his right index finger. As he would make mistakes, he would get frustrated and be forced to start over. After what seemed like several minutes, he finally pressed a button on the other side of the machine. A computer-synthesized voice spoke.

"I do not need a shrink. All I need is a cold beer."

Noah and Mrs. Lange broke into genuine laughter. Meanwhile, Gregory's eyes opened wide and his face reddened with color in what appeared to Noah as an attempt to smile. Noah also noticed that Gregory's moans intensified for a few moments, becoming even more abrasive.

Tuning into Gregory's humor, Noah responded, "I like drinking cold beer myself, but it's a little too early in the day for me. Why don't you and your mom come on back to my office, and we can decide together if you need a shrink."

Gregory responded by shaking his head up and down to indicate agreement. He then grabbed the bandanas and pulled them off over his head. Mrs. Lange reached into her purse and pulled out a bag with more. She exchanged Gregory's old bandanas, placing them in a separate bag that smelled of mildew, and giving him fresh ones to put around his neck. Once they were finished, all three made their way from the waiting area back to Noah's office.

Gregory's Referral

Noah, Gregory, and Mrs. Lange sat together around the small desk. Gregory had the voice machine on his lap, and Mrs. Lange was holding the referral form in her hand.

Noah usually spent the initial session getting into the main issues and reserved filling out paperwork until the next time. It was the agency's policy to complete all paperwork in the first session in order to ensure payment from Medicaid or insurance companies. However, Noah believed that it was important to build the therapeutic relationship in the first session instead of being concerned with forms. Nevertheless, because he did not have the chart, the only thing he knew about Gregory Lange was his name and record number.

Looking to Gregory and his mother, Noah began, " Before we get to the reason you're here, let me ask you both a couple of basic questions—how old are you, Gregory?"

After a few moments of typing, the machine spoke, "I am 15."

"Are you in school? What grade?"

More time passed, and then he replied, "I am at Southwest High School." Another pause, then, "I am in tenth grade."

"He has to have a one-on-one teacher's assistant with him throughout the day," Mrs. Lange broke in, "to help him get to classes and to monitor his eating at lunch."

Noah replied, "Oh, I see." He continued, "What about hobbies? Do you have any hobbies?"

Gregory typed his answer, "I like to read."

Again Mrs. Lange interrupted. "The books he reads are about Satan, and they scare me."

Gregory's eyes opened wide again, and he was shaking his head up and down. He then lunged with his right arm at his mother in what appeared to Noah as a mocking gesture. It seemed to Noah that Gregory enjoyed making his mom feel uncomfortable.

Noah turned to Mrs. Lange, "Speaking of Satan, does your family have any religious beliefs or attend church?"

"We're Southern Baptist," she replied. "Until last June, Gregory used to go to church with me and attend Young Life groups every week. "

"What happened?"

"He started interrupting the service," Mrs. Lange answered. "At first he would get up and wander the aisle during the service. The last time we went he made an obscene hand gesture to the pastor and continually hit me until I took him home."

Noah turned to Gregory, "So church is not a place you look to for support at the present time?"

Gregory's finger moved across the keyboard, "No more."

Concerned about focusing too much on religion, Noah decided to wait until the next session to explore the issue further. "It sounds like this is an important issue we may need to address in a future session. Right now, let's focus on what brings you to see me today."

Mrs. Lange replied, "Dr. Wolfman, from the Duke Medical Center referred us to the Pitt County Mental Health Center so Gregory could be evaluated for depression. Gregory is scheduled to have surgery next month to stop his drooling, but Dr. Wolfman will not operate unless Gregory wants the operation and begins taking better care of himself—Gregory is not eating."

Turning to his mother, Gregory put his right hand up in front of her face and made a sharp moan. He then typed on his machine, "How would you like to eat nutrition shakes made for old farts every single day?"

"I imagine it must get boring," Noah answered, "eating the same thing all the time."

Mrs. Lange broke in, "Well, once he has the surgery next month he might be able to begin eating solid foods again. Right now it's too risky; he can choke because he has a lot of difficulty swallowing. He is also staying up all night. I don't think he has had a good night's rest in the past six weeks."

"What are you doing with your time instead of sleeping?"

Gregory's finger moved slowly over the keys. "I think about ways to die."

Caught off guard by Gregory's response, Noah reacted, "To die?" and then asked, "Is that the best solution?"

"I will not be God's entertainment."

At that point, Noah thought he was beginning to see a pattern to Gregory's anger and beliefs. He thought that although Gregory may enjoy aggravating his mother, his withdrawal from church, his interest in satanic material, and his last comment suggested that religion could be an important issue for him.

Mrs. Lange broke into Noah's thoughts. "He probably would have tried to kill himself by now, but I haven't given him the chance. I guess that is one of the good things about his condition; I don't think he could do anything without my help right now."

Gregory's moans intensified, and he made a sudden gesture with his right arm, attempting to hit his mother. Although he missed, he expressed his anger through the voice machine. "I hate you, bitch."

Noah felt uncomfortable, but at the same time recognized the familiarity of Gregory's emotions.

Noah remembered how difficult it was to be a teenager trying to gain freedom and independence. He couldn't even begin to imagine what it would be like to have to rely upon his mother for everything.

Noah spoke to Mrs. Lange, "Is there anything Gregory can do on his own? It appears to me Gregory's independence is very important to him right now."

Gregory motioned to his mother to let him answer. He then utilized the voice machine to speak, "I want to get a job so I can make some money. I want to go to parties with my friends. I want to drink beer."

"Is there any way he could do some of these things?"

Mrs. Lange answered, "Well, you see he doesn't have great balance and he could fall. He would also need someone to watch him eat and drink to make sure he doesn't choke. Besides, he doesn't have many friends anymore."

Gregory broke in again with a loud moan and by raising his right arm in front of his mother's face. He then typed, "What about Charlie or Thomas?"

Mrs. Lange turned to Noah, "They used to be Gregory's friends when he was 11, before the accident, but they haven't been very close since." She continued, "They are polite to him at school, but they don't really include him anymore."

While Mrs. Lange was speaking, Noah sensed he was being too confrontative with her. He also thought he was losing focus on a holistic picture for the assessment. Therefore, he decided to change the direction of the interview.

Gregory's Accident

"Mrs. Lange, what exactly happened to Gregory?" asked Noah.

Mrs. Lange proceeded to tell the story. "Four years ago, Gregory got hit head-on by a car. It's a miracle he's even alive. He was playing at a friend's house down the road and it was time for dinner. I called over to the house to have him come home. He wanted to stay and eat dinner with his friend and have me pick him up afterwards, but I asked him to walk home. It was Thursday night and his dad used to get off early from work, so I tried to make sure that the family ate together on those nights. Anyway, as he was walking home, a car came

around the curve and hit him." Mrs. Lange looked at her son. "It has really changed him. He used to be very popular in school, made good grades, and loved being around people.

Noah asked, "So is he now considered disabled?"

Mrs. Lange was quick to answer. "Absolutely not. That's part of the problem; everyone wants to treat him as if he were retarded or disabled. He has Traumatic Brain Injury; most people call it TBI. Gregory resents having to do anything with the MR/DD population. You see, I worked as a habilitation specialist for 10 years with clients with severe and profound retardation, so Gregory knows the difference and does not want to be seen that way."

Noah felt embarrassed. He had never even heard of TBI. "Physically," Noah thought, "he looks disabled. But intellectually, he's bright and able to communicate coherently with his voice machine." Noah also admired Gregory's sense of humor and his desire to be independent. Mrs. Lange, Noah thought, loves her son and has nothing but the best intentions for his care. However, it seemed to Noah that she was so involved in her son's life that Gregory felt smothered.

Noah decided that he needed to talk with Gregory alone in order to connect with him and to gain his trust. He carefully constructed the next statement and turned to Gregory. "I apologize for looking at you as if you're disabled. I don't know much about TBI, in fact I have never heard of it before today, but if you're willing to teach me, I am willing to learn so I can help you."

Once again, Mrs. Lange answered for Gregory. "Well, actually there is a TBI association in Pitt County, and we're having a meeting in a few weeks. Congressmen Howard Coble will be there to learn about TBI, too. You're welcome to come as well if you would like."

Noah responded, "Thank you for the invitation. Let's talk about that at the next session." He then got up and went over to his file cabinet, pulled out a family history questionnaire and handed it to Mrs. Lange. "I'll tell you what, if it is okay with you, Mrs. Lange, why don't you give Gregory and I a chance to talk alone. Here, you can fill out this family history form which will provide me with more collaborative information."

Mrs. Lange looked down at the form and smiled up at Noah. "That will be fine."

Noah turned to Gregory, "Is that okay with you?" Gregory moved his head up and down again to indicate agreement.

"Great," Noah said as Mrs. Lange moved toward the door. "We will be done by 11:30."

Alone With Gregory

As Mrs. Lange left the office, Noah considered how to continue the session. Although proficient in a variety of psychotherapeutic modalities, Noah could not help thinking that Gregory's desire to die was linked more to spiritual issues than negative thinking or cognitive distortions. Noah had strong spiritual beliefs of his own that he believed influenced everything he did in terms of his social work practice. However, he worked for a publicly funded community mental health center, and he valued the client's right to self-determination. He also empathized with Gregory's circumstances and could understand why he would want to die. Noah wondered what to say next.

12. teaching note
I Will Not Be God's Entertainment
Michael E. Sherr and Terry A. Wolfer

Case Synopsis

Social worker Noah Andrews was responsible for completing a psychiatric intake assessment with Gregory Lange, an adolescent left severely disfigured after being hit head-on by a car. Scheduled to have surgery the next month, Gregory had been referred to the mental health center to be evaluated and treated for depression. Noah began to explore religious and spiritual aspects of the case, after being intrigued by several references to religion. Confronted by Gregory's overwhelming anger, dependency, and suicidal thoughts, Noah wondered how best to help Gregory.

Learning Outcomes Related to Religion and Spirituality

The case discussion will facilitate the work of students as they

1. Appreciate that competent social work practice may require us to deal with the religion and spirituality of our clients.

2. Gain proficiency in considering how a client's spiritual beliefs, history, and current affiliation interact with other issues involved in a client's case.

3. Become aware of their own spiritual beliefs and examine how those beliefs affect the professional helping relationship.

4. Discover that professional social work requires students to synthesize their awareness of religion and spirituality with broader concepts such as transference and countertransference, self-determination, family enmeshment, and advocacy, in order to assess and intervene with target systems at all three levels of practice (micro, mezzo, macro).

Courses and Levels for Which This Case Is Intended

Written for a master's level capstone course in social work, this case may also be useful at the graduate level for specialized courses on social work practice with individuals, social work practice with families, medical social work, mental health services, or religion and spirituality.

Discussion Questions Related to Religion and Spirituality

Various combinations of the following questions can be used, depending on what aspects of the case an instructor wishes to explore or emphasize.

Establishing the Facts

1. What caused Gregory's current condition?
   At age 11, Gregory was hit head-on by a car as he was walking home from a friend's house.

2. What is Traumatic Brain Injury (TBI)? How is it

different from mental retardation or a developmental disability (MR/DD)?

Mental retardation is a particular state of functioning that begins in childhood and is likely to continue indefinitely. It is characterized by significantly subaverage intellectual capacity, existing concurrently with limitations in two or more adaptive skill areas (communication, self-care, home living, community use, health and safety, leisure, social skills, self-direction, functional academics, work). Developmental disabilities are severe, chronic disabilities attributable to mental and physical impairment, which manifest before age 22 and are likely to continue indefinitely. They result in substantial limitations in three or more areas (self-care, receptive and expressive language, learning, mobility, self-direction, capacity for independent living, and economic self-sufficiency), as well as the continuous need for individually planned and coordinated services. In contrast, TBI results from damage to brain tissue caused by an external force. It can lead to any number of neuropsychological and physiological impairments depending on the severity of the injury. Recovery and improvement in functioning is possible but is a life-long process.

3. What do we know about the religion and spirituality of the participants?

The case mentions that Gregory and his mother are Southern Baptists and used to attend church every week. Gregory also used to attend a Young Life youth group. Gregory's mother tells Noah that Gregory does not currently attend church, and she also mentions that he has been reading satanic material. However, the case never mentions whether Gregory actually believes or participates in any satanic practices. Further, there is no information about Mrs. Lange's current attendance at church.

Noah is Jewish. The case indicates that Noah's religious beliefs strongly influence his social work practice, but the case does not mention his Jewish denomination (reformed, conservative, orthodox) or his current attendance at synagogue. We also do not know what Noah understands about Southern Baptists or Young Life.

4. What is the nature of Gregory's family relationships?

The only family members mentioned in the case are Gregory and his mother. Therefore, we don't know

much about Gregory's father or siblings. "His dad used to get off early from work" is briefly mentioned in the description of the accident, but there are no other details given. Gregory's relationship with his mother appears paradoxical and complex. As with other teenagers, Gregory is an adolescent trying to gain independence. However, Gregory knows that he is dependent upon his mother for his daily functioning. He demonstrated his anger and frustration during the interview. Mrs. Lange apparently feels fortunate just to have Gregory still alive, and she has spent the last 4 years caring for his every need. She wants Gregory to improve, as is evident by the scheduled operation, but appears so involved with Gregory's care that he has little control over major aspects of his life.*

5. What expectations does Gregory have about seeing a psychiatric social worker?

The case indicates that Gregory equates going to see a psychiatric social worker with seeing a "shrink," something that he prefers not to do.

6. What aspects of Gregory's functioning indicate that he may have depression?

The case mentions several symptoms. For example, Mrs. Lange tells Noah that Gregory is not eating or sleeping, and Gregory reveals that while sleepless, he thinks of ways to die. Further, the case mentions that Gregory does not want to have an operation that could improve his daily functioning, possibly allowing him to eat and drink regular food again, a possible sign that Gregory may not have much hope or motivation for the future.

Analysis

7. What evidence is there that Gregory feels suicidal? How do you assess the validity of the evidence? What should Noah do about this information?

When Noah asked Gregory what he does with his time instead of sleeping, Gregory tells Noah that he thinks about ways to die. This is the only direct reference in the case to suicide, but there are several indirect signals and risk factors. Gregory's age, being younger than 19, symptoms of depression, possible rational-thinking loss, and his brain injury, combined with his statement of intent to die, are all warning signals for potential suicidal behavior.

However, the case does not mention any specific plan that Gregory has for taking his life or any actual efforts to do so. Mrs. Lange indicates that he is unable to seriously hurt himself without help, and she assures Noah that she will never give Gregory a chance to act on his suicidal thoughts. In summary, Noah must make a professional judgment about Gregory's suicide risk before he does anything with the information. He must decide if Gregory is a danger to himself or to others.

Based on Noah's decision, there are several ways he can respond. Noah can (1) have Gregory evaluated further by the on-call psychiatrist, (2) take out a petition for Gregory's involuntary commitment himself, (3) talk with Gregory and his mother about considering voluntary commitment, or (4) decide to let Gregory go home, knowing that his mother is watching him. In any case, Noah must consider his agency's policy for dealing with clients who are potentially suicidal.

8. What are Noah's reasons for routinely delaying formal assessment (i.e., paperwork) until the second session? What are the consequences? Do you agree with what Noah is doing? Would you do the same?

The case mentions that Noah usually delays filling out paperwork until the second session because he believes it is more important to build a therapeutic relationship in the first session. However, because Noah does not complete the paperwork during the first session, the agency loses out on billing Medicaid and insurance companies, and if Gregory and his mother do not return for a second session, then the agency will never receive any revenue for serving the Lange family. The case also mentions that Noah does intakes on Monday and Thursday. This means that at least twice a week the agency does not receive revenue for these services. As a professional social worker, working for a community mental health agency, Noah is responsible to many different systems, including the client, the agency, the profession, the community funding the mental health center, and the greater society. He must balance their competing interests. If Noah disagrees with the agency about the need to complete all paperwork during the first session, perhaps he could advocate a change instead of disregarding the policy.

9. What problems are created by the apparent disorganization of the medical records? What might be the cause? How could Noah address this?

The case mentions that for the third time in a month Noah will not have a chart to review before beginning an intake session. It seems that the agency keeps records in different locations. However, the case does not explain why there are different locations. Further, the case says nothing about why the charts were not ready. Noah has thought about talking to the medical records supervisor about the problem but has been unable to find the time, due to his large caseload. The case also does not indicate if Noah has a direct supervisor who might be able to address the issue.

10. As a professional social worker, what is appropriate for Noah to say or do regarding religion and spirituality? What is not appropriate?

As a psychiatric social worker, it is important during an evaluation to gain a holistic and comprehensive understanding of your client and the environment. In this case, it would have been useful for Noah to explore Gregory's specific reasons for wanting to die. Further, it was appropriate for Noah to ask exploratory questions about Gregory's religious participation and spiritual beliefs, and he could also assess Mrs. Lange on the same issues. It is appropriate to assess the Langes' access and willingness to use their church for support, and Noah must be mindful not to judge or discount the Langes' religious and spiritual beliefs. He must also remember that Gregory is a minor. He might need Mrs. Lange's permission to talk with Gregory about religion, depending on agency policy. Finally, it would be inappropriate for Noah to use his clinical role to enter into a theological debate about their religious differences.

11. How do the religious differences between Noah and the Langes affect their relationship? Given these differences, how should Noah proceed?

Through the course of the session, Noah thinks he notices that religious and spiritual issues are an important factor in Gregory's situation. Gregory used to attend church regularly, but now he reads satanic material, has an apparent desire to die, and says, "I will not be God's entertainment." Noah has strong spiritual beliefs, but they are much different from the Langes'. Perhaps the differences prevented Noah from probing for more clarification about Gregory's statement about not being God's entertainment. Should Noah tell the Langes he is Jewish? After the intake process, should he refer the Langes to another clinician for treatment? Social workers are trained to appreciate and have knowledge of diverse populations. Noah could rely on his clinical skills to express his appreciation for their differences but also his willingness to help. In fact, he could use their differences as a rationale for exploring these issues and seeking deeper understanding.

12. How can Noah attempt to build rapport and trust with Gregory? What is appropriate? What is not appropriate?

Noah was shocked to learn that Gregory was his 10:30 intake, and the case makes it clear that he has little knowledge of Gregory's condition. Nevertheless, Noah found several areas to continue to build rapport and trust with Gregory. He could easily identify with Gregory's desire for independence and his struggle for more freedom from his mother. Noah also can continue using basic reflective listening skills to express to Gregory the reciprocal nature of their relationship. In particular, Noah will need to continue to demonstrate genuine interest in learning more about TBI, and Gregory's TBI in particular. Noah's response, talking about the use of alcohol in front of Mrs. Lange, could be considered inappropriate, but it is important to place his response in the context of the session. It may also be inappropriate for Noah to lead Gregory into more discussions about religion without Mrs. Lange's approval. As mentioned above, even with Mrs. Lange's approval, Noah must consider whether he is qualified, given their religious differences. Further, while identifying with Gregory's desire for independence, Noah must be careful not to alienate Gregory or take sides against his mother.

13. Who is the client? What does the client want?

The official identified client, according to the chart, is Gregory Lange. Nevertheless, there are other identified clients, including Mrs. Lange, the Lange family, Dr. Wolfman (the surgeon who recommended the referral), and the Pitt County community and its taxpayers who fund the mental health center. Dr. Wolfman wants Gregory evaluated and treated for

depression to improve his attitude about the upcoming surgery. It appears Mrs. Lange also wants Gregory to have the operation, in order to get "better," and she certainly wants Gregory to remain alive and safe. Although not specifically mentioned, Mrs. Lange may also want Gregory to participate in church again.

Gregory wants to be able to go to parties, to have a job and make money, to take risks and participate in adolescent rebellious behavior. Most of all, he wants to gain independence. In summary, Gregory wants to live as "normally" as possible, given his condition.

14. How does transference and countertransference between Noah, Gregory, and Mrs. Lange influence the interview?

Because of Noah's expectations about the types of clients he serves, he was shocked to find Gregory scheduled for an intake interview. The case mentions that Noah tried to suppress his initial reactions toward Gregory. Further, throughout the session, Noah looked at Gregory as if he were disabled. Noah also has certain beliefs about God and the value of all living beings. His beliefs certainly influence his perception of the issues in the case, as well as his response to Gregory's suicidal thoughts.

The case also indicates that Gregory did not want to see Noah because he felt he was being forced to see a "shrink." This reluctance could influence how Gregory interacts with Noah. Further, Noah can easily identify with Gregory's desire for independence, and this could influence how Noah views Mrs. Lange: perhaps Noah is too quick to judge her as smothering Gregory. Finally, because of the accident and Mrs. Lange's experience as a habilitation specialist, it is important for her that Gregory not be labeled or viewed as disabled. This might influence her willingness to utilize certain resources in the community if they are at all related to serving the MR/DD population. Given the amount of transference and countertransference, Noah would be wise to consult his supervisor and colleagues.

15. Noah interprets Gregory's suicidal thoughts as a manifestation of religious and spiritual issues. Do you agree? Why or why not?

The information Noah has gathered thus far certainly makes it plausible for him to suspect the presence of significant religious and spiritual issues. However, Noah does not know anything about the etiology of TBI, and it could be affecting Gregory's cognitive processes and perceptions. Gregory states that he wants to go to parties, drink beer, and get a job. He doesn't say he wants to talk about religion. Perhaps Gregory is really upset about not being able to become more independent and does not know how to communicate this verbally. In the case, Noah suspects that Gregory likes making his mother uncomfortable. Gregory could be reading satanic material and responding to Noah in such a way to get a reaction from his mother and even from Noah. Finally, Noah has not finished the intake or reviewed Gregory's chart yet. There could be other information that may influence his evaluation.

Action

16. How should Noah continue the interview when Mrs. Lange leaves the room?

   There are various ways Noah could continue the interview. He could further explore Gregory's suicidal thoughts, thoughts and feelings about his relationship with his mother, how Gregory views himself, or how Gregory thinks and feels about the accident. More casually, he could focus on the present and talk about whatever Gregory wants for the remainder of the session. Depending upon his knowledge and competence with different therapeutic modalities, there are many other ways he could continue the interview and work to build rapport.

17. In future sessions, should Noah intervene individually with Gregory, with Gregory and his mother, with his mother individually, or a combination?

   Gregory's individual issues seem to be intertwined with his complex and paradoxical relationship with his mother. When Noah develops a treatment plan with Gregory and his mother, he may encourage intervening with all of the client systems in order to be most effective. However, respecting their right to self-determination, Noah should give Gregory and his mother his recommendations, along with alternatives, and allow them to make an informed decision.

18. What is necessary for completing a thorough intake assessment?

   First, remember that assessment is continuous. Next, it is vital to inquire about Gregory's functioning in all the ways he interacts with his environment. It may help to organize the information by assessing Gregory's functioning at micro, mezzo, and macro levels. At the micro level, Noah needs to understand Gregory's physiological, psychological, social, and spiritual functioning. At the mezzo level, Noah needs to assess the nature of Gregory's relationship with his mother and the patterns of their communication. Further, if he has a father, or siblings, or an extended family, Noah needs to know about those relationships, as well as any with his peers. At the macro level, Noah needs to assess Gregory's functioning with his school, his church, the hospital, the government, the TBI association, and any other agencies that are working with his family.

19. What should we expect psychiatric social workers to know about TBI/MR/DD?

   Social work practice in mental health organizations occasionally involves clients with MR/DD. For that reason, students considering mental health practice should consider taking specific courses or continuing education workshops on social work and MR/DD. Because TBI is less common and Noah has not previously worked with clients suffering from it, it is understandable that he has little knowledge of the condition or of the issues involved in serving this population. Nevertheless, generalist social work knowledge and helping skills are the foundation for competent practice with any client population. Noah utilized his interviewing and listening skills to begin his intake with Gregory, despite not having Gregory's chart or any previous knowledge of TBI.

Teaching Suggestions

   The instructor could begin with a question about Gregory's accident, and discuss the experience of working with clients having Traumatic Brain Injury (TBI). Then, the instructor could probe students' awareness of their own stereotypes regarding people who look and function differently from most others. To deepen students' understanding of the case, the instructor could invite discussion about Gregory's developmental level, current and likely future functioning, whether he is depressed, and his risk of suicide. To explore the interpersonal dynamics of the case, pose questions about Gregory's relationship with his mother, and their relationships with others, including Noah. Once the psychosocial context has been well-developed, the instructor can raise questions about the religious and spiritual aspects of the case. How are these likely related to TBI, depression, adolescence, their social supports, and their hopes and expectations? How do religious differences between mother and son and between the clients and the social worker help or hinder the case? How can these differences be handled? Finally, the instructor may ask students to role-play the end of the interview with Gregory, developing a treatment plan contract with Gregory and his mother, or the next psychotherapy session. Depending on how the remaining topics fit with the purpose of the course, instructors may wish to discuss prioritizing client needs over agency needs, conducting initial interviews without prior client information, advocating for change within a large government agency, and intervening across system levels.

Additional Notes

13.
Why Can't They Make This Place More Jewish?

Evelyn Hoffman and Dennis R. Myers

"Mother is feeling so alone here. She's begging me to let her go back to New York. I don't know how to help my mother laugh again and meet new friends and stop missing home so much." It was the undercurrent of desperation in Jean Rubin's expression of concern for her mother, Myra Golden, that momentarily called Tom Harris's attention away from his routine case planning as a county geriatric social worker at the Central Arkansas Mental Health and Mental Retardation Center. Since his first encounter with Jean over 6 months ago, Tom was not accustomed to hearing this level of frustration in her voice. He thought he had helped in resolving at least some of these feelings around the unrelenting physical decline experienced by her 88-year-old mother, but never had her words contained such sheer hopelessness.

Tom knew that a seamless transition from a cosmopolitan setting like New York to a southern area like central Arkansas, where there was a very small Jewish community, would be difficult for a Jewish older person who was also facing frightening physical challenges. Tom recognized that, in spite of Myra's depression and resistance to the idea, it was time to facilitate her involvement in a setting that would provide peer contact and the possibility of supportive friendships. As he thought about this proposition, Tom had an uneasy feeling that Myra's culture and religion, so different from most of those who lived in central Arkansas, would present a significant barrier for her. Part of him wanted Myra to

minimize these differences for her own good. But Myra would soon show Tom how her religious beliefs and practices would become a catalyst for enriching community social services and, at the same time, present Tom with a difficult dilemma regarding the role of religious diversity in public life.

Myra Golden's Relocation

Jean was aware that the local county Mental Health and Mental Retardation Center had a Geriatric Care Unit and she decided to seek assistance there. Tom, the unit's only geriatric social worker, recalled his first encounter with Jean, when she told him, "I'm moving my mother here to Plainview from New York City, and I need your help to know what's available to make her happy. She absolutely does not want to come. This is a very difficult move for all of us. I just know it has to be, because so much will be different for her."

As a loving Jewish daughter, Jean's passion was to live out the teachings of Torah: "Do not forsake me in my old age." For her, that meant placing herself, her husband David, and their home in the center of any plans for her mother's care. The fact that Jean herself was recovering from cardiac by-pass surgery and was battling diabetes did not detract from her resolve. However, she was facing one of the most difficult challenges of her life. "I thought I would be a *shtarker* (strong, tireless person), but this situation with Mother overwhelms me."

Jean knew that the act of transplanting Myra from her life-long home in the New York City borough of Queens would require the support of a professional. Jean needed someone who could help her plan her mother's relocation and who was knowledgeable about aging resources in Plainview, where Jean herself had moved so long ago. Tom was quite comfortable with such requests, just as he was also prepared to work with adult children regarding the guilt and the unfinished business that often attaches itself to the role of caregiver.

Presenting Issues and Gerontological Assessment

Tom's initial impression of Jean and David Rubin was that they were a mutually supportive couple who had recently celebrated their 50th wedding anniversary. They were both motivated to provide within their home the care that Myra would need. Even though Tom had only recently completed his MSW, his two years of gerontological work with families and caregiving issues had taught him that such relocations were complex. This one seemed no different in that respect. For most of her 88 years, Myra Golden reveled in the web of relationships in her congregation and neighborhood in Queens.

"At home in Queens her days were so full," Jean explained. "Always on the phone with her friends or involved in nonstop bridge games at the Jewish senior center. Seems like if she wasn't at the center she was off with her friends to a Broadway show. She could always be found at weekly Sabbath observances and, of course, there were celebrations of the High Holy Days and Passover."

Myra had been outspoken in her disapproval of Jean's decision to leave the advantages of life in the Big Apple to move to Plainview upon her marriage to David, her World War II sweetheart. Now Jean was insisting that Myra make the same move she had made over 50 years earlier. How ironic it was that Myra herself would be traveling the pathway that created so much friction between her and Jean so long ago.

The decision to move Myra into the Rubin's home was triggered by a stroke that brought with it a severe decrease in Myra's ability to manage independently in her apartment. According to the geriatric assessment that Tom received from her internist in New York, her Cerebral Vascular Accident (CVA), or stroke, affected her ability to prepare her own meals and independently handle personal hygiene. Her comprehensive assessment noted that her "instrumental activities of daily living (IADL) scores reflected moderate impairment and that she had deficits in short-term memory and in the use of her right hand."

Tom also noticed in the assessment that she "was a confident woman who flourished when she had rich human interaction available to her and who highly valued her religious life." Given that she could no longer care for herself and that caregiver support from a family member was unavailable in New York, Tom concurred with Jean's plans to relocate her mother and agreed to facilitate a healthy transition for all concerned.

It did not take very long for Tom to understand clearly that the answer to the caregiver question could never be a nursing home. He knew Jean would say to that possibility, "Not on your life! It will be a *nechtag* (dark night) before I would allow such a thing to happen." Jean's desire to assume the primary caregiver role for her mother was based on more than an adult child's love and gratitude toward her parent. At the foundation of her feelings lay the rich traditions of "caring for your own" and "honoring parents" which are markers of Jewish family life. Although Tom understood that the transition would be difficult, neither he nor Jean anticipated the devastating effects that the change in geography, culture, and religious surroundings would have on Myra's well-being.

The Warren Senior Center

The move itself went extremely well. Jean and David had lovingly prepared for Myra a bedroom with a private bath within their home and had encouraged her to furnish it with treasured items from her New York apartment. For Myra, however, this change was a *nechtag* indeed. She longed for her home and expressed her outrage, frequently wondering aloud what she had done to deserve such a fate as this. Tom recognized the hurt and fear that lay below the anger and helped both the mother and the daughter express the grief, sense of loss, and helplessness both were experiencing in their own way. Tom also knew that he must help Myra form meaningful relationships in the community.

Because Myra was so active, she would need a place to interact and become involved with age peers, a place where recognition, familiarity, and laughter abounded, and a place where she could pursue her enjoyment of bridge. Locating this retreat was essential if there would be any chance for a change of heart about the move. Even more than food, Myra needed daily doses of social nourishment.

Tom recommended that Myra try the Warren Senior Center and scheduled an initial visit with Samantha Ross, the director, who verified many reasons why the senior center environment would be a good fit for Myra. Its membership, in large part, included very active adults who tended to be highly educated. The program was enriched by a nutrition program that included a noon meal Monday through Friday, educational offerings in partnership with the local community college, day trips to scenic and interesting areas of central Arkansas, intergenerational experiences with students from a nearby elementary school, and games and crafts. At the Warren Senior Center, the domino game "42" was the main table game, and Tom thought that it had many of the features of bridge. The Warren Center received its primary public support through the Older Americans Act, with funds channeled through the local Area Agency on Aging on a contract basis to the Central Arkansas Senior Ministry, which operated the senior center as a private, not-for-profit agency of the First Methodist Church in Plainview.

Religious Insensitivity

Initially, Myra's decision to give the Warren Center a try seemed to be affirmed by her reception there. At first, she enjoyed her new friends and the variety of offerings at the center, but it was not long before unanticipated features of the program began changing the senior center into an uncomfortable and alien setting. In the beginning, the unsettling features were only minor irritations, for instance, the center staff's complete disregard for Jewish holidays, such as Passover. It seemed to Myra that she was the only Jewish person coming to the center. One day she came home, and when Jean asked her about her day, she replied, "Very strange! Are people of their faith given instruction on who they can dance with or sit next to? It seems to me that

everyone in the center has a boyfriend or girlfriend and I feel like I should go elsewhere!"

With time, other religiously insensitive factors became increasingly obvious, including differences in dietary requirements for observant Jews and the meals served at the center. Christian prayers and hymns were dominant during mealtimes and sing-alongs. To Myra, these elements appeared to play a major role in the life of the center. Finally, there was the issue of scheduling the center dances—one of Myra's favorite activities—on Friday evening, the very time of worship services at the synagogue.

Making It Better for Myra

Myra wondered aloud to Tom, "Couldn't there be something done to make the place more Jewish?" It was obvious to Tom that something needed to happen. Although he had some concern about the cultural and religious differences Myra might experience when he made the referral, he never imagined that this publicly-funded senior center would be so difficult for non-Christian participants.

"We really want to be as responsive as we can to our participants' individual tastes, but you have to remember that we have our limits," Samantha Ross said in response to Tom's attempt to start a conversation about his concerns. Nevertheless, she agreed to a meeting with Tom, Jean, and Myra "to see what could be done to make things better." She listened intently to Myra's complaints:

"The Friday night dances are at the same time as synagogue services and that keeps me from going and I don't think that's right!"

"Could the bridge players have the use of at least one of the tables?"

"Please provide some lunches for people like me who have religious restrictions on what they can eat. Maybe having something Jewish around here wouldn't be so bad!"

Samantha told Myra that she needed to allow more time for "everyone to get to know her better" and to "realize that central Arkansas can never be like New York City." She explained further that any changes in the program would need the approval of the center's council, an elected body composed of five center participants, two members from the Area Agency on Aging Advisory Committee, and Ms. Ross herself. She agreed to discuss these concerns with the council as part of the agenda for the upcoming week's meeting.

Myra seemed relieved by the opportunity to express some of her concerns, but Tom had an uneasy feeling that the road to making the center more accommodating to ethnic and religious differences would be long and hard.

"How can a senior citizen program that is receiving Older Americans Act monies be so supportive of one religious viewpoint and so unresponsive to those who hold other beliefs?" was Tom's rhetorical question to his supervisor as they reviewed what had become known as "The Myra Case."

Tom's supervisor reminded him that the center's program mirrored the values and preferences of most older people from central Arkansas, and, in that sense, the center was being responsive to the needs of the majority.

"But to what extent must Myra be denied the richness of her personal and religious tradition?" Tom asked himself. He was more determined than ever to do what he could to assure that Myra would have an environment that would embrace, rather than ignore, the traditions and beliefs that contributed so much to her quality of life.

Congregational Solutions

Tom's supervisor recommended that he explore other options for social connection and activity for Myra. Tom thought to himself, "How are older persons who do not attend the Warren Senior Center addressing these needs?" As he made the arrangements for a meeting of the Rabbi, Jean, Myra, and himself, Tom hoped that the local Jewish congregation would have some answers.

Rabbi Rebekah Crystal of Congregation Rodef Shalom listened attentively as Myra and Jean summarized their encounters at the Warren Senior Center, the most exasperating of which were the increasing number of subtle and not so subtle efforts to persuade Myra to convert to Christianity. It seemed to Myra that the future of some of her new friendships depended upon her acceptance of this new religion.

"None of this is a surprise to me," observed Rabbi Crystal, "as frequent attempts at conversion are a way of life for Jews in the South. Some of the local group have even had the *chutzpah* to try to convert me."

Then Rabbi Crystal addressed Myra's predicament. "Though our congregation is relatively small, we have at least 10 older members who, like Myra, need some outlet for their social needs and have not felt welcome at the center."

"What about the possibility of the congregation funding a program for its seniors that would include kosher meals, celebrations of the High Holy days and Passover, bridge and mah-jongg games, Jewish dances, and anything else Jewish?" Tom asked Rabbi Crystal.

Jean mentioned that she had heard of a similar program, called Chavarah, that had been developed in Texas and that could serve as a model. The main challenge to establishing such a program would be funding for a director, a van and driver, and someone to oversee meal preparation. Rabbi Crystal thought that these monies could be provided by the congregation and the local chapter of Hadassah, the Jewish welfare council. There would be enough funding to provide a program for three days per week.

"Tom, we will need to rely on you pretty heavily if this is to become a reality," Rabbi Crystal observed.

How to Proceed?

Following his initial excitement over the new program, Tom began to reflect on what his next steps would be in the quest to help Myra and Jean. His patience with waiting to hear from Samantha Ross was rewarded by a message that reported, "The center council has decided to move the dance to Thursday night and approved some changes in the menu for her benefit. Please call me so we can discuss this."

The realization that the center council was willing to consider ways to accommodate Myra generated a deep sense of satisfaction for Tom and stimulated his dreaming about many other substantial changes that could open Warren Senior Center to the whole community. There could be life after New York City for Myra! Tom thought of her and how pleased she would be with the changes and the sense of empowerment she would feel as a result of her speaking up. Jean had already indicated that Myra appear to feel a bit better about the center and her relationships there.

Tom knew that this dilemma was one of those "soul searching" times in his social work career. It sounded as though the possibility of inaugurating a Jewish senior activity program was very real. However, the request for more cultural and religious sensitivity at Warren Senior Center had not fallen on deaf ears, and there were signs that Myra was becoming more integrated there. "How should I invest the limited time and skill resources I have" was the question most on Tom's mind as he contemplated the difficult choice before him. He wondered, "What would be best for her? For present and future Jewish elders? For other religious and ethnic elders? For the community?"

13. teaching note
Why Can't They Make This Place More Jewish?
Evelyn Hoffman and Dennis R. Myers

Case Synopsis

Tom Harris, a gerontological social worker in central Arkansas, confronted the dilemma of how to help a Jewish client from New York in a publicly-funded senior center program that offered only southern foods and games and Christian-centered programs. As Tom addressed the case, the public senior center became more ethnically sensitive. He also discovered that the local synagogue was willing to consider providing senior center services to their elderly Jewish members. Tom was faced with a practical and ethical dilemma around whether to advocate for ethnic and religious integration or segregation in programs for older persons.

Learning Outcomes Related to Religion and Spirituality

The case discussion will facilitate the work of students as they

1. Understand how social workers are involved in transitions that significantly impact older clients and their families.

2. Develop the capacity to engage in ethical and professionally competent assessment and problem solving when legitimate personal, religious, ethnic, and professional values are in tension.

3. Encounter the issues of federal funding and the separation of church and state.

4. Practice developing religiously and ethnically competent social work interventions at the macro level.

5. Enhance their capacity to understand and assess the strengths of Jewish culture and family life.

6. Assess and clarify the micro, mezzo, and macro practice implications of balancing the competing demands of dominant and minority client cultures.

7. Identify the impact of culture on caregiving in later life.

8. Explore the pros and cons of ethnically integrated versus ethnically segregated social programs.

9. Consider the implications of client advocacy and client empowerment for social work practice.

Courses and Levels for Which the Case Is Intended

This case is appropriate for master's level advanced practice courses to highlight how religion and ethnicity impact micro/mezzo/macro practice within the context of diversity, social justice, and populations at risk. This case is also appropriate for the foundation year of graduate programs, as well as generalist baccalaureate programs, particularly within human behavior and the social environment and practice sequences. It may also be useful for teaching specialized content on rural social work, religion and spirituality, and gerontology.

Discussion Questions Related to Religion and Spirituality

These questions are intended to stimulate exploration of social work practice issues related to ethnicity, spirituality, and religion. Broader questions are also included to facilitate case utilization across a wide spectrum of course objectives and learner needs.

Establishing the Facts

1. Why did Myra Golden leave her home in New York?

2. What is Tom's position at the agency? What are Tom's qualifications for this role? What do we not know about Tom's role and the agency that may be relevant?

3. List Myra Golden's needs and explain how the Warren Senior Center is meeting them.

4. What aspects of the Warren Senior Center program are insensitive to Myra Golden's religious and ethnic beliefs and practices?

5. What role does Tom's supervisor play in the case?

Analysis

6. In what ways is being Jewish both a cultural and religious reality?

    Discuss the interplay that exists between a rich religious tradition and the development of language, symbols, rituals, and family life that may become an important cultural identity separate from individual participation in the religion's congregational practices and adherence to the belief system.

7. What are the family dynamics that Tom addresses as he works with Jean Rubin and Myra Golden? What do you see as strengths in the family? As weaknesses?

One of Tom's challenges is negotiating the tension between Jean's need to care effectively for her increasingly dependent mother and Myra's need for independence. In expressing her role of caregiver, Tom must help Jean temper her sense of responsibility for her mother's happiness and help Myra process the anger and grief connected to the loss of home, relations, and personal efficacy. Myra's adaptation to the Rubin's home can be facilitated by Tom if he enables the family to make this process intentional and ensures this transition does not exacerbate the conflict between Jean and her mother.

Strengths in the family are a loving mother-daughter relationship as well as a supportive spouse. A strong tradition of eldercare and inclusion which marks Jewish family and congregational life is another strength evident in the case. Jean's willingness to seek professional help contributes to easing Myra's transition.

Jean's tendency for overinvolvement with Myra may become a barrier to her personal development and her problem-solving skills.

8. What are the cultural and social changes with which Myra Golden is confronted in the move? How are those the same or different than those made by any senior adult relocating to a new community?

    Myra Golden has moved from a major urban setting with a large Jewish population and multi-ethnic neighborhoods to the rural South. The differences between those two settings are profound. Language differences, including accent and vocabulary, must be accounted for from the start. Food differences, entertainment opportunities, access to diversity, climate, and transportation (taxis and subways versus individual cars) are all potential areas of adjustment for Myra. Certainly any adult moving to a new community has to deal with a new home, new streets, new places to shop, new medical care delivery systems, and new faces, including new neighbors. However, most moves require more than simply adjusting to different cultural expectations, such as Southern cultural practices like waving at everyone and making eye contact. New localities may also shape different life stage expectations like involvement in community life, grandparenting, volunteering, etc.

9. What social work values are in tension?

This is a difficult situation as Tom must balance his ethical responsibilities to his client, his colleagues, his profession (social justice), and to society. His decision to work with the Jewish synagogue could result in services for a number of clients not being served currently and could make a difference for Myra and her needs as she adjusts to her new environment. However, that solution avoids the very important issue of justice for use of federal funds for programming that is not sensitive to diversity and that alienates clients of a faith perspective different than the majority. Tom may also find himself struggling with his own religious worldview and the emerging awareness that the center's programming is comfortable to him personally but does not address the needs of his client. Finally, reporting the agency's failure to provide religiously inclusive programming could result in termination of funding that would compromise services for a number of clients. The tension focuses on determining the competing needs of diversity within client systems and how to maximize competing values at the same time.

10. What are the advantages of the synagogue offering a senior adult program? Disadvantages? How does the presence of nine other senior adults who might come to a program at the synagogue but are not going to the senior center impact your thinking about the appropriate resolution of the dilemma?

    Highlight how the rich traditions of Jewish family, cultural, and religious life can be integrated into a senior center program. Examples are mentioned in the case, such as menu offerings and holiday celebrations. These and many other facets of the culture could be deeply infused, which would contribute to a heightened sense of identity among the Jewish elders within this community that does not highly value Jewish ways of life.

    Discuss what would be lost to the public senior center and to the community if this ethnically segregated approach were adopted (i.e., tolerance and understanding among citizens suffers, the enrichment potential inherent in integration of diverse cultural practices is not permitted to nourish communal life).

11. To what extent should publicly-funded social services accommodate the beliefs and practices of religious and ethnic groups? What legal basis is available to reinforce a demand that public social services accommodate these groups?

    This is the central social policy question raised by the case. It provides the platform for a discussion of the contemporary social issues of equal access to social provision, separation of church and state, accommodation for diversity, and budgetary limitations on social programs. State Units on Aging, which oversee the allocation of Older Americans Act funds, require that agencies which contract for services must provide programming that is ethnically sensitive.

12. What criteria might be applied in deciding whether or not to establish a religiously and/or ethnically segregated social provision?

    The social worker must consider the needs of the clients at the current center, the needs of Myra, and the needs of the other Jewish elderly persons expressing an interest in a senior center at the synagogue.

    Certainly, one consideration must be the cost of providing an alternate site and the possibility that the alternate site administrators may at some point decide to apply for federal and state funding and, in fact, compete for the available funds. Can the community support two programs? Does the provision of a second center ethnically polarize the community further? Might there be ways for two programs to work together on some joint programming? Is it possible to have "both/and" instead of "either/or?"

    Are there licensing or certification issues? Will the kitchen have to be examined by the health department? Does that present other issues?

13. What is the potential impact on his agency if Tom advocates for more inclusive programming at the senior center?

    Publicly funded agencies such as the county Mental Health and Retardation Center must be responsive to the cultural values and practices of the local community. Often Board member appointments and funding of the center are authorized by local public officials, such as county judges who are elected to office. These legal, political, and budgetary connections make agencies and employees susceptible to pressure from citizens if policies or programs are not perceived to be in concert with the community. If Tom presses too much for change at the Warren Center, he may create an unwanted political and economic backlash.

14. How do societal views of aging impact the social worker's perspective on this case?

Attitudes toward the elderly may influence the community's response to Myra's transitional needs. For example, the belief that "all old people are alike" devalues any initiative that seeks to individualize programming. Ageism may further hinder the availability of funding for the level of accommodations that would support an increase in ethnic sensitivity. Viewing aging as a "leveler" further diminishes the importance of ethnic identity in later life.

Action

15. What are Tom's next steps with Myra Golden? With the senior center? With the synagogue?

Hint: consider potential interventions at all three levels (micro, mezzo, and macro) of social work practice Examples of potential interventions:
- *Micro-counseling with Myra to facilitate her relocation.*
- *Mezzo-family intervention to enhance Myra's adaptation in the Rubin's home.*
- *Macro-advocacy to make the senior center more ethnically sensitive.*

16. What work do you think needs to be done with the family of Myra Golden and Jean Rubin?

Highlight the need for work within the mother-daughter relationship. Caregiving and care management issues now, and in the future, require attention to include education regarding community resources, education, and long-range planning.

17. To what extent should Tom take on the role of advocate? How would Tom begin to activate this role? What is at stake if he does? If he doesn't?

Responding to this question provides an opportunity for students to examine the Older Americans Act and how this service delivery system functions. Using this system as a basis, they can be challenged to discover avenues for influencing greater ethnic sensitivity within funded programs.

18. How does Tom deal with ethnic and/or religious prejudice and discrimination that may present barriers to the resolution of this matter?

Lead students into identifying strategies that promote greater tolerance for ethnic and religious differences. Have them consider how focus and dialogue groups might contribute.

19. What kind of consultation should Tom seek as he decides how to proceed? Who are the stakeholders and what available resources could or should be mobilized? How should Myra Golden be included in future decisions and actions?

Make the students aware of how the resources of senior citizen groups and gerontological specialists, such as the American Association of Retired Persons, the Area Agency on Aging, congregational senior adult ministries, and gerontological social workers, can be utilized.

Teaching Suggestions

The case is primarily designed to elicit reflection and conversation regarding Tom's role as a change agent at the macro level of practice. However, there is sufficient information to support discussion regarding assessment and intervention at the micro (counseling and care management) and mezzo (family) levels. Instructors may choose to emphasize a generalist perspective or focus on a particular level of practice. Therefore, alternative instructional modules are provided that can be mixed and matched according to course learning objectives.

Module 1:

Prior to the class, have students read the case and select three or four students who will provide a role play which delivers these foundational elements in an interesting way. Also select two groups of at least four students to plan a debate concerning Tom's next steps (i.e., whether or not he should advocate for more ethnic sensitivity in the public senior center or work with the synagogue to create a new program). In preparing their arguments, have each group review the analysis and action questions and include issues such as, but not limited to, the applicability of social work values, the implications of the course of action for Tom and his agency, community concerns around separation of church and state, and the dynamics of Myra and Jean's relationship. Each group will have an opportunity to rebut the other group's argument before leading the class in a discussion of the issues raised in the debate. The instructor may provide the class with a rating sheet on which they can evaluate the extent to which the groups addressed the issues they were assigned.

Module 2:

Ask the students to read the case before class and have them write responses to these questions. You may wish to collect these without assigning a grade.

1. What is going on here? What is Tom thinking and feeling as he encounters the dilemma in this case? How might Tom's own religious views influence him?

2. What social work practice and value issues does Tom need to sort through?

3. What would you do if you were Tom? What would you not do?

Ask selected students to read their reflections to their colleagues. Use the student reflections to draw out as many issues and action recommendations as time permits. Reach for the basis of the

students' recommendations for Tom's next steps. Draw out potential interventions that will assist Myra and the Rubin family in adapting to the relocation. Identify the arguments for and against the integration of religious or ethnic beliefs and practices in older adult programs. Contrast these with the advantages and disadvantages of religious and/or ethnic segregation in social programs.

Module 3:

Invite an authority on Jewish religion and culture to present an overview of these topics and provide her or his own unique perspective on the case. Lead students into a discussion of how their own faith perspectives and religious affiliations impact interpersonal relationships, music and food preferences, family traditions, perceptions of the elderly, and understandings of other people. Move the discussion to an examination of how faith and religion might impact social work practice.

All Modules:

After the case has been thoroughly discussed and the questions covered, explore the social worker's responsibility for culturally competent practice and the importance of intentionally addressing faith and practice in supervision and collaboration.

Additional Notes

14.

These Things Happen: Confronting Dual Responsibilities

Helen Wilson Harris, David A. Sherwood, and Elizabeth H. Timmons

Hector had gone into the first counseling session with Nancy Mejia thinking that he knew what to expect. Nancy was a 31-year-old Puerto Rican woman, referred by Juan Rodriguez, the pastor of a small Hispanic church not far away. Rev. Rodriguez had been seeing Mrs. Mejia and her husband about their marital difficulties, and he had described her problem to Hector as depression. Only a few minutes into the intake session, Hector realized that the problem was much more complicated than depression and that his intervention could alienate Rev. Rodriguez. He had a difficult decision to make.

Social Work and Ministry

Hector Gomez was both an ordained minister and an MSW, serving as Associate Pastor and Director of Community Ministry at Shiloh Fellowship, a large, multicultural Pentecostal church in Buffalo, New York. Hector had been with the church for 3 years and loved his work, believing that it was a perfect fit for his gifts and his training, both in spite of and because of the unique challenges and opportunities it brought him. Hector chose church social work because he wanted the opportunity to use both his professional skills and his belief in the love and the forgiveness found in a relationship with God.

Shiloh Fellowship was a large and growing downtown church that had made a strong commitment to providing social ministries to the local community, including free counseling, computer classes, day care, after-school tutoring, adult literacy classes, and school-based outreach services. Hector directed these programs and, as a licensed clinical social worker, provided the counseling services.

Nancy Mejia's referral had come from Estrella Sancta, a smaller Hispanic church affiliated with the same denomination. The congregations had developed a reciprocal relationship to meet needs and exchange resources. Shiloh was clearly the larger church in terms of resources, but the Shiloh pastoral staff was strongly committed to respecting and preserving the dignity of Estrella Sancta. The churches had participated together in Bible-school outreaches and community ministry development, which included tutoring, transportation, and other social services. Hector had been a resource for Juan Rodriguez, the pastor at Estrella Sancta, in a variety of ways, including assisting youths who needed services that were available at Shiloh, and providing day care for working single mothers.

As a social worker, Hector was frequently involved in the ministry interface of the two churches and had begun to establish some credibility with the more traditional Pastor Rodriguez. Hector felt like he possessed a deep understanding of the Hispanic church, both culturally and denominationally, because he had grown up in a similarly small and conservative Hispanic congregation. Hector admired the commitment of Pastor Rodriguez to make church and scripture central to the lives of members of the congregation. He remembered with appreciation his own pastor's role as a spiritual mentor while he grew up in the church and when he felt God's call to ministry.

The Referral

On a winter morning, Hector had received a call from Pastor Rodriguez about a family at Estrella Sancta.

"I've been trying to help this couple, the Mejias, with some problems they have been having in their marriage. I thought we were making some progress, but now things have gotten worse."

What do you mean?" asked Hector.

"Well," said Pastor Rodriguez, "I used to be able to really count on Nancy to do the right thing. She is the strong church member in the couple, and I had hopes that we could use this counseling situation to help her husband to take greater spiritual leadership in his home. Ramon isn't really involved in the church, but he needs to be. I know he has his problems and isn't always an easy person to live with, but I think he could be a better husband if he got more involved in the church. In the meantime, if Nancy just set the right example, maybe he would come around and be a better person at home and at church. But the more I've tried to talk with them, the more she has pulled back. Now she just cries and looks at the floor when we meet together. She stays at home except for going to work and to church service. She doesn't even come to the women's activities anymore. I think she's got a problem with depression. That's why I suggested that she come and see you. Maybe you can figure out if this depression thing is serious and help her get more out of my pastoral counseling. I'm getting nowhere right now."

"Would Ramon be willing to come in to see me as well?"

"Ramon said he wouldn't meet with anyone but me," Pastor Rodriguez replied. "He said it was hard enough to admit they had a few problems, and he wasn't going to take it any further out of the family."

"I think it is important for both of them to be involved," Hector said.

"He's beginning to trust me and frankly, he isn't comfortable with you. Hector, you may have family in Puerto Rico, but maybe you don't look very Puerto Rican to him. Besides, as their pastor it's my job to do everything I can to preserve their marriage and help bring him closer to God. You know I am their spiritual covering. I just need you to help her with this depression thing so she will get back on track."

"I'll do everything I can to help. Have you talked with Mrs. Mejia about this?"

"Yes," Pastor Rodriguez said. "I told her I wanted her to see you, and she said she would."

Hector's administrative assistant was able to arrange an appointment for the next afternoon.

My Husband and I Have Been Having Some Problems

When Hector brought Mrs. Mejia into his office and introduced himself, he noticed her subdued, shaky voice. He said, "You seem upset. Can you tell me about what brings you here today?"

Mrs. Mejia said in a soft voice, "My husband and I have been having some problems, and I just don't know what to do."

"Can you tell me more about that?" Hector said.

She started slowly, but gradually the details began to come out. She was 31 years old. Her parents had come from Puerto Rico, but she had been born and raised in the Buffalo area. She had finished high school, gone to work in an office, and started saving for more education, but her parents wanted her to settle down and start a family. She had married Ramon Mejia 6 years earlier, and they had a 4-year-old son.

Mrs. Mejia took a deep breath and continued. "Ramon and I are both Puerto Rican, but in many ways we come from different worlds." She explained that Ramon had come to Buffalo from Puerto Rico as a teenager and was steadily employed as a custodian in a large company. "Ramon works hard every night, but it is so hard to get ahead without an education."

Hector asked gently, "Whatever happened to your plans to go back to school?"

Nancy explained that she decided to go to school part-time after their son was born. She had completed her associate's degree at the community college and for the last two years had been employed as a secretary at a small office-supply company.

"That's when the problems really began," she said tearfully. "Ramon has always been a little jealous, but nothing like this. He accuses me of thinking I am better than him and always wants to know where I am every minute. He seems to get angry a lot, and we've been getting into these fights."

"What do you mean by 'fights'?"

"Well, it's mostly him yelling at me and putting me down. But it is even worse than that. Several times he has hit me. Usually he doesn't hit me, but I never know when he will. And he hits me so no one else will be able to see it. I'm so scared. And our little boy gets so scared when he is like that."

"Have you told Pastor Rodriguez about the hitting?"

Nancy said, "Oh no. I couldn't do that. I just said we fight a little. I'm afraid to tell him any more—Pastor Rodriguez is trying so hard to get Ramon in the church. I think he believes it is my fault that Ramon doesn't come more. I don't want the church to think I'm a bad wife and a bad Christian. I know what they'd say."

"What do you mean, you know what they'd say?" asked Hector.

These Things Just Happen

Nancy hesitated. Hector sat quietly and waited for her to continue.

"There are a few of the other sisters in the church that I feel close to. I told a few of them what has been happening."

Hector asked, "What did they say?"

"They said these things just happen. You just have to live with it. Maybe it's your cross to bear. Maybe God is teaching you something. Just pray that God will give you the strength you need to be a good and patient wife, and pray that God will change him. They said that they would pray for us, and that I should remain faithful to both my husband and God. Our people believe that you have to submit to your husband. That's what they say. And I know Pastor will say the same thing."

She paused again. "They even told me that I should be careful not to involve the authorities in the situation. They warned me that I could end up losing my son if I reported that Ramon was hitting me."

Hector listened quietly as she shared her disappointment that her friends in the church had not offered to help her but had instead told her she would be wrong to try to get away. He was familiar with the thinking that God would frown on a woman who left her husband, the belief that it was part of the woman's job to just take it and keep the family going no matter what.

"That must leave you feeling very stuck," Hector said.

"I'm afraid all the time. I can't sleep. I feel sick to my stomach and I've lost 20 pounds this year. I can't concentrate at work." She began to cry softly. "I'm just so sad. I don't know what to do anymore. I don't know when he is going to start in on me again. I'm at the end the end of my rope. I just wish it were all over."

"You wish it were all over?" Hector asked. "I'm wondering if that means you have thought about hurting yourself."

Nancy sighed. "Two times every day. I drive across a bridge on my way to work, and I get this very strong feeling that I should swerve off the bridge into the river."

"This sounds serious. Have you thought about other ways to deal with this?"

"Leaving," Nancy said, "but that seems so impossible. I'm afraid the church wouldn't understand that. Neither would my family. And even if they did and tried to help me, I'm afraid they might get hurt too. You don't know how angry he can get."

As a Hispanic man, Hector was familiar with the strong cultural admonition for women to submit to their husbands and also to church authority. In some ways there was an interaction between the machismo culture of the Hispanic community and the religious culture of his church that included valuing intact families, the husband's authority in the home, and the importance of discipline and compliance with authority. Hector had grown up in a home where the roles of mother and father were clearly defined. He had found many of those gender roles challenged as he left home and completed his theological and social work education. Hector realized that he had experienced significant changes in his own view of the roles of men and women in the family and in the church. Even so, on holiday visits home he still found that his mother spent her time in the kitchen and waited on his father. His father's word in the home was law, and everyone seemed to know and accept the rules.

Hector also knew that in the Pentecostal church, the authority of husbands in the home was a major doctrinal position. In spite of their relative freedom to assume leadership positions in the church, women were expected to submit to their husbands as the "head of the house." Hector was aware that many in the church were fond of quoting the Bible passage from Ephesians 5:22, "Wives, submit to your husbands as to the Lord."

This Is Serious

Hector's mind was racing as he considered what to do next. He thought, "This is serious. Nancy and the child are at risk of being hurt. And she feels desperate."

He considered several possibilities. "I know I've got a good relationship with the women's shelter and I know there's a family or two here in Shiloh Fellowship who could make room for Nancy and her son for a little while until things get sorted out."

But Hector also could not help thinking, "I know I'm going to have to address this with my pastor and the referring pastor, and I know they may not support me, especially Pastor Rodriguez. In fact, I know that my senior pastor is going to ask if we really have to do this. He'll want to know if there are any other options. When it comes right down to it, will he back me up? I'm afraid that Pastor Rodriguez won't understand at all. He'll probably think that I didn't do what he asked me to do. He'll think that I support the breakup of families. He made it pretty clear that the marital relationship is an issue for him to deal with, not me. Clearly the abuse has not been discussed with him. What will he feel about Nancy telling me and not him? Man, what is this going to do to the relationship between our two churches?"

Hector asked Mrs. Mejia, "I know this has been really hard for you. I need to know how safe you feel now."

Nancy replied, "I'm afraid to go home. He threatened me when I went out the door to come here. I know I'm going to get it if I go home."

"Nancy," Hector said, "there are several options for you. Before I explore them with you, I'd like your permission to discuss our conversation with my senior pastor so we can determine how our church can help. Will that be all right?"

Nancy nodded slowly. "OK. I'll wait here."

Now What?

Hector called Pastor Pevia at home and explained the situation. "So," he concluded, "she is in my office, terrified of going home. She is desperate, and the situation is not safe. I think I can get her into the women's shelter, but I'm concerned about Pastor Rodriguez."

Pastor Pevia sighed. "Hector, you know that this woman is Pastor Rodriguez's responsibility, not yours. Why don't you tell her that she needs to tell her pastor this information? He is going to feel that you took over his authority and interfered with the work he is doing with this family. You know we have a lot at stake here. Think about the children's ministries and the youth. Think about the work you have been able to do with the families from that church. We don't want to jeopardize all of that."

"Yes sir, I know," replied Hector. "I don't want to do anything to alienate Pastor Rodriguez. But Nancy is scared of telling him, and you know yourself that the church's position is for a woman to keep the family together no matter what."

Pastor Pevia's voice rose slightly, "Yes, I do know that. Hector, I have confidence in your judgment, but you need to know that if you go ahead with this, it's going to cost us all a lot of headaches. Are you sure you can't work it out with Pastor Rodriguez?"

14. teaching note
These Things Happen: Confronting Dual Responsibilities
Helen Wilson Harris, David A. Sherwood, and Elizabeth H. Timmons

Case Synopsis

Social worker Hector Gomez served on the staff of a large multicultural, urban church. He received a referral from the pastor of a smaller Hispanic church affiliated with the same denomination. The pastor asked Hector to see a depressed woman, the wife in a couple who had been in the pastor's marital counseling. Hector discovered that the woman was being battered by her husband and was ready to leave. He knew that facilitating this move would be counter to the norms of Hispanic culture and the Pentecostal church, which emphasize keeping families together. Hector wondered how to help his client with the immediate crisis while preserving his working relationship with the referring pastor. Hector knew that it was important to continue the collaboration between the two congregations and to honor the faith tradition of keeping families intact. He also knew that his client's safety could be in jeopardy.

Learning Outcomes Related to Religion and Spirituality

The case discussion will facilitate the work of students as they

1. Understand the cultural and spiritual beliefs of the major players in this case and the impact of those beliefs on the options available.

2. Identify dual roles and responsibilities in congregational social work, specifically the dual roles of minister and social worker.

3. Examine the dynamics of trust and credibility between disciplines, particularly when there are fundamental theological, political, or ideological differences.

Other Learning Outcomes for Which This Case Can Be Used

The case discussion will facilitate the work of students as they

4. Examine values such as client self-determination and confidentiality in a nontraditional social work context.

5. Consider systems impacts in collateral referral agreements.

6. Describe the similarities and differences between formal helping networks (congregational structures and community social service agencies) and informal helping networks (Mrs. Mejia's family and the church "sisters").

Courses and Levels for Which the Case Is Intended

This case was written for a master's level, micro-macro advanced practice course. However, the case may also be useful at the undergraduate and foundation-year level in practice or field seminar courses, and in specialized courses dealing with social work practice in congregational contexts or culturally sensitive social work practice.

Discussion Questions Related to Religion and Spirituality

Various combinations of the following questions can be used, depending on what aspects of the case an instructor wishes to explore or emphasize.

Establishing the Facts

1. What is Hector's position in the church?

2. What is the arrangement for collaboration between the two congregations?

3. What do we know or need to know in order to assess the urgency of Mrs. Mejia's safety issues?

   Hector has determined that Mrs. Mejia is desperate and considering suicide but has not yet completed an assessment of the risk of suicide. This is the most urgent area of assessment. Additionally, there may be concern about the child's safety if Mrs. Mejia is transporting him across the bridge when she is thinking of driving over the edge. If she is not at immediate risk of suicide, her level of depression must be assessed. She may need to see a physician for medication assistance.

4. Who are the persons to whom Hector must relate as he determines that Mrs. Mejia's situation constitutes a crisis?

   Hector knows he will need to talk with both his pastor and the referring pastor as he completes his assessment and begins making referrals for Mrs. Mejia. He realizes as well that he will need to assist her with finding safe shelter, which may mean placing someone else in jeopardy. Additionally, Hector is aware that Mr. Mejia may blame him for Mrs. Mejia's decision to leave and seek shelter elsewhere. Therefore, Hector may find himself confronted by the abusive husband.

5. What do we know or what may we deduce from this case about Pentecostal beliefs and values about marriage, about gender roles, and about

dealing with problems? Is there anything we need to clarify or confirm?

   We may determine from the referring pastor's conversation that he sees the pastoral role as being very important for this family and for the life of the other families in the church.

   Additionally, the role of men as leaders of their families seems to be a belief of both the pastor and the women of the church who Mrs. Mejia consulted. There also seems to be a belief among the women of the church that problems should be managed within the home and church.

   Hector knows that the pastor has been counseling with this couple. His respect for the pastoral role and his reluctance to usurp that role are important. Hector does not know what Mr. Mejia's spiritual condition is, but he recognizes that the pastor is ascribing value to the role of the male head of the family as a spiritual leader. Hector is working as a social worker in a Pentecostal church because he believes that the problems of society are best addressed through the love and the forgiveness found in a relationship with God. He has grown up in the Pentecostal church where problems are addressed "within the family of God." The pastors with whom Hector works seem to share these experiences and beliefs. Hector is not familiar enough with the Mejias to know whether or how deeply they share these beliefs.

6. What do we know or what may we deduce from this case about Hispanic cultural values and beliefs related to marriage and gender roles? Is there anything we need to clarify or confirm?

   The major players in this case are all Hispanic and are living out their own understandings of Hispanic cultural values and beliefs, but they may not all be the same. Hector was reared in a traditional, conservative home but has experienced some changes in perception. He is aware of the emphasis placed on traditional gender roles and is able to ascertain their impact on Mrs. Mejia, who has endured significant abuse, Mr. Mejia, who struggles with the need to dominate his wife even as she makes educational and financial progress, and the referring pastor, who has attempted to preserve this family unit and bring the husband "into the church."

7. What areas of overlap and or distinction do we find between Pentecostal and Hispanic beliefs and values?

There are indications in this case that both Hispanic and Pentecostal beliefs include fairly traditional understandings of families and male authority in the home. Additionally, there seems to be overlap in the belief that problems should be addressed within the family, both in the culture and in the church. Pastor Rodriguez voices the belief that involvement in the church will remediate Mr. Mejia's behavior in the home and strengthen the marital and family relationships.

8. How have religious views and interpretations of the Bible impacted the support available to Mrs. Mejia?

Hector is concerned that Mrs. Mejia has not been offered sanctuary because the women of her church attribute blame to her lack of faith and perhaps even her lack of faithfulness. He realizes that any assistance he provides to her outside of the family unit and the church structure will further distance her from this support network. It seems very significant that the women of the church, to whom Mrs. Mejia feels closest, have given her answers that include their interpretation of scripture, which suggests that she should stay with her husband and submit to the abuse. In these ways she has already lost the support of the congregation.

On the other hand, Hector holds his position because of his church's commitment to providing resources for people in need. He knows of at least some families in his church who would be willing to take Mrs. Mejia and her child into their homes in order to be faithful to their religious views and interpretations of the Bible. It is important to note the diversity between these two collaborating congregations and to be aware that there is likely diversity within the congregations as well.

9. Even though Hector is an "insider" culturally and religiously, what might he still need to learn more about to help Mrs. Mejia, and how might he learn it?

Although it is easy to make assumptions about individuals and groups based on this case or experiences with representatives of a group, it is important that critical thinkers not stereotype clients or client groups by making generalizations. Hector is in a position to understand some things about the family, the culture, and the church. However, he must always find out from his clients and the client systems more about their culture, their spirituality, their religion, and how each is significant in the clients' lives.

Analysis

10. How does Hector's position as both a minister and as a social worker complicate his work with Mrs. Mejia? How does it enhance his work with Mrs. Mejia?

Mrs. Mejia would likely not have gone to see a lay counselor or therapist. Her willingness to see Hector seems largely a result of the referral by her pastor. His dual role, although complicating for him, is in fact a benefit for her. Hector is not only skilled in assessment and counseling, but speaks the language of the church as well. He may also be able to mobilize the resources of the church and effectively negotiate continued support for Mrs. Mejia within the congregation. Hector must include consequences for the church in his assessment and interventions.

11. What difference would it make if the social worker were not a member of either of these two congregations?

There may be both challenges and benefits to the social worker's position as a member of the congregation and of the congregational staff. Certainly Hector is knowledgeable about the language and worldview of the church and can understand and empathize with the Mejias spiritual journey and their work with their pastor. Additionally, Hector understands and can facilitate the congregation's support. There are areas, however, that may be compromised by Hector's church membership. The potential for dual relationships, the challenge of confidentiality, and the concern about the rest of the church and its programs are all particular concerns.

12. How does the concept of "pastoral covering" impact the way that the pastors in this situation might view Hector's interventions and involvement?

The view of the pastor as one who provides "covering" and "shepherding" for his flock is important. Rev.

Rodriguez may perceive Hector's intervention as violating the expectations he had when he made the referral, which jeopardizes the sense of responsibility Rev. Rodriguez may feel for what happens with the Mejias. Additionally, if Mrs. Mejia leaves her husband, even temporarily, Hector may be perceived as violating other beliefs about families and husband-wife relationships that Rev. Rodriguez values. Hector may share with Rev. Rodriguez and Rev. Pevia a belief in pastoral responsibility, but he may also believe that other values take priority in a situation such as this one. Rev. Rodriguez may believe that he needs to be in charge of the helping process, and Rev. Pevia may be caught in the middle, supporting the principle that the Mejias should be considered Rev. Rodriguez' pastoral responsibility, but also respecting Hector's judgment and skills regarding what may be needed in this case. Hector will need to fashion his intervention to respect this pastoral principle as much as possible as he goes along, and to work to overcome any negative consequences that may weaken the relationships between the pastors and the congregations. Hector believes the pastor's investment in his congregants is very important to the spiritual care of the Mejias, and, Rev. Rodriguez has been working with Mr. Mejia to get him more involved in spirituality and in the life of the church. He may believe, with the pastors, that a referral outside of the church will damage the opportunity to share the love and the forgiveness of Christ with this young man.

13. What sources of strength might be available to Mrs. Mejia from her church and faith network?

Mrs. Mejia will benefit from awareness that there are church members who are willing to help her through the crisis. Additionally, Mrs. Mejia's values, beliefs, and attitudes are important to her and are grounded in her culture and in her faith. She, like many clients, may find strength in her religious beliefs and in the support available to her through the church. Hector believes he knows people within the church who will be willing to provide her temporary shelter, financial and material support, and emotional and spiritual support.

14. What are the systems concerns and issues here?

Hector's church is larger, multicultural, and a partner with the smaller Hispanic church. The churches have worked together on several projects, and a misstep here could jeopardize the collaborative work being done with Hispanic youth and other groups.

There are additional larger concerns, including the question of mandated licensing requirements to report suspected abuse or neglect.

15. What are Hector's conflicting interests regarding the client, the churches, and the referring pastor?

Mrs. Mejia is Hector's primary client. As a pastor and a church staff member, Hector must consider the impact of his decision on the joint ministry of the two congregations and the youth who are the primary beneficiaries of that collaboration. His pastor, Rev. Pevia, may not be supportive of his intervention in this case because of the church's emphasis on solving problems within marriages. His pastor may also have concerns about alienating Pastor Rodriguez. Pursuing a referral resulting in Mrs. Mejia's departure from the family could jeopardize Hector's work in the church and could in fact jeopardize his position. There may be much at stake for the church as well, when the traditional positions of male authority and female submission are challenged by presenting alternatives. The referring pastor, Rev. Rodriguez, has been working with this couple and may feel embarrassed or angry about Mrs. Mejia's decision to withhold the domestic abuse from him. One of Hector's interests is to take care of the client while preserving the working relationship with the referring pastor. This cannot happen if the pastor loses face in the transaction.

16. What does it mean when women in a church are afraid that reporting beatings could result in losing their children to the authorities?

The possibility exists that this fear and concern might be related to the women's experiences directly or indirectly with immigration and naturalization. Might these women have fears of governmental authority and intervention? This might partially explain the reluctance to "tell" about the abuse. It is possible for a culture of fear to be developed when members of a group have stories about maltreatment at the hands of "authorities."

17. What does it mean when generations of patriarchal authority have resulted in the sense that "it has always been this way?"

Generations of patriarchal authority seem to be reinforced by both the culture and the church. Mrs. Mejia learns from the "other sisters" in the church that women are expected to "take it." She is told that this is her "cross to bear" and is reminded that women have been subjected to this behavior for generations. We are not told the ages of the women she consulted, but there does seem to be a sense that her supporters or mentors crossed generational lines. It seems significant as well that she does not believe there will be any significant help available to her from her family. In fact, she worries about their safety.

18. How does Mrs. Mejia's history of growing up in the United States compare with her husband's past, in which he came to the mainland as a teenager?

    It is very possible that Mrs. Mejia's youth in the United States has contributed to her willingness to seek further education and to now consider going against the traditional gender roles and leaving her husband. Is it possible that Mr. Mejia's arrival in the United States as a teenager may have impacted not only his education, but also his adjustment to the new country and his subsequent relationships? Is it possible that the culture in Puerto Rico is more traditional in ascribing gender roles than even Puerto Rican culture in the United States? If so, Mr. Mejia's youth in Puerto Rico may be part of the difference in the couple's opinions of education, women working outside the home, and so forth.

Action

19. If you were Hector, what would you do? What are the major alternatives you have for the next step? What are the pros and cons and any ethical concerns for each option?

    a. Assist Mrs. Mejia with a plan for leaving or for safety the next time her husband becomes abusive. This option includes providing Mrs. Mejia with phone numbers for emergency assistance.

    b. Refer this situation back to the couples' counselor. Call Pastor Rodriguez and enlist him to confront Mr. Mejia and meet with the couple.

    c. Call Mr. Mejia and request he come to the office for a meeting.

    d. Assist Mrs. Mejia with calling her family for help leaving.

    e. Assist Mrs. Mejia with a safe place in the congregation and a referral to the Women's shelter.

    f. Send Mrs. Mejia for a psychiatric assessment for antidepressant medication.

    g. Others?

20. What structural arrangements or working agreements might Hector develop to facilitate referrals and case ownership in the future?

    One of the challenges in congregational social work is the informality of the context. It is not known in this case if Hector has a job description outlining his duties as a social services minister in the church. It is not known what Pastor Rodriguez or Pastor Pevia understands about social work as a profession, about professional licensure, and about reporting mandates. Certainly it would make some sense to consider formalizing this information for the pastors, deacon bodies, and church staff who might make referrals between the churches. Frank discussion between Hector and the referring pastors will make a real difference in avoiding similar dilemmas in the future.

21. How can social workers educate congregations about issues of family abuse using methods that are sensitive to the diversity of the group and that recognize and utilize the strengths of the church's commitment to intact families?

    Education of the congregation is an approach that may or may not impact the Mejias but will likely help the pastors and the congregations with future situations like this one. Information about the frequency of abuse, discussions regarding gender roles, and the use of scripture to address injustice would be a beginning. Sensitivity to scripture that celebrates the value of each human being would enable the congregants to continue to depend on the Bible and their spiritual experience to define family and family relationships. It is certainly possible that the commit-

ment of the churches and pastors to the integrity of the family could lead to the provision of support and services that would help this family and others get needed help. Premarital and marital counseling and enrichment groups might be one approach to providing this information in an interactive format.

22. It appears that Mrs. Mejia has decided that things must change even if it means leaving her husband. What should Hector do if he finds this decision to be in conflict with his own perceptions of what should be done and if he believes that he could not in good conscience support it?

    The standard answer for social workers when their values come into conflict with a client's values is to refer that client to another service provider. Although this may be a possibility in this situation, it may also be impossible to refer the case to another Protestant church social worker. One option is for Hector to clarify for the client his own value position, help her explore the pros and cons of each possible decision, and endorse the social work value of client self-determination.

Teaching Suggestions

This case enables students to explore both the challenges and the opportunities in congregational social work practice. Encourage students to be careful when they explore stereotypical thinking in the church, and equally in themselves, as they examine these complex issues. As students lay out the facts of the case and explore the issues in depth, they will be able to frame the problem and decide how they would respond to the situation. The discussion should include an examination of how Hector's training as a social worker enabled him both to discover the crisis of domestic violence in the Mejia family and to confront the issues of church support during his first interview with Mrs. Mejia. Students should be encouraged to explore the dual roles that Hector Gomez has in the church setting and the competing needs of this client and the clients who benefit from the collaboration of the churches. As students discuss the facts of the case and the complexities of the competing value systems, they will be able to identify the options available to Hector and to discuss the pros and cons of each. Additional areas of discussion could include the benefits of social workers as ministers in the congregation and the challenges of dual identity. Consider discussing "what ifs": What if Hector were Anglo or African American? What if these two congregations and pastors were Catholic or Jewish instead of Pentecostal? Would the dynamics be the same? These "what if" discussions could be done in small group discussions, enabling a broader inclusion of perspectives on the impact of spirituality and ethnicity on social work in congregations.

Additional Notes

15.

Reason to Believe

T. Laine Scales, Linda B. Morales, and Elisabeth Kenny

In the spring of 1992, Carla Shepherd, a Child Protective Services worker in Waco, Texas was assigned to investigate allegations of child abuse among members of a Branch Davidian religious community living in the county. After a thorough investigation, Carla needed to decide how to write up her investigation of this unusual group. She wanted to be objective, but rumors around the town about abuse, and pressure to either find something or close the case immediately, made writing the report difficult. Carla needed more time to explore the community, but deadlines were inevitable.

Carla was a licensed social worker who had been employed for over 10 years by McLennan County Child Protective Services. This job was her first after completing her BSW degree at Baylor University, and she had become very skilled at working with children and their families. She was known in the agency as a good social worker who had the ability to get children to open up to her. When she first came to the agency, Carla was assigned to "in homes" casework, but she had eventually been assigned as an investigative social worker, sent to probe potentially difficult cases, like this one.

The Case Is Opened

On February 26, 1992, Carla's supervisor, Darlene Starr, called Carla into her office and handed her a file. "We have a report from a court in Michigan that there is physical and sexual abuse

going on out there with the Davidians. The allegations came out during a custody battle up there."

When Carla heard the word "Davidians," she knew immediately that Darlene was referring to the religious community of Branch Davidians who were living a few miles outside the city. The group had been featured in the local media 4 years earlier, in November 1987, when a skirmish between the leaders ended in gunfire. The two feuding men had been arrested, and the situation was resolved when George Roden was declared mentally incompetent and his opponent, Vernon Howell, assumed leadership of the group, changing his name to David Koresh. The Davidians kept to themselves, so until the shoot-out, most Waco citizens had not heard of the group and did not know they were living in the surrounding countryside. Now and then, someone might mention the Davidians in passing, and Carla remembered hearing the Sheriff characterize Koresh as "a good ol' boy." But occasionally, people showed fear or disdain for the "fanatics living out there."

Now someone had filed a report. "I want you to go out there and investigate these allegations" said Darlene, "and just to be sure that there is no trouble, I am going to go with you and we will take two deputies from the Sheriff's department."

"Wow!" said Carla. "Do we really need all that? Do you think anyone will be willing to talk openly if we bring 'the law' with us?"

Darlene reminded Carla of the skirmish that had been all over the news. "We want to be safe rather than sorry. The deputies will stay outside; we just want to have them there."

The Branch Davidians

This subgroup of the Branch Davidian religious community had existed in Waco, Texas since 1935 when its founder, Victor Houteff, brought his ministry from California. Houteff had attempted to establish his group by drawing converts away from the Seventh Day Adventist Church. He preached millennialism—the idea that the "end times" would be coming right away and would be announced by a catastrophic event aided by superhuman agents. Millennialist sects live in a constant state of readiness for the apocalyptic end of the world, building temporary homes and often separating themselves from mainstream society.

After realizing that most Seventh Day Adventists in California were not receptive to his message, Houteff decided to move with his followers to the city of Waco, Texas. A few years later, the group purchased 77 acres of land outside Waco, and built a community which they called Mount Carmel. Houteff and his followers lived at Mt. Carmel until his death in 1955, at which point, his wife, Florence, took over the leadership of the Davidians.

The sect continued seeking new recruits, especially among members of the Seventh Day Adventist churches in California, Australia, and England, as well as local community members in Texas. In 1987, in the wake of the shoot-out, Vernon Howell of Palestine, Texas, took over the leadership of Mt. Carmel from George Roden. Howell then took on the name "David," suggesting the renewal of the Old Testament Israelite kingdom, and the name "Koresh," a derivative of the Biblical "Cyrus," after the Persian king who had defeated the Babylonians and allowed exiled Jews to return to their homeland.

David Koresh proclaimed himself "messiah" and "anointed one" from the Biblical House of David and claimed he had been sent to open the Seven Seals that signaled the coming apocalypse, as promised in the New Testament Book of Revelation. Koresh was known as a charismatic leader who exerted a great deal of authority over his group of followers.

Child Protection and Religious Beliefs

In her 10 years of service, Carla had become very familiar with the policies of Child Protective Services. She knew that CPS policy was very clear in its requirements that workers respect the religious beliefs of the families with whom they come into contact, and it was very important to her that she clearly understand these policies before she went out to do the investigation. So on February 25, as she was preparing for the Branch Davidians home visit, she spent some time looking through the CPS manual for guidance.

The manual contained one section called "Investigation of Lack of Medical Care Because of Religious Beliefs." Defining medical neglect was the most common area of conflict between child protection and religious beliefs. In these cases, medical experts had established that a procedure or intervention was necessary for a child's health, but sometimes the parents' religious beliefs prohibited the procedure. The manual described various processes in cases of alleged medical neglect, but Carla did not believe this situation would pertain to the Branch Davidians, because the allegations were not related to medical neglect. But she did note this phrase at the end of the section: "If the worker determines that the child is otherwise abused or neglected, the worker gives a disposition of Reason to Believe (RTB) to allegations other than medical neglect." Carla knew her job was to determine if there were any reasons to believe that the allegations about child welfare were true.

Carla also knew that CPS had been involved in further disagreements about other additional areas of treatment of children, which had led to reports and a subsequent investigation of religious groups. For example, she had read about an incident in another state involving a 15-month-old boy who had been taken out of a 3-hour-long church service because he cried. The boy was spanked by his parent under the supervision of a deacon, and investigations revealed that the child had bruises on his thighs and buttocks.

"Will I find something similar at Mt. Carmel?" Carla wondered. In cases like the one she had read about, there were two concerns raised. First, a 15-month-old child was not developmentally ready to learn such compliant behavior as being quiet in church. Second, the degree of correction—leaving bruises—was out of line. Carla believed that workers needed to respect the scriptural justification often quoted by the parents: "Spare not the rod from your son lest he die." But respecting their beliefs did not mean that CPS would tolerate abuse.

Investigations Begin

Typically, CPS workers arrive unannounced on the first visit to investigate a home and then announce any subsequent visits. When Carla and Darlene arrived at Mt. Carmel on February 27, 1992, David Koresh had gone into town. Carla and Darlene interviewed one child, Cyrus, who was the 5-year-old son of David Koresh and his wife, Rachel. Rachel was very pleasant to the two social workers and readily gave permission for them to interview Cyrus alone. As she closed the door, she instructed the boy, "Answer whatever questions these nice ladies ask you."

A few days after Carla and Darlene visited Mt. Carmel in February, David Koresh came to the office of CPS to talk to Carla. He made it very clear that the CPS workers were welcome to come back any time and talk to anyone in the community. "We have nothing to hide," he said. He was very cooperative, and Carla recalled the Sheriff's description of this "good ol' boy." She saw in him the charisma that drew followers to his cause. While sitting in Carla's office, Koresh began to speak about his doctrine of the Seven Seals, based on the Bible, and in particular, the Book of Revelation. Carla's Sunday School class had actually studied this prophetic text a few years before. The class members and the teacher had agreed that it was difficult, confusing, and not easily discerned.

Carla had been raised in the small town of Comanche, Texas, by devout parents who regularly attended the Mt. Olive Church of Christ. She studied the Bible regularly, but many of the gloomy revelations about the "end times" were beyond her comprehension. Carla felt uncomfortable when Koresh quoted scripture in her office, and she did not know how to respond. He referred to himself as "the anointed one," which in her experience was a term that referred to Jesus Christ. He also believed, as millennialists do, that the "end times" were coming right away.

As Koresh left her office, she said to herself, "I have to separate my personal convictions from theirs, and most important, I must separate what I believe from what I know my job is in this situation. I *must* remain objective!"

The original 30-day deadline was nearing. Carla did not have enough information to write her report so she asked for, and was granted, an extension of one month. She wanted to visit Mt. Carmel again and to try to gather more information.

The Interviews Continue

On the second visit, April 6, 1992, Carla took a co-worker, Paula, to help with the numerous interviews. Darlene, her supervisor, came along as well and spoke with some of the adults in the community. The Sheriff's department escorted the workers, remaining outside during the investigation. As the three social workers entered Mt. Carmel, they had to wait a few moments while a Bible study ended. As Carla stood in the doorway listening to the sermon, she realized that so much of the scripture Koresh was preaching sounded familiar to her from her own church experience. "When I talk to the Davidians, their sincerity and strong belief really come through," she thought. "Both the children and the adults I have met here seem sincerely convinced that their way of life is the true path."

"When I first heard of Mt. Carmel, I thought they were dangerous fanatics," Carla mused. "But I have seen that their belief is strong and steady. And they certainly do study it a lot!"

After the Bible study ended, the interviews began. While Darlene talked to the adults in the community, Carla and Paula interviewed about fifteen children. The workers talked to the children as a group, building rapport by being friendly and trying to demonstrate that they could be trusted. Carla and Paula asked the children questions about their daily lives, asked if they had been physically punished, or touched in ways that made them uncomfortable. They asked questions such as, "What happens when you get in trouble? Who disciplines you when you do something wrong? In what ways are you disciplined?" to give the children opportunity to report physical overcorrection and to give an idea of what behavior might be corrected by adults in their community. However, the children did not report any activities that indicated abuse. The children had memorized Bible verses and quoted them. It seemed to Carla that they were repeating what adults had taught them to say. She wondered if perhaps they had been coached for these interviews.

There was never a time during the interviews when any child made a statement that Carla considered evidence of abuse. Still, Carla continued the investigation, feeling that the children were not trusting her and longing for more time to gain their confidence.

"You are a Babylonian! Are you going to take us away?" asked Mark, a 4-year-old boy.

"You are safe with me," said Carla. " I will not hurt you." She could not contain her curiosity. "Why do you call me a Babylonian?" she asked. "What is a Babylonian?"

"A person who lives out there," replied Mark. "A person who is not one of us."

It became clear to Carla that without the children's trust she would have a difficult time getting information from them.

Searching for Evidence

Carla and Paula returned to Mt. Carmel one more time, on April 30. On this visit, the workers particularly wanted to speak with the teenage girls, as some of the reports alleged that the teenage girls were taken as "wives." According to Texas law, a young woman must be 18 years of age to legally consent to sexual relations, but girls may obtain parental permission to cohabit or marry at age 14. Carla interviewed five adolescent girls and not one of them made any statement that indicated they were having sexual relations with Koresh, that they were considered his wives, or that they were in any way abused. The adults never referred to any of the teenagers as wives of Koresh. Carla still had no proof that the allegations were true.

The workers also asked to tour the facilities in order to examine the living conditions and to make an assessment of hygiene, nutrition, and overall safety. Perhaps the children were being neglected or endangered in this manner. As she walked around the house, Carla thought that she was in a maze. Rooms and hallways had been added on and, without a guide, it would have been easy to get lost.

The religious practices of the Davidians required that the men and the boys sleep in a dormitory-like facility on one floor of the two-story house, with the women, the girls, and the small boys sleeping on a separate floor. There were no indoor bathrooms in the home, and members of the family used chamberpots and buried their waste outside in a back lot. Carla was amazed that there were no unpleasant odors in the home, and she determined that the facilities were adequate and sanitary. In fact, all of Mt. Carmel was very clean.

Next, Carla and Paula examined the kitchen and food storage areas. The group kept their food in large coolers, and there was plenty of it. In fact, Carla had never seen so much food all in one place! In addition to the large stores of food, the group kept a supply of military rations (MREs or "meals ready to eat"). Carla knew that millennialists lived in constant readiness for the "end times," and therefore the use of MREs fit into their theology.

Finally, Carla and Paula knew they had to investigate the weapons that were on the premises to see if they were kept out of reach of the children. "It is not against the law for a family to keep weapons," Carla reminded herself, and she knew that it was not her responsibility to determine how many weapons were allowed. But the two social workers did need to be sure that the weapons were kept safely away from the children. Koresh offered to take them down through the trap door into the place where the weapons were kept in a bus that was buried underground. Carla and Paula crawled into the area, examined it, and determined that the weapons had been safely secured and were not accessible by the children.

By the end of the third visit, Carla still had no evidence of any abuse or neglect. As they drove back to Waco through the Texas countryside, Carla said to Paula, "It really frustrates me that we have only been able to speak to each child one time. I really do have suspicions that something is going on. But I can't put my finger on it and we have absolutely no solid evidence that anything is amiss. I wish I could come back and make a few more visits." David Koresh had assured Carla that she was welcome any time and that she was invited to attend religious services or to visit as much as she needed. But if no allegations could be substantiated, agency policy required that the report must be written right away and the inquiry must be closed.

"I think if I could just begin to build more rapport with the children, I might be able to get more information."

How Do I Write the Report?

The day after the third visit, Carla sat down at her desk to write her final report to be turned in to her supervisor. Her head was swimming with questions and doubts. She knew that, in some ways, she was expected by people in the community, and now by this court in Michigan, to substantiate the long-running rumors that Koresh was a crazy lunatic who abused children. But Carla had witnessed a peaceful community raising its children in a strict, but loving environment. With no abuse substantiated, CPS policy dictated that the case must be wrapped up within 30 days of its beginning, and one extension had already been granted.

Carla could hear the words of her supervisor, Darlene Starr, ringing in her ears, "In this business our reports cannot be based on intuition! We have to have hard evidence and if there is none, we must follow procedure and close the inquiry, and soon."

Carla knew that she could not write a report substantiating abuse if she had not found any. But was there any way to keep this case open?

She began to feel a gnawing in the pit of her stomach. She worried that if she could not find abuse now, something worse might happen to the children later on. "If only there were no CPS deadlines!" she said to herself. "If only we could observe for a while longer. There are very clear laws about what is allowed in terms of caring for children, and I have an uneasy feeling that something is amiss, and no one will tell me. But I have absolutely no evidence to prove these suspicions."

Perhaps there was a way she could describe the home or the rituals in terms that might raise a red flag, even though she could not report actual abuse. "Then maybe the case could stay open a bit longer," she thought. "But am I being biased and judging these folks on their religious convictions about discipline and marriage, just because they are different from my own? Am I letting the unusual nature of this group influence my decision?"

Carla would have to decide how to write the report. Could she give a disposition of "Reason to Believe" for these allegations?

15. teaching note
Reason to Believe
T. Laine Scales, Linda B. Morales, and Elisabeth Kenny

Case Synopsis

Carla Shepherd, a Child Protective Services worker in Waco, Texas was assigned to investigate allegations of child abuse among members of a Branch Davidian religious community led by David Koresh. After a thorough investigation, which revealed no evidence of abuse but made her suspicious, Carla had to write up her results. She wanted to be objective, but writing the report was difficult because she had to either find some evidence or close the case immediately. She needed more time to investigate, but she had already received one extension and was out of time.

Learning Outcomes Related to Spirituality and Religion

The case discussion will facilitate the work of students as they

1. Consider the importance of respecting religious diversity.

2. Analyze how agency policies may guide a social worker's decisions regarding religious communities.

3. Differentiate between what is illegal (child abuse) and what is legal (spanking) in terms of a religious community's beliefs and practices regarding discipline.

Other Learning Outcomes for Which This Case Can Be Used

The case discussion will facilitate the work of students as they

4. Understand the importance of meticulous and ethical reporting and record-keeping practices.

5. Recognize both freedoms and restrictions that stem from necessary agency policies.

6. Analyze how the media may influence the way in which a social worker's assessment is viewed by the public.

Discussion Questions Related to Religion and Spirituality

Establishing the Facts

1. Who is involved in this case?
    The instructor may wish to use the board to outline the major players in the case.

2. What does Carla know about the Davidians before her first visit to Mt. Carmel?
    See the section on Branch Davidians. Students may be tempted to bring in knowledge about Branch Davidians or this case, based on what they have read or heard. Remind them that they must stick to the facts as presented in the case. Carla did not

have the benefit of hindsight and had to make her assessment based on the facts as she saw them.

3. What guidance does the CPS manual offer Carla as she investigates this religious group?

    Refer back to the paragraph in the case that quotes the CPS manual. How is this helpful? How might the manual be written to be more helpful in this case?

Analysis

4. What is Carla's task for investigating this religious group? What types of evidence must be present for Carla to substantiate abuse?

    Instructors may wish to lead students in a examination of various textbook definitions of child abuse, or examine the laws of their own states and discuss what may constitute evidence. Carla used definitions and policies applicable to Texas, which can be accessed online at http://www.state.tx.us. Follow the links to "Criminal Justice and Law" and find the family code or the criminal code. Other states have similar information on state websites. Students could be divided into teams to examine these policies.

5. What pressure is Carla feeling in this situation?

    Looking back at the list of major players that the class has generated, analyze how each one may be expecting a certain outcome from Carla.

6. Is there anything that Carla is sure about so far? What is she uncertain about?

    Carla has determined that the children are not being neglected in terms of food, in terms of being cared for, and in terms of sanitary and safe conditions in the home. Carla has not been able to substantiate abuse, but has a "gut feeling" that something is not right. She needs more time, but her agency's policies require that she close the case right away if no evidence of abuse is found. The religious community is tightly-knit, and she feels that as an outsider she has not had time to gain the trust of the children.

7. What measures might Carla be using to determine if the children are being abused?

    The instructor may lead students in examining definitions of child physical abuse. Workers must

differentiate between spanking and abusing. Look at definitions in textbooks used in your social work program, as well as related laws in your state. Keep in mind that Carla is investigating two types of abuse: physical abuse of smaller children and sexual abuse of teenage girls.

8. What are the rights of a spiritual leader such as David Koresh in defining relationships (i.e., between husband and wife) when those definitions are opposed to state law (in this case, the Texas Family Code)?

    There are some religious groups that allow polygamy and "early" marriage. The community acknowledges marriages, but these may not be legal marriages if the bride or groom is already married to someone else, is underage, is marrying without necessary parental consent, or is marrying to obtain legal status in the USA (such as a green card). The worker must understand the law and know what is legal in his or her state and county.

Action

9. Can social workers allow clients to be self-determining when the client's decision is against the law?

    Lead students to differentiate between what is legal, what is ethical, and what is a matter of religious or spiritual preference.

10. To what extent can a social worker (representing a governmental agency) mandate behavior of a community with strong religious convictions about child rearing and physical discipline?

    In this context, the CPS worker represents the law. The social worker is there to determine what actions are legal. She or he must respect the beliefs of the religious community and should act in ways that communicate this respect. But the worker must also separate the right to freedom of religion from legal obligations.

11. The Branch Davidians were not the only religious community in the U.S. in which multiple marriages (polygamy) were quietly condoned. Should multiple marriages or cohabitation with minors within religious communities be viewed

differently by helping professionals than multiple marriages among secular groups? Why or why not?

Often religious communities, as well as some other cultures around the globe, interpret the age of marriageability for females as coinciding with the onset of puberty (early teen years). Child welfare policies and laws in the United States consider sexual relations with underage females as abusive.

Reflecting on the Outcomes of the Waco Standoff

At some point, after the class has analyzed Carla's situation using only the knowledge available to Carla at the time, the instructor may lead students to use the following questions for reflection based on the hindsight that we now have. Instructors and students will find many written accounts of the Waco story, with a variety of interpretations of these events. You may use archived editions of your local newspapers to examine how the media in your area reported the unfolding events, or students may examine back issues of national news magazines. Internet searches also produce interesting views on the case, often with extreme bias. Whatever the source, instructors should urge students to critically evaluate the point of view.

Instructors should keep in mind that students will have a varying range of memory and knowledge of the case. A traditional-aged undergraduate student may have been 8 or 10 years old at the time these events occurred, while a nontraditional student may have been 40 years old.

12. How did media coverage affect the outcome of events as they were unfolding?

Because the Waco incident became a matter of national attention, it is public, documented knowledge that Carla and her colleagues reported no abuse at Mt. Carmel (see Report of the Department of the Treasury referenced below). Unless they have studied the governmental reports, students are not likely to know this information until they read this case. Once the incident was made public, media sources typically accused Koresh (implicitly or explicitly) of abusing the children and the teenage girls. Government officials explained that their actions were motivated by their duty to defend the children who were being abused. What do you think happened? Do you think government offi-

cials read Carla's report? Did they believe Carla's report was correct? Was Carla's report correct? These questions do not have easy answers.

13. The NASW Code of Ethics states that the profession has a clear obligation to change patterns of discrimination and to break down barriers that impede the rights of members of minority groups, including members of religious minority groups. Did the social worker fulfill her obligation to protect the rights of minority religious community members in the case of the Branch Davidian families?

The instructor may compare the Davidians to other members of minority groups. Use the facts of the case to discuss how community rumors and other serious allegations may have added pressures for Carla. Discuss how Carla's dilemma may have been augmented by her obligation to protect the minority group from discrimination.

14. Why must social workers take their record keeping seriously?

Carla had no idea that her report would become a matter of national significance and that the findings would became a matter of public record. It is clear that Carla deliberated over her report and took it very seriously. It is also clear that she faced a dilemma as she wrote the report and wished for more time to resolve that dilemma. The final outcomes of the Waco tragedy may have been altered if Carla's report, which reported no abuse, had been interpreted differently or utilized in a different way by government officials. Instead, government officials continued to state that there was abuse at Mt. Carmel. In addition, Carla or her agency may have been legally liable if it was determined that she was negligent in her reporting or record keeping.

15. During the Waco tragedy, Carla watched the unfolding events as a handful of the children she interviewed were rescued from Mt. Carmel, but many died in the fire. Today, as she reviews her actions in the investigation, what do you imagine she might be thinking or feeling? What would you think or feel today if you were Carla?

Instructors may ask students to reflect on this question verbally or to write a response to turn in or to share in small groups. Students may be asked to create an "empathetic journal entry" in which they imagine Carla's thoughts in 1992 during investigations, in 1993 after the fire, and this year, as she remembers the incident.

Teaching Suggestions

This case is different from most others in this text because the ending of the story is known (though many who have not researched the case may mistakenly believe that abuse was documented). We suggest starting out with a discussion that is limited to information that was available to Carla at the time. After the case has been analyzed with this limited information, students may want to bring in information that they possess about the final outcomes of the case. The instructor may spread the discussion over two class periods, using this division. Assigning students to research the events will heighten their interest and help them to learn about the role of the media in shaping public opinion about religious communities. Guide students toward a variety of points of view and remind students to consider the sources and critically analyze what they read. Instructors may use an "empathetic journal assignment" in which students try to imagine the feelings of the worker after learning of the deaths of many of the children she interviewed.

Additional Notes

For Further Reading

Lewis, J. R. (1994). *From the ashes: Making sense of Waco.* Boston: Rowman and Littlefield.

See especially the sections, "Dynamics and Impact of the Media" and "Polygamy and Accusations of Child Abuse." Two other provocative essays are, "Suffer the Little Children," and "Who was abusing the children at Waco?"

Wright, S. A. (1995). *Armageddon in Waco.* Chicago: University of Chicago Press.

U.S. Department of the Treasury. (1993). *Report of the Department of the Treasury on the Bureau of Alcohol, Tobacco and Firearms, investigation of Vernon Wayne Howell also known as David Koresh.* Washington, DC: U.S. Government Printing Office.

See especially timeline in Appendix D to consider CPS as one of many agencies involved over time.

16.

A Tale of Too Many Relationships: Bonds, Boundaries, and Borders

Raymond Lisauckis, Carol A. Sherwood, and David Davis

Kay Jenkins was a master's level social worker in a private practice that focused primarily on sexual abuse and domestic violence. She received a referral from Ed Javits, a local pastor and former colleague. Four months into the counseling relationship, the case took an unexpected turn. The client revealed that she had had sex with Ed.

A Small Private Practice

Kay and the pastor, Ed Javits, were both members of the same conservative Christian denomination, but were involved in different congregations. They had worked together for several years at Oak Valley Family Counseling Center, a family-preservation agency where Ed was still employed when he had referred this client to Kay. Kay had been the director and Ed's supervisor at Oak Valley. They had worked together at the center for 6 years before Kay left to open her own practice, and they had seen a variety of families and clients, many of whom were referred to them through the state's child protective services. Ed's master's degree was in Pastoral Counseling. Kay had grown to appreciate his clinical judgment and skills, and he worked well with clients and families. He was intelligent, witty, insightful, and an easy person to like.

When Kay left the Family Counseling Center to begin her private practice she was also raising three young children and was not eager for the practice to be very large. She had primarily limited advertising to word of mouth. Kay and Ed still regularly consulted with one another on cases, and it was not unusual for

one to ask the other to take over a case when a specific need made it appropriate. Kay did not have any supervision or professional consultation because of the small size of her practice and because there were so few master's level social workers in her area. Kay was pleased when Ed called her with a referral.

The Referral

Jessica Peterson had been a member of Cornerstone Community Church for 7 years. Ed had moved his family to this small-town church 6 years ago to become an associate pastor. Jessica quickly became a good friend of Ed's wife, Marla. They had children of similar ages and frequently provided childcare for each other. About 5 weeks before Ed made the referral to Kay, Jessica had begun talking with Ed about her difficult past, which had included parental alcoholism and an abortion when she was a teenager. Jessica shared with him that she was beginning to recall memories of childhood sexual abuse that had been perpetrated by her grandfather. As Jessica began to remember more details of the abuse, her emotional stability became more fragile.

Jessica lived with her mother and her two children. She was divorced, and her former husband had disappeared from her life several years earlier. Jessica was afraid that her mother would become angry with her and blame her if she told her about the sexual abuse. Jessica was feeling increasingly unable to take care of her children, so Jessica, Ed, and Marla had agreed that until she was feeling more stable, she could stay in the guest room at their home. Jessica's mother lived nearby, so Jessica was able to see the children easily.

As Jessica's memories became more real to her, she had become more self-destructive and at times exhibited psychotic symptoms. She began cutting her wrists and hallucinating about blood in the room where she was staying. Ed had convinced her to enter the hospital, but she only stayed a couple of days and was released when she refused medication and appeared stable enough to return home.

Jessica had been in Ed's home for approximately 3 weeks when he called Kay with the referral.

"I think you are the best person to work with this case," Ed had explained. "I know what a good therapist you are, and because you're a Christian, too, you will be better able to understand where she is coming from."

He told Kay about Jessica's abuse, her self-destructiveness, and her recent hospitalization. "I would like to keep in touch with you for a couple of weeks regarding Jessica," Ed suggested to Kay. "I would like to do this even after you start seeing her. Marla and I don't mind her being with us, in fact she is a great help to Marla right now, but we feel she should return to her mother's home as soon as possible. We would like for you to make that one of the treatment goals."

This Is a Nightmare

In Jessica's fourth month of therapy with Kay, she again began having difficulty controlling the urge to cut herself. As they searched for a precipitating cause, Jessica confided in Kay.

"I need to tell you that while I was living with Ed and Marla, Ed and I had sex about five or six times. Sometimes Marla would be upstairs sleeping. Marla assumed we were downstairs talking about the abuse." She added, "He did not force himself on me, but I am not real sure how it all really did happen. It all seems very confusing now that I have had some time to think about it."

She explained that she had thought that Ed loved her, but now she was not sure. Their sexual encounters had occurred during Jessica's most unstable periods and had continued after Ed had referred her to Kay for therapy.

"Ed doesn't know that I'm telling you about this. I don't know what he would think or do. And I can't bear the thought of Marla knowing. She is my best friend. Knowing Marla has changed my life. She helped me find myself after the divorce, and I don't know what I would do without her. I can't believe that I have been involved in something that would hurt her so much if she knew about it."

Cornerstone Community Church was Jessica's support and an important spiritual resource. She was afraid to talk to anyone in the church about the incidents because Ed was one of the pastors and was so well-liked, and because she was not sure what the people in the church would think of her. Jessica was confused about what had happened to her and was not sure what she should do next.

"I feel confused," she told Kay. "I hate it that we committed adultery like that. I feel guilty, but I also think I might have been taken advantage of. Do I need to forgive Ed? Will Marla ever forgive me?"

As Jessica revealed her relationship with Ed, Kay thought to herself, "This is a nightmare. What have I gotten myself into? What needs to happen next between Jessica and Ed? What would be the most therapeutic way for me to intervene in this mess? Could a soap opera be any more enmeshed?" As Jessica related more details of the story, it became increasingly apparent to Kay that Ed had not told her nearly enough of the truth when making the referral. Ed had been having sex with Jessica for at least four weeks prior to the start of her therapy with Kay, and the relationship had continued for another two weeks after that, until the two of them mutually decided to end it.

Affair or Abuse?

After Jessica's session was over, Kay realized how upsetting Jessica's disclosure had been for herself. She was furious with Ed. Kay felt that he had completely abused the trust that Jessica had placed in him, had taken advantage of his relationship with Jessica, and had also betrayed her own trust in him. Kay immediately called and told Ed that she wanted him to come to see her. He agreed to do so.

"Ed," Kay began, "Jessica has been to see me this week and has told me that during the time she was living with you and Marla, the two of you had sex several times in your home."

Ed did not deny that it was true. "It did happen. We just seemed to be drawn to each other. She was hurting so badly. I don't think either of us wanted it to happen, but it was hard to stop. I knew it needed to stop. That was part of why I wanted you to start seeing her and to work with her to help her get back to her own home."

Kay responded, "Ed, I can't begin to imagine what you were thinking! Jessica was ill. You were a spiritual counselor to her and you are a therapist. You took complete advantage of both of those roles."

Ed's response shocked Kay even further. "I know that what we did was wrong, but we were two consenting adults. I was never her therapist. She trusted me and told me things, but I knew that I could not be her therapist. I never saw myself as that. It is surprising to me that you don't see it as I do. It was just a very stupid and unfortunate thing for us to do."

Kay responded, "I think the church needs to know because you were her pastor. I'm not sure what should be done in regard to informing Oak Valley."

"Please, Kay," Ed pleaded, "don't make this worse than it is already."

Although Ed was adamantly opposed to informing other people, he wanted to tell his wife Marla immediately. Marla was 7 months pregnant with their third child at the time of Jessica's disclosure to Kay. Jessica insisted that she did not want Marla to know until after the birth of the baby because this pregnancy had been difficult, and the doctor had warned her that stress could make it even worse. Jessica had been helping her out quite a bit with her housework and childcare. Jessica's sense of responsibility and guilt would not allow her to force Marla to deal with this issue in this vulnerable time. Because Jessica was again becoming self-destructive, Kay felt she had no choice but to go along with Jessica's decision, even though she knew that they were just prolonging the inevitable. Kay was a firm believer that keeping secrets only made things worse.

Who Needs to Know?

During the few months of therapy following Jessica's disclosure to Kay, treatment focused primarily on understanding what had happened between Jessica and Ed. Kay attempted to help Jessica see the role that Ed played in her life. They also explored the responsibility Ed had, both as a leader in her church and as a professional therapist, not to abuse the power and trust that his professional roles gave him.

Eventually, Jessica became less self-destructive

and made the decision that after Marla's baby was born she wanted Ed to tell her what had happened. She also wanted the other leaders in the church to know. Jessica felt that the leaders should make a decision as to whether or not Ed should continue in his roles at the church. When Kay told Ed, he agreed that he wanted his wife to know, but he did not agree that anyone else in the church should know.

"It's really not any of their business," he said. "I agree that I should step out of my leadership roles at the church for a while, but that is all I will agree to. Nothing like this has ever happened to me before, and believe me, it will never happen again. I want you both to believe me and to just let it end there."

Jessica was clear that she wanted the church leaders to know, but she did not want to hurt anyone more than necessary. "I am of afraid of being perceived as an unstable divorced woman out to get a man. But I have to tell my side of the story. I don't want to feel guilty, and I want to feel more in control of my own life. At the same time, I don't want to hurt Marla and the rest of the Javits family."

Kay supported Jessica's decision that the church leaders should be told. She was not sure that something like this would not happen again between Ed and someone else. And he was a person who played a prominent role in the church. How would he possibly convince the church to let him just drop his responsibilities temporarily without telling them why?

Kay also continued to wrestle with the dilemma of what, if anything, needed to be done in regard to Ed's professional status as a therapist. As a pastoral counselor, he was not licensed under any state board, and what had happened had not been in the context of his work at the Oak Valley Family Counseling Center. He continued to stand firm on the argument that he had not been Jessica's therapist, and that his professional self was not in any way involved in the incidents.

"Sometimes I feel like I should just march into Oak Valley," Kay thought, "and tell his supervisor that Ed took advantage of one of my clients—had sex with her. What exactly are my professional obligations? And what is going to be the best thing for Jessica? I wish I had someone who could help me sort all of this out."

16.teaching note

A Tale of Too Many Relationships: Bonds, Boundaries, and Borders

Raymond Lisauckis, Carol A. Sherwood, and David Davis

Case Synopsis

Kay Jenkins, a social worker in private practice, was shocked to learn that her client, Jessica Peterson, had been having an affair with Ed Javits, who was Jessica's pastor, Kay's friend and former colleague, and the counselor who had originally referred Jessica to Kay. To further complicate matters, Jessica was best friends with Ed Javits's wife, and had been staying with them while she recovered from the emotional strain of past sexual abuse.

Learning Outcomes Related to Religion and Spirituality

The case discussion will facilitate the work of students as they

1. Understand that social workers often interact with pastoral counselors and faith-based organizations, and that sensitivity to and knowledge of church polity and functions have implications for consultation, referrals, and effective use of these resources.

2. Explore how ethical decision making can be challenged by a social worker's personal involvement and investment of feelings, including religious beliefs and moral views.

3. Learn to value the importance of supervision for persons in clinical practice and persons in pastoral roles.

4. Consider responsibilities, guidelines, and cautions when consulting or collaborating with unlicensed or unregulated workers in faith-based agencies.

5. Distinguish between legal, moral, and ethical issues in clinical practice settings and churches.

6. Explore the potentially abusive or destructive power of those in positions of authority, including church leaders.

Other Learning Outcomes for Which This Case Can Be Used

The case discussion will facilitate the work of students as they

7. Discuss how work with clients can lead to the unexpected, and how practice standards guide difficult decisions.

8. Understand the complexity of professional boundaries and limit setting when social workers are dealing with multiple relationships.

9. Discuss how we need to consider both the needs of individual clients and the greater needs of society.

Courses and Levels for Which the Case Is Intended

This case should be used for MSW-level courses, because it involves a social worker in private practice. The course may be used to cover content on values and ethics, mental health, legal issues, spirituality and religion, faith-based organizations, and use of supervision and consultation.

Discussion Questions Related to Religion and Spirituality

Establishing the Facts

1. Students may be asked to develop a visual representation of the persons involved in the case and their various relationships with each other.

2. What guidelines and standards does Kay have available to her to help her determine her actions regarding Ed's behavior?

   The NASW Code of Ethics provides principles and guidelines regarding client and colleague relationships, referrals, collaboration, and sexual behavior. Kay, like any social worker, was also profoundly influenced in her evaluation of the situation and her behavior by her own worldview and values—her philosophical, spiritual, and religious assumptions and beliefs. The guidelines in the NASW Code of Ethics could be helpful, but these require interpretation and do not always provide unambiguous direction.

3. What systems does Kay need to learn more about to help clarify her decisions?
   - *Church or denominational structures or policies which may or may not be available in this case.*
   - *The Javits family system and Jessica's involvement in it.*
   - *Legal systems which may or may not be relevant or available.*
   - *Professional licensing and sanctioning systems.*

4. What questions would you ask Ed if you were Kay? What would you ask Jessica?

Analysis

5. What were the circumstances that established the professional relationships and the ethical, moral, and legal boundaries around the relationships in this case? How were the boundaries established and understood? How were they crossed or ignored? Are there differences in the establishment of professional, ethical, legal, or moral boundaries?

   Informal boundaries were established based on friendships and personal relationships. Professional boundaries existed based on a history of working together, including the current referral. Professional ethical standards provided guidelines for conduct and expectations. Beliefs about values, spirituality, and religion defined moral boundaries. Legal boundaries were set by statutes and court interpretations.

6. What is the difference between a moral issue and one involving professional ethics?

   Although Ed did not fully excuse his behavior, he expected the consequences of his moral indiscretion to come from his church and his family, not from his profession or the courts. Kay was concerned about appropriate consequences sufficient to address Ed's unethical conduct as a professional.

7. What care must be taken by social workers in dealing with spiritual and religious issues raised by clients?

   For example, if a client wants to engage the worker in a religious dialogue involving forgiveness, reconciliation, and grace, what is the appropriate role for the worker? Social workers must always engage in an assessment process which tries to understand what the meaning of the request has for the client and what its effect on the helping process would be, much like any other request that a client might make. This would include an honest appraisal of the worker's competence to respond, its appropriateness to the helping process at that point, and the potential for unethical exploitation of the relationship. Even in explicitly faith-based agencies, the same sort of assessment must be made. For example, if a Christian client asked a Christian social worker in a faith-based agency to pray with her, the appropriate response is not intrinsically obvious. The social worker would need to assess whether or not this would be a helpful support of client strengths and resources or a form of enabling that allows the client's characteristic dysfunctional use of religion to avoid dealing with needed issues.

8. How might the fact that the social worker shares a number of spiritual and religious values and beliefs with both the client and Ed facilitate effective practice on the one hand, and present potential challenges on the other hand? How might Kay's own religious views influence her practice and her response in this case?

These shared values can provide both insight and blinders. The worker's own understanding of the church, its customs, rituals, traditions, and teachings can be used to formulate the approach to working with clients and making decisions. Kay must consider whether she is responding to Ed's conduct with her personal feelings of being betrayed, with her own set of moral standards which describes his behavior as sinful, or with the guidance of her profession's ethical responsibilities.

9. Confidentiality must be considered in this case in order to protect whom? When do the rights of the greater society and other potential clients outweigh the right to confidentiality of an individual client or fellow worker? What is best in the long run for both Ed and the church and what are Kay's responsibilities in the matter?

If Jessica had refused to move to confront Ed, or if she refused to allow Kay to share case information, what options would Kay have in responding and reporting Ed to either the agency where he is employed or the church? There may be a need to report his actions in order to protect others who might be vulnerable. What if the client does not agree with this course of action? What consideration should be given to Marla or to the congregation?

10. What clinical issues complicate dealing with this situation? How do they affect assessment, planning, and decision making?

Jessica has a history of mental illness issues, including post-traumatic stress, self-destructiveness, hospitalization, and reluctance to take medication. It appears that she has developed a high degree of enmeshment with the Javits family at all levels, which greatly affects her decision making and behavior. It is not clear how the dynamics of the family system and Jessica have interacted with each other. Therapy has enhanced Jessica's ability to make choices regarding her involvement with the family, but it is not clear how

far she wants to go or should go in that process. Jessica wants to challenge Ed, but she does not necessarily want to make a permanent break with either the family or the church.

Action

11. What are the next steps that Kay should take in order to respond appropriately to Ed's involvement with Kay's client? What are the choices she faces? Why are they in conflict? What makes the choices involved uncertain? How is your opinion affected by:
    - *Ed's attitude toward his culpability*
    - *Your own religious or moral views*
    - *The fact that the indiscretion involves sex*
    - *The fact that Ed is not a licensed social worker and is not subject to social work standards of conduct*

12. If the church leaders do not think that Ed needs to resign or be disciplined, what do you think Kay should do next? How involved should Kay become in helping the church leaders deal with the situation?

13. What would Kay need to know or to explore about denominational structures to understand her options in acting as an advocate for Jessica? How does church polity enter into the discipline of its leaders (i.e., pastors, priests, rabbis)?

14. Ignoring the problem is a decision. Is it a viable option?

15. What options might be developed for an isolated social worker in Kay's situation to have access to professional supervision or consultation?

Teaching Suggestions

Begin by noting that improper sexual relations with clients are one of the most common causes for sanctions by professional governing boards, including social work. The duty to protect clients from improper conduct by social workers extends to colleagues from other professions as well.

After the case has been thoroughly discussed, explore how workers can become mediators and advocates for clients who might have to deal with the power and abuse of those in authority, even in a faith-based setting. Just as workers are required to be aware of the quality of services and resources available in a secular agency, workers must also be sufficiently aware of the organization and functions of faith-based agencies when making effective use of those resources.

Additional Notes

17.

A Cursed Child?

Ann Fleck-Henderson and Michael P. Melendez

Sandra breathed a sigh of relief when Ruby Malcolm left her office. She had stalled for time because she needed to think. Tomorrow morning, Ms. Malcolm would be back, expecting some professional direction and advice about what to do with her defiant 14-year-old daughter. Right now, Sandra had no idea what that advice should be. Clearly, she needed to consult with her mental health team. A lot would depend on how she presented this situation to them.

Sandra Kaplan and Urban Family Services

A 28-year-old white Jewish woman, Sandra Kaplan had focused on multicultural clinical work and had become fluent in Spanish during her master's program in social work. She had graduated 2 years ago and had moved to Easton, Massachusetts to work at Urban Family Services (UFS). She loved this job, especially because of the racial and ethnic diversity of the people who came to the clinic for services.

In addition, UFS had a certain prestige as a traditional treatment center. It was an old agency, affiliated with Downstate Medical Center, a major teaching hospital in Easton. Sandra had access to excellent medical consultation, psychological testing, and in-service education. The agency had long-standing relationships with local schools and child protective offices. Sandra felt proud to be at UFS and believed her clients received excellent clinical services.

Case Review

Sandra looked at her notes from Ms. Malcolm's first visit, 4 months ago.

Referral from Dr. Peters, eldest daughter's pediatrician, for anxiety.

Presenting concern of client: Anxiety, "near the end of my wits," due to second daughter's behavioral difficulties.

Household: Ms. Ruby Malcolm – 32 y.o. Haitian American, divorced
  Maria – 16 – diabetic. H.S. junior
  Irene – 14 – behavior problems. 9th grade
  John – 13 – 7th grade.
Maternal parents live in adjoining unit, own both housing units.

Ms. Malcolm is employed as nursing aid, has GED and steady job. Support from parents, friends at work, and church.

Assessment: Anxiety due to family stress, particularly inability to control Irene.
Plan: Supportive counseling. Consider referral for medication evaluation. Connect to resources.

Sandra reflected on her past work with Ms. Malcolm. She felt they had developed a solid and trusting relationship quickly. Ms. Malcolm knew what she needed: "I just need to talk this out," she would say, and Sandra would listen, facilitating Ms. Malcolm's understanding and problem-solving processes.

Defiant Daughter

"I don't know what is wrong with Irene. Nothing makes her stop. She says things to me no one in my family has ever said to their mother or to anyone. She skips school. Maybe she's on drugs—I don't even know."

Sandra had listened carefully as Ms. Malcolm described Irene's sudden outbursts of temper. Irene would let out a volley of swear words and threaten to run away or to hurt someone in the family. These outbursts often followed requests that she do her chores or complete her homework, but sometimes they seemed to come from nowhere. There were also days when she did not respond violently, and Ms. Malcolm could see no logic or pattern in her behavior, except that it was getting worse. After the outbursts, Irene would run from the room weeping or muttering to herself. Nothing seemed to console her or stop her outbursts. In addition, Irene was cutting school and would not say where she had been or what she had done.

Ms. Malcolm felt as if she had tried everything. She had never had such troubles with Maria, and she was worried about John being influenced by seeing Irene behaving so badly. She reasoned with Irene in calm moments, offered rewards, threatened punishments, grounded her, held back her allowance—nothing seemed to make a difference. "I feel like hitting her, but I know that won't help," Ms. Malcolm said. She talked about the differences between her way of dealing with children and her own parents' ways. She saw her parents' ways as traditional, hers as more American. "My parents would have given me a good sound whipping if I had behaved like that, and I know that's what they think I should do with Irene. But I don't think that's right, and in the U.S. you are not allowed to hit your kids. I thought if I came here to UFS, you could help me. You would have a more scientific approach."

Escalating Efforts

In consultation with her supervisor and team, Sandra supported Ms. Malcolm's restraint from physical punishment of Irene and her efforts to get help from relevant agencies. Over the ensuing weeks, Ms. Malcolm met frequently with Irene's counselor at school, but these meetings did not seem to help. Irene rarely came to scheduled meetings, and when they did meet, Irene was sullen and noncommunicative.

Finally, as what seemed like a last resort, Ms. Malcolm contacted the child protection agency, with support from the school counselor and from Sandra, and filed a petition for Children in Need of Services. That was about a month ago. The court assigned a probation officer to Irene, but she was still defiant. Ms. Malcolm was clearly discouraged and feeling helpless. Sandra, too, was beginning to feel helpless.

Ms. Malcolm continued to manage her work and her household, but she was having trouble sleeping, was crying a lot, and often felt nervous. Sandra offered the possibility of medication, but Ms. Malcolm refused. "As long as I can talk with you, that's enough. I don't believe in drugs." Also, Ms. Malcolm did not seem to get support from her parents. "They have different ideas. They're old-fashioned," she said.

Two weeks before today's meeting, the school counselor had taken an out-of-control Irene to the hospital emergency room, from which she was admitted to an adolescent in-patient unit for evaluation. At first, Ms. Malcolm had been relieved. Irene would get the expert help she needed from one place. Sandra and her team had also been relieved. Sandra felt she could now focus on helping Ms. Malcolm without feeling vicarious responsibility for Irene's situation.

The relief was short-lived, and last week Ms. Malcolm was very distressed again. She had been to the hospital daily and had met with the social worker there. "The hospital social worker says Irene is getting treated for some imbalances in her brain," she reported. "But, Irene is not better. She is acting bad there, too, and she looks like a zombie. They put her on one drug, and now it's another one. I don't know what they are doing to her."

Subsequently, Sandra spoke to the hospital social worker who acknowledged that Irene was not better. The staff there were mystified about the nature of her disorder.

Today's Questions

Today Ms. Malcolm seemed subdued as the session began and unusually distant. "Nothing is helping," she said quietly. Sandra felt inadequate, knowing she was part of what was not helping. "My mother says we've gone on with this long enough. She has a different idea about what is wrong with Irene. Maybe she is right. I should have listened to her sooner. The hospital can't keep Irene if I don't let them, can they?"

"Probably not," Sandra replied, "unless Irene is a danger to herself or someone else. Do you want to take her out?"

Ms. Malcolm hesitated. " I don't know if you will understand," she said, "but Irene was fine until suddenly all these troubles began about a year ago." She continued tentatively. "When there is such a change, and the behavior is so angry and bad, it is likely someone put a curse on her. This happens a lot, and sometimes you don't know who put the curse on or why. If the hospital had found an illness, I would have believed that, but the hospital can't find the problem, so it is most likely a curse. No medicines will help with this, and the drugs will maybe hurt Irene. There are wise women, sometimes we call them witches or root women, who can lift the curse. My mother knows these people, and she can help me now."

"I see . . ." Sandra responded. "I don't know much about that. I'd like to understand."

"Just tell me it's O.K. to go ahead and take Irene out of the hospital. I don't want to do the wrong thing, but I feel in my bones that this is the only way."

Sandra felt torn. "We have only a few minutes left," she said, "and I need to think about this. Could you come in early tomorrow, so I can give it some thought?"

Ms. Malcolm agreed.

Sandra's Quandary

Sandra was left with a dilemma. She wanted to support Ms. Malcolm's decision to take Irene out of the hospital, but she was not sure she could give any rational justification for that inclination. It would be hard to defend, and if she wanted to go that way, she would have to justify her support. The mental health team had its weekly meeting this afternoon, and with a complicated issue like this, she had to consult the team. The safe thing to do with Ms. Malcolm was express no opinion—just encourage her to do what she felt was right. But if that meant tacitly supporting taking Irene from the hospital against medical advice, she was not sure it was a good move, clinically, for Irene. Irene was not responding to counseling, probation, or (so far) medication. She was obviously seriously troubled. It would be hard to convince the team, especially the psychologist, who was even more committed to neurological explanations of behavior than the psychiatrist, that Irene's trouble was a curse.

17.teaching note
A Cursed Child?
Ann Fleck-Henderson and Michael P. Melendez

Case Synopsis

Sandra Kaplan, a Jewish social worker with a fairly recent MSW, held a clinical position at a prestigious and traditional family service agency. Her client, Ms. Malcolm, was a Haitian American woman troubled by her 14-year-old daughter's defiant behavior. Many approaches had been tried unsuccessfully with the daughter, and finally the school's intervention had the child hospitalized for psychiatric evaluation. When this hospitalization did not appear to be working either, Sandra was faced with Ms. Malcolm's request for support in removing her daughter from the hospital and taking her to a "wise woman," in the belief that a curse would be the only way to explain the child's behavior. Sandra was inclined to support Ms. Malcolm, but was not sure she could justify this position and doubted that the mental health team at the agency would concur.

Learning Outcomes Related to Religion and Spirituality

The case discussion will facilitate the work of students as they

1. Consider the implications of culturally competent practice in a situation where traditional beliefs of an immigrant client conflict with the beliefs of Western medicine and psychiatry.

2. Understand that modern medicine is also a belief system, not an ultimate truth.

3. Assess the risks and benefits of a treatment plan that is not supported by the beliefs of a patient's primary group.

Other Learning Outcomes for Which This Case Can Be Used

The case discussion will facilitate the work of students as they

4. Consider the issues of responsibility, liability, and autonomy (or lack thereof) in working with a team.

5. Increase their understanding of acculturation to the dominant culture as a process that does not eradicate earlier meaning systems from cultures of origin.

Courses and Levels for Which the Case Is Intended

Because of Sandra's role, the case is probably most appropriate for the graduate level. It can be used in course material on ethics, multicultural practice, spirituality, psychiatric social work, medical social work, children and families, and human behavior in the social environment.

Discussion Questions Related to Religion and Spirituality

Establishing the Facts

1. Given Sandra's role, what is her responsibility to Ms. Malcolm and to Irene?

    Ms. Malcolm is the client, and Sandra is hired to help her manage her anxiety. She has no direct responsibility for Irene.

2. What do we know about Ms. Malcolm's relation to traditional Haitian beliefs?

    Ms. Malcolm was raised in the United States and distances herself from traditional Haitian child-rearing practices. We know that she has a church affiliation. We do not know her relation to traditional Haitian spirituality.

3. What does Sandra know about traditional Haitian beliefs?

    Very little.

4. What interventions have been tried with Irene, and with what success?

    Counseling, child protective system, juvenile justice system, and now psychiatric evaluation and medication.

Analysis

5. Why is Sandra even considering supporting Ms. Malcolm's decision to remove Irene from the hospital if she, herself, does not believe in curses?

    Sandra has a special interest in cross-cultural work. She believes that every culture's ways of understanding life and illness have legitimacy and value.

6. Are there any Western arguments for supporting Ms. Malcolm? That is, arguments other than Irene might really be cursed and need intervention from a "wise woman"?

    Yes. Ms. Malcolm needs the support of her parents, and potentially her Haitian community, as she feels desperate about Irene. Ms. Malcolm does not believe in using drugs and has a right to make decisions about her child. Irene's condition may worsen if she experiences her family in conflict with the hospital's treatment.

7. Is the team's belief in biological causes of Irene's behavior any more justifiable than Ms. Malcolm's belief in curses? If so, how?

    This question will probably be debated in terms of scientific evidence for the biological bases of behavior and the efficacy of neurological treatments versus the lack of scientific evidence for curses. Ultimately, the team's belief in science is probably not more justifiable than a belief in curses. However, the team makes its decisions within a cultural and institutional belief system, with which it must be consistent. Ms. Malcolm essentially bought into that system of belief by seeking help at UFS.

8. Does it make a difference in Sandra's thinking that Ms. Malcolm has been raised in the United States and sees her parents as "traditional" and in many ways different from herself?

    Yes. If Ms. Malcolm were a completely traditional Haitian American in her perspective, she probably would not feel she needs Sandra's blessing to take Irene to the wise woman. Ms. Malcolm is caught between belief systems. Sandra may be able to help Ms. Malcolm negotiate these two ways of thinking and believing.

Action

9. With whom must Sandra consult before responding to Ms. Malcolm? Is that her choice or required?

10. What arguments can Sandra make for supporting Ms. Malcolm in seeing the wise woman with Irene?

11. What arguments can Sandra make for telling Ms. Malcolm that she cannot support that decision at this time?

12. If the team members cannot agree with Sandra that she should support Ms. Malcolm, what are Sandra's options? What should she do?

Teaching Suggestions

The instructor might begin the discussion by asking students to identify what they see as the most important issues in this case. Some students may see the main issue as a political one: how to persuade the team. Others will perhaps see the main issue as educating Ms. Malcolm about her daughter's condition and persuading her to accept the hospital's interventions at least for a while longer. Sandra does have some conflict herself between her openness to other cultures and support for Ms. Malcolm, on the one hand, and her Western rationalist beliefs, on the other. Some students may see the issue as a conflict of cultures. Ms. Malcolm, and now Sandra as her ally, are caught between Western rationalist beliefs and traditional Haitian culture. These students may be looking for a compromise position, such as giving the hospital a little more time. In our experience teaching this case, Sandra's dilemma raised a lot of issues about responsibility and accountability.

Information on Traditional Haitian Beliefs

It may be useful for the instructor to share some information about traditional Haitian beliefs related to illness. A good source is Paul Farmer's *AIDS and Accusation*, published in 1992 by the University of California Press in Berkeley, California. If a person suffers a sudden setback (medically or in other areas), it is often seen in this culture as having supernatural origins. One possible origin may be a

Additional Notes

curse from a person taking revenge on the individual or the family. In that case, it is important to combat the curse, which means discovering who did it and either neutralizing it in some way or by taking revenge. Priests, priestesses, or voodoo practitioners, may be consulted. Because Haitian Americans see voodoo as stigmatized in this country, they are unlikely to use that term in talking with an Anglo person or to acknowledge voodoo practices. Haitian people may also use charismatic Catholic or Protestant leaders to deal with a curse.

A root woman is an herbalist, who may or may not be a priestess. Herbalists are another source of traditional healing. The interactions between traditional herbs and psychoactive medications are unknown.

The experience of clinicians in one clinic serving a Haitian population here in the United States suggests that a traditional, or charismatic Christian, healer may bring temporary alleviation of psychiatric symptoms. However, if nothing else in the patient's life is changed, and the stresses remain as they were, the relief is quite transient. (From a personal interview with Mel Schmid, clinician at the Haitian Mental Health Clinic, The Cambridge Health Alliance, Cambridge, MA.)

18.

Grace
Claudette Lee and Terry A. Wolfer

"Well," Grace Johnston wondered, "what should I do? I need to talk with someone. I don't know if I can stay in this practicum. It was so great at first, but now I just don't know."

Grace thought about her strong desire to be a social worker. It was November of her final year of college and she was in a practicum that she really enjoyed initially, but now felt unsure about completing. She was very distressed about the recent turn of events. She needed to make a decision and planned to call Dr. Jones, her faculty field liaison, tonight.

Background

Grace was from Midlands, a small town of about 10,000 citizens on the flat, sparsely-populated plains of central Nebraska. Most of her family lived within a 20-mile radius and they visited each other often. She had 2 uncles, an aunt, and 15 cousins in addition to 3 younger brothers and sisters. The whole family attended Lutheran Church of the Master and they were all active, singing in the choir, ushering, and participating in many of the volunteer ministries run by the church.

Grace had attended Central Community College in her hometown for her first two years of college and then had transferred to Hastings College, a small Lutheran school with a social work program. The college was located about 75 miles from Midlands in Hastings, a larger town of 32,000 inhabitants.

Grace had done volunteer work in her home church while attending Central, and she continued this practice at a church in Hastings. She had enjoyed working with the elderly at the Midlands Elder Care Center and had also enjoyed being a scout leader with the Girl Scouts. She told a friend, "I really enjoy the volunteer work I do and have decided to become a social worker so I can continue helping people." Her decision was strengthened her first year in the social work program when she met other students who seemed to feel just as strongly about helping people. She began volunteering in Hastings by serving dinner at a homeless shelter on Wednesday nights and reading to the elderly at a local nursing home each week.

Practicum

In her senior year of college, Grace pursued a practicum at the Hastings Family Service Center (HFSC), a faith-based agency. Agency goals included empowering their clients to lead productive lives by providing services that would give them interpersonal and vocational skills. Services were provided in the areas of shelter care (foster children, battered women), childcare, and family, individual, and group counseling. HFSC also had a grant from the state to work with a public shelter which housed the homeless, many of whom were non-English speaking Hispanic workers attracted to the community by a meat packing plant. HFSC's mission affirmed "the value of all human life, respect for the dignity of all people, and a commitment to help people achieve their full potential."

During her screening interview, Grace told her practicum instructor, Pam Brown, "I've never worked with or seen homeless people before, and I've never had an opportunity to work with the Hispanic population. I would really like to learn more about them."

The Break Room Incident

Grace had begun thinking that she had really chosen the perfect practicum when something happened that caused her to begin to think differently. She was in the staff break room one day when Marti Byers and Dave Hinton, two of the agency therapists, came in.

"Hi, Grace. How's it going?" Marti asked.

"Great," said Grace. "Pam told me I could sit in on your Thursday group if it was okay with you."

"Fine with me," Marti shrugged, "but it's not the best group we've had."

"That's right," added Dave. "This group whines about everything. The room is too hot. The room is too cold. The refreshments are stale. I hate when people whine! And then there's that woman who must be colorblind. You should see the colors she wears together. And she thinks she's quite stylish!" Dave snorted, and Marti laughed in agreement.

Caught off guard by these comments, Grace didn't say anything. But she thought, "I'm really shocked at their attitudes."

"Anyway," Marti continued, "you're welcome to come to some sessions. We meet Thursday nights at 6:30. Just let us know when you're ready to sit in."

Getting Help

After leaving the break room, Grace thought further about the comments made by Marti and Dave and how they had shocked her. She decided to find Pam, her practicum instructor, and talk with her about them. Grace liked Pam and felt comfortable talking with her about anything at the center.

After describing the incident to Pam, Grace explained, "It really bothered me to hear them talk that way. I have heard other staff members joke about client situations at times and wondered why they do it. It just doesn't seem right to me. I don't think it shows respect for their clients or that they

value or care for them. How can you help someone who you don't respect? And what if the clients overhear them?" Her voice quivered a bit as she spoke.

"I'm sure they were just letting off steam," Pam responded, "and not really making fun of their clients. Marti and Dave are both excellent therapists. They care for their clients and would do nothing to harm them. Maybe you should have confronted them about their comments. That's generally the best way to handle that kind of situation."

Pam paused for Grace to respond, but when she didn't, Pam continued. "I know you work hard, and I think you're doing a fine job. But I wonder if other things may be bothering you also? How are you handling the stress that comes with working in an agency like this?"

"I know I stay busy," Grace countered, "but I thought I was handling things okay. I really enjoy what I do here and what I'm learning."

"You look a little tense," Pam prodded. "Perhaps we should talk about ways of coping with stress. People have different ways of handling stress. One of the methods I use is prayer and meditation. I take advantage of the chapel we have in the building and start my day by spending 5 minutes there saying a prayer each morning. It helps me tremendously. You should try it sometime."

Although Pam invited Grace to join her at prayer several more times over the next 2 weeks, Grace declined. It disturbed her even more when she was also invited to attend morning prayer by two other staff members. Grace began to wonder, "Is everyone talking about me? Did Pam tell other staff about our conversation? I thought our discussion of personal issues was confidential, I thought I could trust Pam. And I don't like being pressured about morning prayer."

Grace finally felt so uncomfortable about the situation that she began to think about leaving HFSC and doing a practicum somewhere else.

Moving On?

Grace called Dr. Jones, her faculty field liaison, and left a message saying, "Things have changed since your last visit, and I need to talk with you as quickly as possible." She did not know Dr. Jones very well, but other students had told her that Dr. Jones was very nice, easy to talk with, and a fair person.

Grace had liked the way their first visit had gone. Dr. Jones had made her feel good about what she was doing in the practicum.

When Dr. Jones did not call back right away, Grace became anxious and called again. This time, Dr. Jones answered. Grace said simply, "I would like to make an appointment to speak privately with you. I am feeling very uncomfortable at HFSC, and I am not sure I want to stay."

Dr. Jones seemed puzzled by Grace's comments and the urgency in Grace's voice. But Grace did not want to say any more on the phone, so Dr. Jones agreed to set an appointment the next afternoon.

When Grace and Dr. Jones met, Grace was almost in tears as she began talking. She related to Dr. Jones what had been happening and how she felt about her situation.

"Well, Grace," replied Dr. Jones, "You seem very upset. I think we need to meet with Pam to sort through this situation before making a final decision. First, though, we can talk about how you would like to handle that meeting. Is that okay?"

Grace nodded.

"What do you think your options are besides leaving, and what do you think needs to happen for you to continue?"

18.teaching note
Grace
Claudette Lee and Terry A. Wolfer

Case Synopsis

Grace was a senior BSW student who had sought out a practicum that would not conflict with her values. She chose a faith-based organization where she would receive a variety of experiences, including work with a diverse population. The agency mission stressed the value of all human life, the dignity of all people, and the importance of helping people to achieve their full potential. Therefore, Grace expected to find committed and caring helping professionals whose values and behaviors reflected both her own ideals and the agency's mission. Instead, she was stunned to find several of her colleagues making derogatory jokes about their clients. When Grace tried to discuss her feelings with her practicum instructor, she was further disturbed by her instructor's defense of her colleagues' conduct and by the suggestion that she needed to learn to handle the stress of her job. Finally, Grace became extremely uncomfortable when the staff at the agency began to harass her about joining them for prayer to relieve some of her stress.

Learning Outcomes Related to Religion and Spirituality

The case discussion will facilitate the work of students as they

1. Identify ways that spirituality and religion overlap with professional life, both providing support and creating challenges for practice.

2. Describe how personal religious and spiritual practices can both support and conflict with social work values and ethics.

Other Learning Outcomes for Which This Case Can Be Used

The case discussion will facilitate the work of students as they

3. Identify how preconceived ideas about agencies, agency values, and agency staff can present challenges.

4. Identify alternative ways for dealing with interpersonal differences and conflict, especially among professional colleagues.

Courses and Levels for Which the Case Is Intended

This case is written for both the bachelor's level and the graduate foundation level. Although spirituality and religion are prominent issues, the case can also be used to discuss social work values and ethics, confidentiality, student expectations, relationships with colleagues, and professional mentoring.

Discussion Questions Related to Religion and Spirituality

Establishing the Facts

1. Who are the major participants in this case?

    Grace, Pam, Dr. Jones, Marti, Dave, and other agency staff.

2. What led Grace to choose a practicum at this particular agency?

    Grace learned that the agency had a variety of programs and helped people in many ways. She wanted the opportunity to work with populations with whom she previously had no contact. She also felt that the basic values of the agency matched her own values, something that was very important to her.

3. What is known about the agency and how it is set up? What is not known?

    It is a faith-based agency and Grace thought it would be a good fit for her because of the values they advocate. Agency values include empowering clients to lead productive lives by providing services that would give them vocational skills. Services are provided in the areas of shelter care, childcare, and family, individual, and group counseling. The mission of Hastings FSC states that the agency values all human life, respects the dignity of all people, and would help people to achieve their potential. More concretely, it has a staff break room and a chapel.

4. What happened to Grace that made her begin to feel uncomfortable?

    Grace was in the staff break room one day when two of the agency therapists came in and talked negatively about the clients in a group they were facilitating. Grace was upset and decided to talk with Pam, her practicum instructor. Pam defended the therapists and then suggested that Grace might be struggling to handle the stress of working in the agency. Pam suggested that Grace attend morning prayer as one method to help with this stress. Grace chose not to go and began to feel pressured about praying when two other staff members invited her to go. She suspected Pam had betrayed her confidence and told other staff about their private conversation.

5. How did Grace handle her indecision and feelings of discomfort?

    Quite appropriately, she discussed it with her practicum instructor and then decided to call her faculty field liaison.

Analysis

6. What is the nature of Grace's relationships with various staff members, and how do these differ?

    Grace liked her practicum instructor, Pam, and felt comfortable with her and trusted her. She appeared to have a comfortable relationship with Dave and Marti and called them by their first names. There is no indication of specific relationships with any other staff. Grace does indicate that she was beginning to think she had picked the "perfect practicum," probably a sign that she was getting along well with everyone. Grace also had liked the way her first visit went with Dr. Jones, her faculty field liaison, and felt at ease with her enough to call her to talk about the situation.

7. How does Grace interpret the comments by Dave and Marti? Do you agree or disagree? Why?

    She was disappointed, even shocked, by their comments and interpreted these as evidence of negative attitudes.

8. How does her response help or hinder the situation?

    Grace's response is an emotional one, which means it may be more difficult to reason with her. Also, it suggests that other concerns (not apparent) must be discussed to get to the core of the problem.

9. Is there any indication that Grace may be examining or giving some thought to her values and those of the agency?

    She decided to discuss her discomfort with her practicum instructor and to call her faculty field liaison. She does some serious thinking about this before making her decision to call. She became very emotional when talking with her faculty liaison. But her concerns are not well articulated.

Action

10. What are the dilemmas that Grace faces?

    Whether and how she should respond to negative behavior and attitudes exhibited by professional colleagues. Whether she can continue to work in an agency where she perceives the staff does not behave in ways consistent with the mission of the agency and her own values. How to approach the social work department at her school if she does not want to continue with this practicum.

11. How do Grace's values relate to the social work Code of Ethics? Have these values caused problems at any time? What did they do?

    Her values, which are stated in the case, are the same as those stated in the social work Code of Ethics. Because of her strong religious background, she may possess additional values which may be in conflict with those expressed in the Code.

12. In what other ways could Grace have responded? And what might the consequences have been?

Additional Notes

Grace might have confronted Dave and Marti in the break room by saying she was surprised to hear them talk about clients in such a manner. Consequences could have been as follows:

1. They may have become defensive and not invited her to sit in on their group.

2. Although they may have considered her naïve, they might have apologized and talked about the group in a more professional manner.

Teaching Suggestions

Start by asking the class about their values and whether their values have caused them problems at any time. Have they had to reevaluate these values since being in school? Are their values very strong, fairly weak, or somewhere in between? Have they had to stand up for a value when everyone else had different ones? Ask if they think that Grace overreacted to the situation and the other staff were just trying to be helpful by demonstrating a method that had been helpful to them in reducing stress. Did any students have any strong reactions when reading this case? Why?

19.

Not in My House!

T. Laine Scales

"How will I respond to Li's request?" Carolyn wondered aloud as she pulled into the driveway at 221 Elm Street. She had been pondering that question for more than 24 hours, and now she had to make a final decision. In 8 years of working as a social worker at Hospice of Branch Springs, she had to make decisions like this frequently, and it never seemed to get any easier. Yesterday, Li Nguyen Johnson, a Vietnamese American patient who was dying of cancer, asked Carol to find a Buddhist monk to perform a ritual for the dying, but Li's husband and primary caretaker, Raymond, swore he would never allow it. Carolyn felt caught in the middle.

Turning Toward Home

On a crisp October day, Carolyn pulled into the leaf-sprinkled driveway of the Johnson home. Carolyn had come for her weekly visit with Li.

"I'm so glad you're finally here!" Raymond said in a panicked voice when he and the little dog, Corky, met Carolyn at the door. He showed Carolyn into the living room while pleading with her, "See if you can make sense of what she is saying—I've tried and I can't. I'll leave you two alone." Raymond called Corky out of the room and closed the door.

Carolyn turned to find Li crouched in the middle of the hospital bed that had been placed in the living room so Li would not have to climb the stairs. As she came closer, Carolyn saw that the tiny woman was actually on her knees, with her face buried in the white sheets. Suddenly, Li crawled around and faced the opposite direction, raising her hands up in the air as she turned. Her long black hair fell around her as she again buried her face down into the bed.

Carolyn imagined Li was trying to find a comfortable way to lie down. "Can I help you get settled?" Carolyn asked. "Here, would you like a pillow?"

"I must get to the East!" Li cried. The urgency in the woman's voice, along with the anxious look on her face, told Carolyn that she was quite upset.

Carolyn had seen this situation many times in her 8 years with Hospice. Dying patients often hallucinate and imagine being somewhere else. "She is in a different reality," Carolyn thought, "imagining she can somehow get herself back to her homeland with this repositioning of her body." Carolyn usually found it was best to go along with the illusion rather than argue with the patient.

"Do you mean you want to go to Vietnam? Is that where you are trying to go?"

Li was silent.

Meeting the Johnson Family

Carolyn had met Li for the first time 4 weeks earlier, when Carolyn had come to the house for the initial intake for Li to receive hospice services. She was surprised to find a younger-looking woman, even though the file said that Li was 48 years old. Although her small, pretty face did not show it,

Carolyn imagined that Li must be in pain. She was neatly dressed in a blouse and a skirt with stockings, and her long black hair was pulled into a tight bun. Carolyn was accustomed to seeing patients in casual clothes or dressing gowns, but she remembered that such formality with "guests" may be in keeping with the Vietnamese woman's customs. Li was sitting on the sofa in the small but neat living room, where a hospital bed had been put in front of the fireplace. Li smiled and motioned for Carolyn to sit down.

Raymond stood in the doorway. "Can I get you anything, my love?" he asked.

"No thank you," she responded, "let me talk to our guest." Carolyn heard Raymond step out onto the front porch where he sat in the swing and quietly talked to Corky.

Li's Story

Li's story fascinated Carolyn. In 1967, Li and Raymond had met in Saigon during the Vietnam War, when he was stationed near her home. They had fallen in love, though they had to hide their relationship from Li's parents, who worried that an American soldier could not be trusted. Li and Raymond were secretly married in Saigon.

When Raymond's tour of duty took him back to the United States in 1969, he began the long process of arranging for Li to join him. Finally, in 1973, Li was able to leave Saigon. Her parents objected so strongly to her marriage and to her departure that they disowned her. They had not spoken to her since, and they did not respond when she had repeatedly tried to contact them throughout her first 8 years in the United States. She imagined they must be dead now, but she did not know for sure.

When Li arrived at their first home on an army base in Ft. Knox, Kentucky, she spoke very little English and did not understand American ways. She was only 21 years old at the time, and although she loved Raymond, she missed her parents and two younger sisters. Even more stressful was the fact that she represented an enemy to the Americans: she was a *gook*. She hated the angry looks of the people on the base and in the town of Branch Springs where she shopped. Fortunately she met Mi-Ling and Sina during her first year at the base. These women were also wives of soldiers and had endured many of the same hardships that Li experienced. The women bonded almost immediately, as they spoke the same language and understood each other's ways. "We were family for one another," Li remembered.

Mi-Ling was the first of the Vietnamese women to become involved in the Covenant Baptist Church near the base. Soon, all three friends were attending regularly, and Li convinced Raymond to attend with her. He doted on Li and would do just about anything she asked. He found it easy to return to the routine of church-going that his family had followed when he was a boy, and Covenant was a church that was easy to love. It offered acceptance to this group of women who were so different in a town with very few Asians. The Christian message they heard at church was quite appealing as well. "Come unto me all you who are weary and heavy-laden and I will give you rest," Jesus said. It was not long before Li, Raymond, and the other Asian American women joined the church and Li was baptized, a big step, as she had been reared in a Buddhist home.

"But what did Buddha offer to a woman who was so far from her homeland?" she asked Carolyn, as she continued her story. "The church has taught me that there is one God, and by trusting in one God and his son Jesus, a person can go to heaven." The women trusted in Jesus, leaving behind the religion of their childhood. Li said none of the Vietnamese women ever spoke of Buddha again.

Raymond and Li moved around a variety of army bases for the next 20 years. Li made other acquaintances, but none like the surrogate sisters she had found in Kentucky. In 1993, Raymond retired from the army, and Li was thrilled when the couple returned to Branch Springs, to Covenant Baptist Church, and, best of all, to Li's friends. "It was like we were never apart!" she said. "We are still like sisters after 27 years, and now that I am sick they come to visit and bring me food every day."

That was 7 years ago. Now Mi-Ling and Sina, along with a few other Vietnamese women who had joined the church, helped Raymond to nurture and care for Li. Raymond was quite tender with her. "Their love has withstood so much over the years," Carolyn thought, as she heard Li's story. "Losing her could be devastating for him."

Receiving Hospice Services

After hearing Li's story, Carolyn had returned to the Johnson home once a week for the past 4 weeks. When a family signed up for Hospice services, the focus was on caring rather than curing and, in most cases, care was provided in the patient's home. Typically, a family member, like Raymond, served as the primary caregiver and, when appropriate, would help make decisions for the terminally-ill individual. The philosophy of Hospice was that every person has the right to die pain-free and with dignity, and that families would receive the necessary support to allow this to happen. Members of the Hospice staff made regular supportive visits to the clients' homes to provide additional care or other services. The Branch Springs Hospice team was composed of the patient's doctor, three nurses, several trained volunteers, a chaplain, and Carolyn, the social worker. The Hospice staff was on call 24 hours a day, 7 days a week.

The staff also provided a "life after loss" program, including counseling and support groups for grieving persons. When dealing with death, patients and their families often discussed spiritual matters. Although the chaplain was available if clients requested his services, Carolyn had no problem talking about spirituality and she was especially at ease with Li, as Carolyn was a Baptist herself. In fact, her own Baptist church had been involved in some evangelistic projects with Li and Raymond's church, so she was familiar and comfortable with their "church language."

Carolyn knew that when Li was gone, Hospice would continue to offer bereavement services to Raymond, and he would have the freedom to choose the amount of his contact with Hospice as he grieved. Watching his tenderness with Li, and even with the little dog, Carolyn guessed that he was likely to need and to want assistance.

Li Asks for Help

Carolyn's thoughts returned to the situation at hand as Li flailed around in the bed. Still trying to determine Li's wishes, Carolyn asked," Are you trying to go to Vietnam? Is that what you want?"

"No! No!" Li cried. "I must turn toward my homeland to pray the Buddhist prayers!"

All at once it became clear to Carolyn what the repositioning was about. Li was fervently praying in the Buddhist tradition, which certainly surprised Carolyn. Once she understood, however, Carolyn was able to figure out which way was East by looking out the window at the church steeple, and she helped to reposition Li on the bed. As she moved her frail limbs, Carolyn could see pain in the small face, but there was no complaint. Carolyn sat quietly on the sofa while Li repeatedly bowed down into the bed and chanted. The woman she saw kneeling with such devotion did not seem anything like the person who had declared 4 weeks ago, "by trusting in one God and his son Jesus, a person can go to heaven." Now she seemed to be drawing on another faith tradition, one that was completely unfamiliar to Carolyn. Nearly lost in her thoughts, Carolyn barely noticed when the chanting stopped.

"I can't remember," whispered Li, her tone revealing her frustration. "I can't remember!" As Carolyn walked toward the bed she could see tears in Li's eyes. "I can't remember the prayer for the dying. Can you tell me how it goes?"

"No, I'm sorry, I don't know the particular prayer you're asking for. Can I pray another prayer for you?"

"No! It has to be the Buddhist prayer for the dying! Please, this prayer will allow me to join my ancestors!"

Carolyn pondered this for a moment. Her gut response would be to reply, " Jesus is the way to go to heaven and join your loved ones." After all, Li had said those very words to her a few weeks before. If Carolyn were to say that to Li would she be evangelizing? "I know I am not supposed to evangelize at all," she thought. "But Li had been a baptized Christian for more than 25 years! Surely it wouldn't be trying to convert someone if you knew they were already a baptized Christian." Carolyn did not know what to say, so she stayed silent.

"The prayer for the dying, I want to see a Buddhist monk! He will do a ceremony for me; this is what we do when we are dying." Carolyn was startled by the word "we." Had Li forgotten that she was a Christian? Just then Carolyn looked up to see Raymond in the doorway. He looked completely stunned as he heard Li's words.

"Please help me find a monk, Miss Carolyn! He will tell me the prayers!"

Carolyn walked to the doorway and she and Raymond stepped into the kitchen. Before they could sit down at the kitchen table, Raymond had turned red. "Not in my house!" he said through gritted teeth. He tried to keep his voice down, but his anger was taking over:

"We are *not* having any heathen ceremonies in our home!"

"Okay, okay," said Carolyn. "Let's discuss this calmly. I don't know if I can even find a Buddhist monk in all of Kentucky. Besides, this may pass. She may forget all about it and return to being a Christian in a few hours. Why don't you go in and try to comfort her. It's probably better not to argue with her. I will come back tomorrow and we will talk about it."

Carolyn's Dilemma

Carolyn spent the rest of the afternoon and the evening trying to figure out what she should do. Would there be a monk available? She called Mi-Ling because she was listed on the Hospice intake form as a supporting friend. Carolyn explained the situation and asked Mi-Ling where she might locate a Buddhist monk.

Mi-Ling became very agitated. "What! She is a Christian woman! If she stops being a Christian I cannot visit her anymore. How can she even be thinking of this? It must be the medicine she is on. I don't think I can stand to see her like that."

Now Carolyn was more confused than ever. That night during dinner she considered her options. She realized that if she helped Li contact a monk, she might alienate the Vietnamese "sisters" and other church friends, damaging the support system already in place to help Li now and to help Raymond after the loss. Carolyn knew that bringing a monk would also make Raymond angry. Hospice served families and Raymond was a client, just as much as Li. If she responded to Li's request would she be undermining the chance that Raymond would seek help for his grief after Li's death? And yet, the philosophy of Hospice called for helpers to do everything they could to make the dying person comfortable. She knew that it was quite normal for the dying to return to their childhood memories and longings. Carolyn thought of herself as a compassionate, open-minded, and caring advocate. Did she not have the responsibility to advocate for Li with Raymond and her friends?

"Who is my client?" Carolyn asked herself as she pulled into the driveway of the Johnson home.

19.teaching note
Not in My House!
T. Laine Scales

Case Synopsis

Carolyn, a hospice social worker, was visiting Li, a Vietnamese woman who married an American and had lived in the United States for over 25 years. Li had established herself with a group of Vietnamese American friends who together became very involved in a Baptist church. Li was terminally ill with cancer, and she asked Carolyn to find a Buddhist monk to perform a ritual for the dying. Li's husband, Raymond, refused to allow Carolyn to bring a monk into the home. Carolyn had to decide how to respond to Li's request.

Learning Outcomes Related to Religion and Spirituality

The case discussion will facilitate the work of students as they

1. Describe ways in which social workers may be called upon to deal with issues of religion and spirituality in end-of-life care.

2. Articulate a variety of options social workers may consider when issues of spirituality and religion become salient.

3. Identify ways in which religion can serve as a resource as well as a cause of ethical tension in social work practice.

4. View religious and spiritual experiences as dynamic, rather than static (i.e., a client's spirituality may change greatly over time).

Other Learning Outcomes for Which This Case Can Be Used

The case discussion will facilitate the work of students as they

5. Identify strengths and resources within a client's social system and consider how they may be utilized in the helping process.

6. Discover the complexity of situations with multiple clients and learn methods of balancing the strengths and needs of each client.

Courses and Levels for Which the Case Is Intended

This case may be used at either the bachelor's or the graduate foundation level to present content on religion and spirituality as a strength and resource for clients, spirituality over the life course, social work values and ethics, race and ethnicity, oppression and power, marriage and family, death and dying, religious diversity, social networks, and skills of engagement, assessment, and intervention.

Discussion Questions Related to Religion and Spirituality

Establishing the Facts

1. What do we know about Li's spirituality?

    It has changed over the life course; it was affected by her relocation to the United States and now by her impending death; her religion has been a source of strength and community; religion is very important to her now. However, religion is also a great source of anxiety for her friends and family, as Li may be moving away from the spirituality of those who surround her.

2. What do we know about Carolyn's spirituality?

    She is Christian, very religious, participates in a traditional church, and feels community with those who believe as she does.

3. How might a person's mental or physical condition at the end of their life affect their practice of spirituality?

    Religious and spiritual beliefs may become very salient as individuals face death. Clients may return to religious traditions of their youth, and these may be different from their religions of later life. Physical frailty or mental confusion may also affect a client's ability to practice rituals and to make these choices.

Analysis

4. In what ways might Carolyn's spirituality be affecting her decision making?

    She may believe that Jesus is the one way to heaven, or she may be hesitant to find a monk if she is unfamiliar with or resistant to Buddhism. She may be hoping that Li's desire is a passing illusion; she may believe that Li's salvation experience is everlasting and eternal and therefore end-of-life struggles are not problematic, or she may affirm a variety of paths to salvation. However, Carolyn's inclinations are not apparent in the story. Students must guard against stereotyping Carolyn and Raymond as they also guard against stereotyping Li.

5. Who should Carolyn consider when making a decision? What tensions are present as she considers what is best for each party involved?

    Carolyn must consider Li as a dying person with last wishes. She must consider Raymond as a long-term client who will need bereavement services. She must consider the Vietnamese friends as an important resource and community for both Li and Raymond. Tensions are present in each relationship as Raymond uses his power as spouse to forbid the monk, and the surrogate sisters use their power as caretakers to resist the monk.

6. How might the Hospice organization be involved in Carolyn's dilemma?

    The team approach utilized by Hospice may function as a wonderful resource for Carolyn. There is a chaplain on the team who may advise Carolyn or may even become involved with the family. Hospice's mission of helping persons die with dignity may persuade Carolyn that she is obligated to search for a monk. Yet Hospice's mission to serve the family after the patient's death compels Carolyn to avoid alienating Raymond and the surrogate sisters. If students suggest that Carolyn find a monk, help them to see ways that the Hospice team might help Raymond and the surrogate sisters to cope with Li's wishes.

7. How does Li's ethnicity impact the situation? How does Raymond's and Carolyn's ethnicity impact the situation?

    Li is Vietnamese in an environment where White individuals are in the majority. Raymond and Carolyn are both White and part of the power elite. Li is in a more vulnerable position in many ways.

8. How would Li's situation be different if she had gone home to Vietnam to die? If her extended family were available and supportive?

    Li's attachment to a less-understood religion may stir up feelings of religious prejudice. If Li were in Vietnam, Buddhism would be an easily-accepted form of religious expression, and a monk would be readily available to perform the ceremony. If her family were supportive, the role of the "surrogate sisters" might become less important. Christians would be in the minority, and therefore Raymond may not be empowered in a traditionally Buddhist family. Raymond would have less power in terms of who comes into the home, as they would be in her family's house.

9. What role do the "sisters" play in this situation? How might they be utilized in the helping process?

The sisters form a much-needed support system for both Raymond and Li. Raymond may also depend upon them after Li's death. They represent Li's homeland, traditions, and native language. In these ways, they serve as an important emotional resource. If they reject her based on her religious traditions, her connection to her homeland is lost at this important time of life review. Yet the sisters have feelings of their own. They may feel threatened and frightened that Li's illness could result in a "regression" to her past religious traditions. They may be frightened that they will undergo a similar process as they age or get ill.

Action

11. Should Carolyn look for a Buddhist monk to come to the home?

Carolyn has a choice to either advocate for Li's dying wishes or to honor Raymond's resistance. The dilemma is complicated by the fact that Li may be experiencing delusions common among dying clients. If Carolyn follows Li's wishes, she may alienate Raymond and the sisters, not only from herself as the social worker but, more importantly, from Li. This alienation may damage the much-needed support system that Li has in place. The dilemma may be further complicated by Carolyn's own feelings and religious beliefs. As a social worker, she has been trained to believe she must be objective. Is that possible? There is no easy answer.

12. How would Carolyn's dilemma be affected if there were no monk available at all in this rural area?

Is she absolved from responsibility if she looks for a monk and does not find one? Does that solve the dilemma? Not really. Family and friends still object to Li's religious expression, which has changed in her last few weeks of life. The dilemma remains.

13. What else might Carolyn do to help all the people involved with these divergent spiritual needs?

Each actor in the story is deeply religious, and each has her or his own beliefs (and possibly fears) about death and about life after death. Carolyn must help each person involved to deal with these emotions and fears. She must also deal with her own feelings elicited by this case. Luckily, she has other helping professionals to assist her. She might choose to involve the Hospice chaplain, the pastor of Li's church, or volunteers who have experience in this area. She also needs to educate herself about Buddhism.

14. What should Carolyn say now?
   - To Raymond
   - To Li
   - To the surrogate sisters
   - In her report to the Hospice Team

   Here the instructor may want to divide students into groups to respond to different aspects of the question or to assign a writing assignment that could be formulated around Carolyn's options. For example, students may be asked to take on the role of Carolyn and write up case notes about the actions they took and their rationale for choosing those actions. Alternatively, students may be asked to create a process recording detailing Carolyn's conversation with Raymond or with the surrogate sisters.

Teaching Suggestions

The instructor could start the discussion with a factual question about the spiritual and religious beliefs of Li and of Carolyn. Help students move to a deeper level of analysis by asking questions related to Li's migration away from her homeland, as well as the importance of the support systems provided by Raymond and her surrogate sisters. Probe issues of diversity in terms of race, nationality, and spirituality. To move the class to consider the question "Who is my client?" and to struggle with the action dilemma, the instructor may divide the class into groups to consider a variety of possible actions, or may assign written responses that require students to place themselves in the role of the social worker.

Additional Notes

20.

Sugarland's Dilemmas

Harvey Stalwick and Doreen L. Holding Eagle

In November 1996, Emily Fisher had an inspiration. As a church social worker at Grace Baptist Church in the Houston suburb of Sugarland, she decided to link members of her congregation with the Texas Family Pathfinders, an established mentoring program that helped welfare recipients find employment. Her invitation to potential volunteers read, "Many of us have said for a long time that there needs to be reform in the welfare system. Now, the opportunity has come to us to be involved in helping reform take place. This is a wonderful ministry opportunity for us." Volunteers responded with enthusiasm.

By May 1999, two teams of mentors had been actively involved with two welfare clients. The church's first partner family had been every volunteer coordinator's ideal, but the second family left the congregation feeling as though it had failed to help. The current situation came into focus at a recent Houston Family Pathfinders coordinators meeting, where Emily learned that after nearly 3 years of volunteer mentor efforts in this large metropolitan area, a total of only 35 welfare clients had been involved. Why so few? Emily was worried that this approach to citywide social ministry was too slow and was possibly standing in the way of reform. She was not sure what to say at a forthcoming meeting of Grace Baptist volunteers, who had recently been recruited to form a third mentor team for another welfare recipient.

Family Pathfinders Program

In 1995, the Texas legislature had passed an extensive and resolute back-to-work welfare reform law, which was based on the "A Partnership for Independence" report by the State Comptroller of Public Accounts. This law created the Family Pathfinders program, a statewide network of volunteers from churches, civic clubs, synagogues, and other community groups to mentor and support individual welfare recipients as they moved along the road to self-sufficiency. Many argued that welfare spending was out of control, and the Family Pathfinders program was seen as the solution. The Pathfinders brochure stated the objective to "help neighbors restore the kind of self-respect and family values that strengthen the community as a whole." This Texas reform preceded national welfare reform and, in the minds of many politicians, was a model to follow.

Grace Baptist in Sugarland

You could not miss the church. The two-story red-brick building with massive white columns supported a tall, graceful spire and was the focal point of a sprawling campus. First-time visitors were also impressed with the parking lot—a sea of upscale cars and sports utility vehicles. Sugarland consisted mainly of upper-income White families who were living well in the economic boom. The congregation, which filled the 1,700 seat sanctuary, was able to support 10 full-time ministerial staff members. It was a busy place with a wide range of educational programs and services. Members referred proudly to the church's letterhead motto, "A Community of Discovery and Good Neighbors." In Emily's experience, members were open to new ideas and committed action.

Emily Fisher

Emily began working as a church social worker at Grace Baptist in 1995. Her official title was Minister of Missions, but when asked, "what do you actually do?" she would reply with conviction, "I try to move people from inside the four walls to outside the four walls to actively live a faith of loving one's neighbor."

Since graduating with a BSW degree in 1975, Emily had been a rural health worker serving primarily African American families, a day care case manager, and a community worker for a church-based inner-city program. It was all hard but rewarding work. Along the way, she attended seminary and blended religious study with her social work education.

When Emily joined the staff of Grace Baptist, she was impressed with the congregation's many outreach activities and intentions, which made her volunteer coordinating role exciting. The varied array of services included inter-faith transitional housing, Habitat for Humanity youth projects, food pantry and second-hand clothes depots, as well as an Albanian refugee resettlement program. This full mix of volunteering and fund-raising experience seemed to be a good fit for the Family Pathfinders program that became available in 1996.

Family Pathfinders at Grace Baptist in Sugarland

When introducing the Family Pathfinders program to Grace Baptist, Emily realized that educating the volunteers about welfare cuts, welfare-to-work, and the social conditions of poverty had to be done less by talking and more by showing. "They didn't have a clue. They wanted welfare cut, but they didn't know the issues," she said to a colleague. It was a challenge, but Emily was determined. She believed what she wrote in the church newsletter: "This is a way to be part of the solution, one family at a time."

The way the program worked was that the Workforce Community program, which carried out this statewide welfare reform initiative, would pre-select suitable welfare recipients and distribute names to the various volunteer mentor teams. The state provided training and orientation for the volunteers that consisted of being briefed on the culture of poverty, job-finding resources, resume writing guidelines, and pointers for dressing smart for interviews. Methods for providing motivational support and inspiration for achieving goals ended this one-day training workshop. The state also held monthly planning meetings for volunteer coordinators throughout the Houston metropolitan area. These training sessions and meetings made Emily's job easier because she could concentrate on providing on-going pastoral support of the volunteer teams, as well as client contact.

Grace Baptist's First Welfare Client: Evelyn

Evelyn was a 27-year-old African American single mother of three children whose ages were 3, 5, and 8 years. She had completed high school in a rural community and had taken computer classes since coming to Houston 6 years ago. Her stated motivation at the time of applying to the Family Pathfinders program was "to find a job to do better for my children."

Grace Baptist's first experience in the Family Pathfinders program was reported in a local paper: "Former welfare recipient Evelyn got a job as a file clerk at a downtown law firm. . . . when the job offer came to her by phone she said, "I didn't even want to hear the salary; all I wanted to know was that I was going to work."

Getting started with Evelyn had been awkward at first for most of the all-White volunteer team who had never had such close contact with an African American. The volunteers found themselves meeting in restaurants in African American communities, finding street addresses in neighborhoods foreign to them, and gradually becoming self-conscious about their lifestyle differences. They provided help in many practical ways: childcare during job interviews, resume writing advice, and friendship. In addition to the activities of the volunteers, Emily found herself increasingly involved with Evelyn through phone support and through assisting the volunteers sort out their attitudes and their "what next?" questions.

A breakthrough in this mentoring project came when the volunteer coordinator's husband found a job for Evelyn in his law office. The job came when Evelyn was only days away from losing her regular welfare check and it replaced $130 in monthly welfare benefits with a monthly salary of $1,700. After a year in this new job, Evelyn was able to purchase the first house she had ever owned. The volunteer mentor team, joined by other church members, hosted a potluck house-warming celebration. Encouraged by this success story, the Grace Baptist Family Pathfinders program eagerly formed a second volunteer mentor team. As before, the state program provided the name of a welfare family with whom the church could partner.

The Second Welfare Client: Kenyatta

Kenyatta, who was 19 years old, and her two sons, 3 years and 10 months old, had moved from rural Mississippi the year before. This resettlement had taken courage, despite the comfort and support of her former hometown pastor and his family, who had moved to the Houston area before Kenyatta arrived. Pastor Wright led a small Pentecostal congregation made up of primarily African American members and welcomed Kenyatta into the fold where she sang in the choir and taught Sunday School. The Wright family occasionally provided financial assistance and care for Kenyatta's children. Over the years, Pastor Wright had encouraged and supported many others like Kenyatta by saying, "It's your time to make the move to Houston."

When the Workforce Community Agency referred Kenyatta to Grace Baptist as the second client in their Family Pathfinders program, they noted she had completed her GED in two months, was good with numbers, and had taken some computer classes in high school. She had expressed an interest in a nursing career, but at present she had no real desire to return to school. The Family Pathfinder volunteer mentor team for Kenyatta was led by Martha Reid, the same coordinator who had successfully found the law firm job for the first welfare client. According to Emily, Martha was well known in Grace Baptist circles as "a quiet dynamo

who gets things done." Martha felt very linked to the program and cherished this experience as a way to live out her Christian calling. When recruiting new volunteers and giving talks in church, she often remarked how volunteering had deeply enriched her life and was a way of giving back.

Our Way or Your Way?

It worried the volunteer team that Kenyatta found a job on her own in a small privately-owned day-care center that paid minimum wage, only $5.15 an hour. The team was even more concerned by the day-care program itself. Visits by volunteers to provide support and advice to Kenyatta revealed the poor quality of care for the children. Martha, as coordinator of the mentor team, confronted a social worker from the Department of Human Services and said, "that place is a slum and health hazard. How can anything be accomplished with a staff-to-child ratio of 1:25? Those children are simply being caged in a shabby building without decent playground facilities." Martha was not satisfied with the social worker's noncommittal response, and the Grace Baptist Family Pathfinders program submitted a written complaint to the state child protection services.

Determined that Kenyatta could and should do better than work at this run down day-care center, the mentor team tried exploring options with her. These included employing a vocational tester, providing budget management counseling (one of the volunteers was a Certified Public Accountant), and pairing Kenyatta with Evelyn who, by this time, was about to purchase her first home. The vocational testing seemed to lead nowhere. The volunteer who helped administer the tests at Grace Baptist Church expected Kenyatta to follow up by completing job applications or appearing for recommended job placement interviews, but she did nothing. Later, Pastor Wright explained that the only thing Kenyatta would say about these visits to Grace Baptist was, "they put a lot of pressure on me and I just felt lost in that place."

Emily's discussions with this volunteer mentor team were so different than her experiences with the previous year's team and Evelyn. Instead of being upbeat and confident, the volunteers seemed flat and discouraged. Emily reflected with them and emphasized that they had to wait for Kenyatta's pace, ask themselves whose values are most important, and spend more time listening and recognizing that she is doing what feels most comfortable. "We have to honor Kenyatta's choice of staying in the day-care job," Emily reminded the team members. "She seems to be working on her own terms even though the job isn't ideal or what you had hoped it should be." Did they understand? She was not sure.

However, in private she was haunted by the thought that she should have done more with Kenyatta. There was a delicate balance between direct client involvement and trying to encourage and empower volunteers. What seemed to bother the mentor team most was Kenyatta's statement that, "God will take care of me . . . whatever happens, happens—God will take care of the rest." Frustrated, volunteers regarded these remarks as trite and one even said, "I think she is just putting us on." These comments bothered Emily as well because they seemed so naïve. But even she was not sure she understood Kenyatta's level of faith. Nevertheless, mixed messages from the present volunteers and her own misgivings about the overall impact of welfare reform efforts had left her uncertain about whether or not to form a third volunteer mentor team. What should she do?

20. teaching note
Sugarland's Dilemmas
Harvey Stalwick and Doreen L. Holding Eagle

Case Synopsis

Emily Fisher, a church social worker at Grace Baptist Church in the Houston suburb of Sugarland, welcomed the Texas Family Pathfinders welfare program as a way to actively involve church members in social ministry. Volunteer mentor teams would be recruited to join with families on welfare to help them move from welfare dependency to the self-sufficiency of adequate employment.

After 30 months of volunteer effort, two teams of mentors had been involved with two African American welfare mothers. The church's first partner family had been a success, but the second family did not achieve the result for which the volunteers had hoped, and the congregation felt as though they had failed. Emily was concerned that the volunteers were becoming discouraged. She also pondered the direction that welfare reform was taking—it seemed too slow and complex. How could volunteers in this suburb of Sugarland make a significant difference in the lives of welfare clients? Emily believed strongly in the church's role in social ministry, but what direction should it take?

Learning Outcomes Related to Religion and Spirituality

The case discussion will facilitate the work of students as they

1. Develop an understanding of the spiritual motivation for generalist social work practitio-

ners located in churches, synagogues, and other communities of faith.

2. Critically analyze nationwide social policy shifts to increase faith-based voluntary sector participation in social programs.

3. Identify the spiritual values that drive a renewal of public social-advocacy roles for churches, synagogues, and communities of faith.

4. Critically explore practice elements framed by person-in-environment considerations, populations-at-risk vulnerability, and whole person spiritual dimensions. Pros and cons of the mentoring role of volunteers could be examined in this context.

Other Learning Outcomes for Which This Case Can Be Used

The case discussion will facilitate the work of students as they

5. Identify with the need for culturally respectful anti-racism analysis in the design of social programs, specifically concerning the reform of public assistance.

6. Understand social class misconceptions and related values embedded in contemporary religious experience.

7. Appreciate the nature of entitlement as a social contract and the importance of human rights.

8. Recognize that sometimes the ideals of reform stand up better under more flexible conditions.

Courses and Levels for Which the Case Is Intended

This case provides bachelor's level attention to public-assistance social welfare issues and to specific aspects of generalist social work practice in a religious context. At the graduate level, this case may be used in social policy and community-organizing courses to provide attention to social contract and entitlement, to nongovernmental delivery of services, to subsidiarity (devolution of social programs to lower, more immediate levels of administration), to human-rights monitoring, and to values in a democratic society.

Discussion Questions Related to Religion and Spirituality

If this case study is viewed as an example for post-2000 social work with the poor in the United States, instructors and students may become more aware of certain aspects of religion and spirituality. Discussion of possible responses to these questions may also be guided by a view of civil society creation in which advocacy is a third force, beyond governmental and private market interests, and one that embraces the spirit of service found in all religions. Or, the instructor may choose to discuss various definitions of social purpose. One interesting definition is found on the cover of each edition of *Tikkun: A Bimonthly Jewish Critique of Politics, Culture and Society*, published by the Institute for Labor and Mental Health: "to heal, repair and transform the world. All the rest is commentary."

Establishing the Facts

1. What initially motivated Emily to become involved in the Texas Family Pathfinders program?

   Emily's main motivation was a desire to raise social awareness by moving church people "from inside the four walls to outside the four walls to actively live a faith of loving one's neighbor."

2. What expectations, based on her experience, did Emily have for the social ministry conducted by members of her church?

   She expected that there would be a great need for raising social awareness, based on years of community work with clients struggling with basic survival needs. Emily realized that the suburb of Sugarland's economic prosperity would limit people's understanding of social needs.

3. How has Emily's church acted toward social concerns in the past?

   Many congregational members possess a service perspective which they frequently act on, including affordable and transitional housing provisions, charitable food and clothing activities, and work with refugees.

4. What social work practice values does Emily urge volunteers to respect?

   Emily, a social worker, insisted that the volunteers respect the values of self-determination, dignity of the client, and nonjudgmental relationships. She was also an educator trying to find effective ways for congregational members to learn through experience about a largely distant world of welfare, the social conditions of poverty, and forms of social advocacy.

Analysis

5. Why has the mentoring program been less successful with Kenyatta?

   Emily implies she should have spent more time with Kenyatta, as her needs were possibly beyond what the volunteers could provide. Or, what may have been overlooked were the many strengths of Kenyatta's contact with Pastor Wright, his family, and the congregation in which she was involved. Sugarland's offer of good will and mentoring was possibly viewed as an imposition.

6. How do you explain the different responses from Evelyn and Kenyatta?

7. To what extent will the Pathfinders program increase "living wage" employment and reduce poverty at a community level?

8. What prompted Emily to pause and question the outcome of the Family Pathfinders program as meaningful welfare reform?

    Emily becomes aware that welfare reform is going slowly. After 30 months of the Family Pathfinders program, only 35 clients have been involved in the Houston metropolitan area.

9. What are the different dilemmas (personal, societal, related to social work practice) found in this case study?

    The main dilemma involves Emily: Should they continue with volunteer mentors, and form a third team, or possibly expand the program? Martha faces a dilemma as well: How should she respond to Kenyatta who seems unwilling to try harder to "get ahead" and leaves everything in God's care? At a societal level there exists a major dilemma well beyond the Grace Baptist Church membership—a dilemma of social class differences in Sugarland. The welfare reform mentoring experiences of volunteers have revealed the shortcomings of any quick fix for the gap between the rich and the poor. The age-old distinction between charity and social justice implicitly presents itself in this case. A final, and possibly more significant dilemma is the "two-ness/double consciousness" faced by the two African American welfare clients. In their struggle as clients they have to respond to both the upper middle-income values of the volunteers for financial betterment and to their own culture and values. Perhaps Kenyatta (seen as a failure) rather than Evelyn (seen as a success) is the individual who comes out of this experience more intact as a person.

    W.E.B. DuBois writes eloquently about the dilemma of "two-ness" in 1903: "One ever feels his two-ness—an American, a Negro; two souls, two thoughts, two unreconciled strivings; two warring ideals in one dark body, whose dogged strength alone keeps it from being torn asunder." And further, he continues: "To be a poor man is hard, but to be a poor race in the land of dollars is the very bottom of hardships." He also tackled the issue of double consciousness: "A sense of always looking at one's self through the eyes of others, of measuring one's soul by a tape of a world that looks on in assumed contempt and pity." Dubois, W.E.B. (1903). The souls of Black folk. *Chicago: A. C. McClung and Co.*

Action

10. Emily is impatient with the slow progress of the Grace Baptist Family Pathfinders program—only two welfare-to-work partner families in almost 3 years. Should Emily urge the expansion of their volunteer mentor team involvement? Would two or possibly three partner families this next year be a realistic goal?

11. Emily and Martha, her volunteer coordinator, are bothered by the limited citywide impact of the Family Pathfinders program. To date only 35 welfare-to-work families have been assisted. What strategy should they consider for raising this issue at the next Houston volunteer coordinators planning meeting?

12. To what extent should the volunteers' experiential learning be shared with Grace Baptist Church members? Specifically, what would have the maximum effect for improving the Family Pathfinders program at Grace Baptist and within the state?

13. What unique role do social workers like Emily have in bringing about social change?

Teaching Suggestions

Before opening up the discussion of Emily Fisher's role and the various questions she is facing, it may be helpful for students to understand the context of this case by reviewing the Family Pathfinders website (http://www.dhs.state.tx.us/communitypartnerships/familypathfinders). Students could reflect on similar welfare reform programs in their community and state.

An appreciation of Emily's role may be guided by a brief historical discussion of how the origin of the social work profession witnessed the contribution of many influential persons who combined spiritual and social analysis perspectives as the basis for social change and progressive social education. This blend gave social work the necessary direction to move ideas about helping beyond charity and moral suasion. Emily, in her career and her dual education in social work and in religious studies, represents this blended perspective.

Classroom discussion of the suggested questions could be followed by an assignment to write an epilogue for the case. This assignment could be done on an individual or group project basis and feature the following:

a) What happens at the next Grace Baptist volunteer mentor team meeting and at the next Houston volunteer coordinators planning meeting?

b) What was the welfare-to-work experience like for the participants as told in their own words?

Within advanced and graduate social policy studies, this case could be used as a discussion-trigger for focusing on such current issues as the "charitable choice" provision of the Personal Responsibility Work Opportunity Reconciliation Act of 1996 (See Section 104 of H.R. 3734). Further, the case study offers a personal aspect to the recent history of welfare reform initiatives and welfare "language" introduced by the publication of N. Gingrich, B. Schellhas, E. Gillespie, and D. Armey's 1994 *Contract with America: The Bold Plan by Rep. Newt Gingrich, Rep. Dick Armey, and the House Republicans to Change the Nation* (New York: Times Books). The Senate-based Temporary Assistance for Needy Families (TANF) programs also reflect this personal aspect, in which social legislation appears directed primarily to time limits, reliance on return-to-work solutions, and an increasing dependence on the voluntary and philanthropy sectors. Related social contract and human rights issues could be explored as well as community-organizing strategies.

Additional Notes

21.

Seeking, But Not Finding

Miriam McNown Johnson

Because of a voice-mail message she had received that morning, Betty Hunter knew that there would be a last-minute item added to the agenda for Kristen Larsen's routine treatment-plan review at the Crestview Residential Treatment Center. Stephanie Gonzales, the cottage supervisor, had reported that the teen was demanding to be allowed to attend the funeral of a local "acquaintance" who had been slain at a party in a possible gang-related shooting. "Kristy's desperate to go. Just thought I'd let you know so you could be thinking about it," Stephanie's message concluded, "because we have so many issues to cover in the meeting."

"There's an understatement for you," Betty thought to herself. Try as she might, Betty could not bring herself to be optimistic about Kristen Larsen's future. Kristen's case was one of the first assigned to Betty when she started her new job as an MSW social worker at the Mesa County Social Services department. Betty had been Kristen's Special Services worker for almost three years now, and it seemed as though Kristen had been losing ground rather than making progress most of that time.

As Betty made the long drive to Crestview, she thought through the immediate challenges of the case. At 17 years old, Kristen was significantly behind in school. She certainly would be unable to complete the necessary credits to graduate before her 18th birthday, and if it looked like she could not do it by the time she turned 19, then she would not be eligible for further support or services from the child welfare system. Because she had been diagnosed with schizo-affective disorder 2 years previously, there was some hope that her case could be transferred into the Adult Services Unit. Both the school and the cottage staff reported that Kristen regularly experienced audio and visual hallucinations. Given that she refused to take her prescribed psychotropic medications, Betty felt that a referral for continuing services through the Adult Unit was certainly justified. Unfortunately, Kristen had no desire to move into a halfway house or to have a case manager "telling me what to do." A talented artist, Kristen argued that she could support herself "painting store windows" or "designing tattoos" while living with friends and casual acquaintances, a lifestyle choice probably inspired by her footloose mother.

A History of Abuse, Neglect, and Multiple Placements

Kristen had entered state custody when she was 13. One of her girlfriends, after spending the night at Kristen's house for a slumber party, reported to the authorities that she overheard Mr. Larsen trying to slip into bed with Kristen. She said that she heard Kristen beg her father to go away, saying, "not tonight." Then Mr. Larsen tried to get into bed with one of the other girls. When the police and Child Protective Services (CPS) came to investigate a few days later, he barricaded himself in the house with Kristen and her sister. Eventually, he was persuaded to give up and was taken to jail, and his children were removed from the home.

Kristen denied being sexually abused by her father for the first 3 years she was in agency custody. The notes in the case file, meticulously recorded by Ruth Gibson, the first worker assigned, indicated that Mr. Larsen had himself been sexually abused as a child. He was diagnosed as being severely depressed and had a long history of threatening violence against family members and public authorities. Approximately a year after Kristen was removed from the home, he committed suicide by driving his car into a tree. Kristen's last contact with him involved an argument over her choice of outfits. After the funeral, a great aunt cleaned out the one-room apartment he rented in the poorer part of the city. Kristen regretted that she was given nothing of his as a remembrance. All she had were a few stuffed animals he had bought her and an old T-shirt she had once borrowed and forgotten to return.

Ruth Gibson said that her clearest memory of Kristen's mother was from Mr. Larsen's funeral. While a sobbing Kristy sought comfort in Ruth's lap, Ms. Larsen appeared to be totally indifferent to her daughter's pain. Betty thought of Kristen's mother as a burnt-out, middle-aged "flower child." Bright and talented, Ms. Larsen attended the local community college sporadically and was frequently unemployed. Although arguably a very gifted fashion designer, she was unable to focus on either a career or her children's needs. She seemed satisfied leaving her children to be raised by her ex-husband.

According to the case file, Ms. Larsen became addicted to methadone during the time that Kristen was in custody and failed to contact her daughter for extended periods. Although she was unable to offer her daughter either minimally adequate care or emotional support, Ms. Larsen had earned a reputation at the agency for demanding to be involved in case planning and being harshly critical of most of Kristen's caseworkers, therapists, and caretakers. Sometimes she hired an attorney to challenge the agency. The case record indicated that Ms. Larsen had been diagnosed with "narcissistic personality disorder."

When she came into state custody, Kristen had three older siblings who were already young adults and alienated from their parents. Her other older brother, who was still a minor, was placed with relatives out-of-state. The record indicated that there was a long-term rift between Ms. Larsen and these relatives. Kristen sided with her mother and thus was cut off from the rest of her family.

Like many youngsters in foster care, Kristen had experienced several moves, and for her, these were always to a more structured, restrictive environment. When Betty got the case, Kristen was still in her first placement, a small, family-run community-based group home that was licensed for four youth. Kristen developed a strong attachment to the houseparent couple and took a nurturing role with the other pre-teens. Her attachment to them was evidenced by the fact that in most of her conversations with Betty at the time, Kristen talked constantly about the kids who had moved on. Unfortunately, the houseparents left soon after Betty took the case and were replaced by another couple.

Kristen was a cute and appealing child at 14. Betty remembered her bed being covered with stuffed animals and Kristen's endless fascination with them. "See this bear? I got him from my father. He helps me sleep by keeping away bad dreams at night. And this dog? His name is Fuzzy. He was my sister's once but now he's mine. He guards my stuff. And this other one . . . ." Each animal seemed to be imbued with meaning and power for Kristen, who noted emphatically, "Some people don't believe me, but I just tell them to go to hell." Betty was always careful not to challenge Kristen's beliefs or to act condescending.

Kristen's other characteristics were not so endearing. She would tune out others by pulling her long hair down over her face and hiding behind it. If Betty persisted in trying to make conversation, Kristen would growl, "I'm getting pissed off now," and resort to making noises. She emulated the language and graffiti of the local *cholos* (Latino gangs), scribbling threats on the back of the seats in the school bus and sending intimidating letters to her relatives about how her "posse" would shoot them if they set foot in the county. Kristen told the other kids she could "feel" her dead father's presence in her room, but the houseparents interpreted it as a pre-adolescent scare tactic. Nevertheless these creepy admissions, combined with frequent temper outbursts both at the group home and at school, kept peers at a distance.

At this time, Kristen was visiting her mother every other weekend. Ms. Larsen often complained to the houseparents about Kristen's behaviors at home, such as staying out overnight. She usually ignored the therapist's suggestions, preferring instead to focus on the variety of diagnoses Kristen had been given over the years. "It's this mom who is 'crazy-making'," the therapist told Betty.

Eventually, the school system tired of Kristen's constant angry outbursts, the houseparents tired of dealing with the school system, and the group-home therapist tired of battling with Kristen's mother and her attorneys. So in the first of several moves, Betty took Kristen to a shelter facility while she sought a new placement. Even in the short 3 weeks that Kristen was in the shelter, she seemed to be deeply affected by the comings and goings of other children, talking constantly about them: "Tiffany is leaving. I don't think they found the right kind of place for her. Betty, can you call her social worker? Do you think Tiffany's new foster parents can bring her here to see me?"

Kristen lasted about a year in her next group home, an eight-bed facility, for girls only. Betty regretted that it had rotating staff, rather than a consistent houseparent couple. It was described as possessing a "therapeutic milieu." Kristen's escapes and admission that she wanted to find a boyfriend and get pregnant were not unusual client behaviors in the facility, but she soon developed other problems. Betty was not the only one who noticed that whenever people were conversing, about any topic at all, Kristen always assumed she was being discussed, or even secretly plotted against. "Stop fucking talking about me!" she would yell from an adjacent room. She began speaking to herself and laughing inappropriately. When she repeatedly reported seeing her dead father and hearing him talk to her, the staff felt they could not keep Kristen safe any longer and asked that she be moved.

Another short stay at the shelter facility and then assignment to Crestview Residential Treatment Center completed Kristen's placement history. Betty was pleased that she was able to get the center to make a commitment to keep Kristen as long as necessary. Her agency had a strong philosophy against hospitalizing children unnecessarily, and they worked hard to keep them in the least restrictive setting and to get them back into the community. The center was able to put her into a special school setting where the staff said that they could handle her when she was hallucinating or paranoid. On the downside, the center's plans to help Kristen develop skills for independent living seemed haphazard and thrown together.

On the Road With Kristen

Although many of her colleagues found transporting clients to be burdensome, Betty knew that teens often feel more comfortable talking in a car or a fast-food restaurant than a therapist's office. Despite being difficult, Kristen was one of Betty's more interesting cases, and Betty never minded spending time with her. It gave her a chance to observe as well as to counsel.

Described as a "classic Nordic beauty," Kristen probably inherited her looks from her father's side of the family. Tall and blonde, with striking blue eyes, she also knew how to flaunt her attributes, including her fully developed figure. Her tight shorts and midriff-baring "crop-tops" invited admiring stares from males of all ages. Kristen usually sought to emulate a tough "street look" with heavy eye make-up and dark lip liner.

Sometimes Kristen chose the destination when they went out. Betty remembered the time, more than a year ago now, when she gave in to Kristen's unrelenting demands and agreed to take her to her mother's house for an impromptu visit. Although no one answered the doorbell, Kristen insisted that her mother must be at home and tried to peek between the closed blinds into the darkened rooms. "I think she's in there, Betty. I know she's in there." Finally, in response to their repeated banging on the door, a thin, disheveled figure appeared. Judging from Ms. Larsen's greasy, unkempt hair, rumpled clothing, bloodshot eyes, dilated pupils, and the sores on her arms, Betty guessed that they had awakened Kristen's mother from a deep, drug-induced slumber. Squinting into the sun-drenched doorway, Ms. Larsen mumbled an unlikely excuse about having a bad case of the flu. In barely audible, garbled language she admonished Kristen to "be a good kid" and promised to arrange a visit when she felt better. As her mother hastily shut the door, Kristen mumbled, "Sure, okay. See ya."

"Never gonna happen," Betty thought to herself. Usually, she could see the strengths in her clients' parents, but not this time. "This kid's got no one and she knows it. Bummer of a way to start out in life."

Back in the car, Kristen stared out the window. "Why me?" she asked. "Why does all this happen to me?"

Betty did not answer.

Kristen usually directed her anger at "the system" rather than at the family that had failed her. In fact, usually she was protective of her parents and their reputations. She maintained the tough, adolescent bravado so typical of foster children who have experienced repeated separations and losses. Betty recalled only one instance when she had seen Kristen openly express strong feelings about her family history. It happened during a special talent show at the center, when someone played the guitar and dedicated the song, "The Wind Beneath My Wings," to her parents. Kristen suddenly burst into tears and wailed so loudly that Betty had to take her out of the room to a quiet place where she could regain control. "Why doesn't *my* mother love *me*? Why doesn't she ever visit? Can't she even write me a letter?" Kristen sobbed.

Another time Betty took Kristen to visit her father's gravesite. Kristen was harboring a grudge against Betty that day, because she had not been allowed to bring a friend along. Kristen did not want to hear any explanations about policies and having to plan ahead. And Kristen knew how to hold onto a grudge. After a few minutes alone at the grave she returned to the car and announced to Betty, "I put a curse on you over my father's grave. I said I hoped you got a fever and you got very, very sick, and you had to go to the hospital and you died."

Betty always responded to such threats with a mix of humor and respect. "I don't believe in curses," she said, "but I think I'll take some vitamin C." Betty did not think of herself as being particularly superstitious, but she did take the vitamin C when she got home—no need to take chances.

Such incidents did not bother Betty as much as seeing evidence of Kristen's decline in functioning. On a recent outing with Kristen they had stopped at a restaurant specializing in Mexican food. Kristen started to order her favorite, a burrito, but got flustered when the counter attendant did not understand her, and then was unable to repeat her request. "I can't do this. Betty, order for me, order for me!" she urged with a note of panic. Betty worried that such cognitive difficulties would multiply in the future, leaving Kristen unable to manage even the simple skills of daily living. Already the school reported that Kristen could not make it through an entire day without needing to be removed from class for angry outbursts or having hallucinations.

Kristen's Search for Meaning and Connection

Betty remembered being surprised the first time Kristen announced that her background included a significant Native American element. She said her mother had both Cherokee and Navaho ancestors. (Betty checked and was unable to find either Kristen or Ms. Larsen on any Native American registry.) Nevertheless, Kristen shared her mother's interests in exploring and adopting Native culture. Ms. Larsen had sometimes taken Kristen to powwows with her, and she had made her daughter a dream-catcher to hang over her bed. These experiences, and the family's Mexican American tradition of making tamales together for Christmas dinner, were Kristen's most meaningful connections to her mother.

The case record listed no religious affiliation for Kristen. She had briefly attended a Catholic church with another child in her first group home placement, but that was the only history that indicated any link to formal religious organizations.

Betty thought about how Kristen's deep sense of spirituality was reflected in the small "shrine" she had set up on the dresser in her room at the center. A bright plastic Virgin Mary votive candleholder was placed prominently in the middle of the display. Around it, Kristen had arranged a collection of items that held special meaning for her. Among the informal snapshots of school chums and group-home friends was a magazine photo of Selena, the promising young Tex-Mex singer who had been tragically killed by a deranged fan. Letters, small stuffed animals, bits of sage, and colorful rocks filled the remainder of the space.

Kristen continued to believe that her stuffed animals had special powers, and she sometimes "made wishes on them." The center's consulting psychiatrist often referred to Kristen's "immature superstitions" and her propensity for "magical thinking."

Betty preferred a more positive outlook on Kristen's thinking and behavior. For example, Kristen collected the sage plants in the hilly area behind the Crestview grounds. She explained to Betty that it was a Native American custom to never remove something from the wild without leaving something else in return. Kristen, who did not smoke, borrowed cigarettes from her friends, took them apart, and left a small pile of tobacco as a "thank you" for the sage. Although Betty did not see herself as experiencing any kind of "spiritual quest," she did feel admiration for Kristen's sense of ritual and connection to nature.

Betty also remembered that Kristen had pleaded for permission to add candles and incense to her homemade altar. Betty was sympathetic to the idea, but understood that licensing rules forbade anything that could be a fire hazard. The same rules made it impossible for the staff to accommodate Kristen's request to conduct a traditional "smudging" ceremony. (A smudge stick is a small, tightly-bound bundle of sage and cedar. The smoke from the smoldering, aromatic branches is used by Southwestern Indians to bless dwellings and repel evil spirits.) Kristen had learned the practice from her mother.

Betty had a difficult time categorizing herself in terms of religion. She was beginning to feel "more spiritual" than in her past. Certainly not a traditionalist, and clearly not a member of any denomination, she was not exactly into "New Age" culture either, but had read some books on Native Americans and liked "connecting" with nature.

Betty did not feel that her support for spiritual practices was supported in her work. Although there was no formal agency policy, religious discussions with clients, and even between colleagues, were clearly discouraged. Betty felt a vague annoyance that the public child welfare system was doing nothing for foster children to help facilitate spiritual development. Kids could request to be taken to church services, but often these outings were seen as an important *socializing* opportunity, rather

than a religious or spiritual experience. And in the larger group homes, staffing shortages and transportation problems were used as excuses to overlook such requests.

The Meeting

Kristen ran out to the car as Betty pulled into the parking lot at Crestview. She pulled a rumpled newspaper clipping out of her pocket. "See, the service is tomorrow. Please, *please* let me go," she cried hysterically. "I promise I'll behave."

"Take it easy, Kristy. It's not up to me alone," Betty reminded Kristen as she walked her back to her room, "but I know it's important to you."

Betty recognized everyone in the conference room attending the review meeting. Representing the center staff were Pat Harrison, Kristen's regular therapist; Tom Fischer, Kristen's teacher; Lupe Garcia, the teacher's aide; Jack Spencer, the clinical services director; and Stephanie Gonzalez, the cottage supervisor who had left the phone message earlier. Also present was Judy Cohen, representing the County Mental Health Center.

Jack opened the discussion by asking the question that was on everyone's mind: "Who was this dead boy? What is Kristen's connection to him?"

Stephanie responded that as far as she knew, Kristen had met him on one of her recent escapes. She was enthralled with his talk of gang activity, but had not had any ongoing contact with him, as far as the staff knew. No phone calls, no letters. She had learned from a staff member a day or two earlier that he had been shot. She saw the obituary in the newspaper and clipped out the information about the scheduled graveside service.

Stephanie reported that the cottage staff were concerned about the safety risks involved in taking Kristen to the service—Kristen might run away, or she might get caught up in gang-related violence. "Who would take her? What if she needs to be restrained? How can we justify sending the two or three staff that might be needed to keep her safe and to make sure she gets back to the center?"

Pat expressed concerns about Kristen's behavior. "I think this boy is just another one of Kristen's inappropriate attachments. She doesn't know how to behave at a funeral. What if she wails and carries on? What if she throws herself on the coffin? This boy's parents probably don't even know who she is. Is it fair to them to have a stranger there, disrupting the service? I just don't think we should let her go."

"What if she gets into one of her 'conversations' with her dead father? What if she starts that weird laughing? She does that almost everyday at school, right in the middle of class, you know," Tom grumbled. "I tell you, I wouldn't want to have to handle it."

"Kristen already has a plan. She said she wants to put a single red rose on the coffin," Stephanie reported. "Of course, she also says she wants to have this guy's name tattooed on her thigh. She is really stuck on making this a significant event in her life—as if she didn't already have enough baggage of her own."

"Kristen has so many unresolved loss issues," Betty noted, "it's obvious that grief is a huge, ongoing issue for her. I think she's searching for some kind of ritual to express her emotions . . . not just about this kid, but for all her losses: her father's death, her mother's disappearance, her alienation from her siblings. It would be nice if she could have something that's related to her own beliefs, like the smudging ceremony or something else religious or symbolic. She's always been interested in the mystical, and. . ."

"Well," Stephanie said, "I don't think you could do a real smudging ceremony inside the cottage." At least she seemed open to the *idea*.

Betty persisted, "It doesn't matter if we follow all the ritual 'rules' as long as Kristen believes in it."

"Are you saying we should encourage her delusions and magical thinking?" Jack asked. "Isn't she confused enough as it is?"

"That's not what—" Betty started.

Lupe jumped in, "Kristen doesn't know what she's doing with all that Indian hocus pocus stuff. I think she makes it up as she goes along. Isn't she really a Catholic? She's always talking about wanting to go to Mass. I say let her attend the regular funeral service. It'll be good for her."

"I disagree," Pat shook her head. "There are real safety questions."

"I don't know much about Catholicism, but I'd be happy to take her to Mass on Sundays occasionally if nobody else can," Stephanie offered.

"I think that a lot of what Kristen does, what you want to call spirituality, seeing the ghosts, hearing her father's voice, are really part of the schizo-affec-

tive disorder," Judy interrupted. "I'm really sorry to change the subject, but I think we have more important, umm, *practical* issues to cover today. Look, we've got a 17-year old high school sophomore, probably sexually active, with no family to speak of, who's seriously mentally ill, refusing to take her meds, and refusing to discuss realistic plans for her future. She's in a bad way and she's running out of time—fast! If she's going to transfer to adult services we've got to start planning for it."

"As her teacher," Tom started, "I think I need to point out that this kid is in no way close to being ready to take care of herself or live independently. In fact, she's getting nuttier every day, if you'll excuse the expression." He seemed to share Judy's concerns.

"And her attorney says that legally we can't make her take the medicine if she doesn't want to," Judy added. "At least not here. She'd have to be put in the hospital."

Betty bit her lip. In her opinion, while making sure Kristen had the basic necessities and treatment, the system had nevertheless failed to help her deal effectively with important issues in her life: abuse, abandonment, lack of self-identity, lost connections to significant others. Betty deeply respected Pat's professional expertise and would never think of asking that Kristen be assigned a different therapist. "But darn it," she thought to herself, "this child has never exhibited much intellectual insight and probably never will. She has only limited cognitive capacity for making sense of all that has happened to her. She needs to be given some constructive way to deal with her feelings about this, now and in the future—no matter where she ends up."

"Listen," Betty said, out loud this time. "I agree that taking her to the funeral might not be a good idea, but she needs *something*. I know that Kristy's 'religion' is a hodgepodge of bits and pieces she has collected along the way. But it has meaning for her and I think we could work together to fashion a ritual that could help her. Maybe we could design some ceremony she could take with her, along with her 'artifacts.' It could provide some continuity, some stability. . . . She needs some structure in her life."

Pat smiled indulgently. "Let's move on, shall we? We need to talk about her medications. I've got her most recent psych eval here. Did you see it?"

Betty sighed.

21.teaching note
Seeking, But Not Finding
Miriam McNown Johnson

Case Synopsis

Social worker Betty Hunter had to decide whether to press her professional colleagues to give serious consideration to addressing the spiritual needs of Kristen Larsen. This 17-year-old, who had a history of mental illness and parental abuse and neglect, would soon be ineligible to continue in residential group care, and therefore the interdisciplinary treatment team was faced with many competing concerns.

Learning Outcomes Related to Religion and Spirituality

The case discussion will facilitate the work of students as they

1. Recognize the importance and potential of rituals and understand that being a competent social worker requires respect for diverse spiritual paths and openness to transpersonal realms of experience that are healing and transformative.

   Perhaps because we live in a relatively young society, many Americans value science, logic, progress, efficiency, and practicality over aesthetics, sentimentality, spirituality, mysticism, ritual, and reverence for the natural world. Although we may use religion and ritual to imbue or to find meaning in traditional rites of passage (e.g., christenings, graduations, weddings, funerals), the nontraditional transitions experienced by many youngsters in the child welfare system (repeated

separations, removals, visits, placements, termination of parental rights, etc.) are often carried out in haste and "processed" only much later, if at all, in therapy. The functions that are routinely filled by religious or other formal ceremonies—acknowledging, celebrating, or mourning life-changing events, dealing with loss, accepting (if not understanding) what cannot be explained logically, and experiencing a meaningful connection to other people (or to other elements of the natural world)—are notably absent in the lives of these children.

2. Support a perspective that considers both client strengths and environmental factors when making assessments.

   Although diagnostic categories may be used to assist practice, the social worker should reject a medical model that simply reduces service consumers to mere pathological labels. Certainly some mental disorders involve delusions and hallucinations, but the DSM-IV cautions clinicians to take into account religious and cultural contexts when making mental health assessments.

Courses and Levels for Which the Case Is Intended

Written for a master's level capstone course in social work, this case also may be useful at the graduate level for specialized courses on social work practice with individuals, mental health services, child welfare services, religion and spirituality, and cultural diversity.

Discussion Questions Related to Religion and Spirituality

Various combinations of the following questions could be used, depending on what aspects of the case an instructor wishes to explore or emphasize.

Establishing the Facts

1. What do we know about Kristen's religion and spirituality?

   It appears that Kristen has had very limited exposure to formal religion. Nevertheless, she has a long history of seeking transpersonal experiences. Her adoption of Native American customs and apparent respect for the natural environment are augmented with a childlike belief in the mystical. Like many people, she is struggling with understanding, accepting, and coping with the many losses in her life without a spiritual framework to help her.

Analysis

2. In what ways might we feel differently about the case if Kristen were a member of a mainstream religious denomination and used more traditional practices? Would we have a different opinion about Kristen's spiritual practices if she were a Native American rather than a Scandinavian?

   Human beings practice a very wide variety of spiritual expressions. Despite the tragedy of continuing wars between ethnic and religious groups, respect for cultural diversity is growing to include respect for different spiritual traditions. Nevertheless, many American social work students may feel more comfortable with religious expressions drawn from the Judeo-Christian tradition, if not from their own denominational background. In addition, it may be more difficult to respect spiritual expressions that the client "borrows" from another culture rather than those that come from the client's own ethnic heritage. We need to remember that experimenting with different personal identities, including religious affiliation, is common among adolescents.

3. Would we assess Kristen's spirituality differently if she were a mature adult rather than a teenager?

   There are several stage-based theories of spiritual development, just as there are stage-based theories of cognitive and moral development. Although students may not be familiar with them, they may naturally assume that Kristen's belief system is somewhat immature or primitive because of her age, her level of education, and her lack of exposure to formal religious teaching. More significantly, students may believe that Kristen is using spirituality in a manipulative way to meet a common adolescent need for attention and control. In any event, we may lend less credibility to a teenager's spiritual requests than we would for an adult with the same concerns.

4. How would we assess Kristen's spirituality if she did not exhibit signs of mental illness?

   Kristen has a history of auditory and visual hallucinations and has been diagnosed with a mental illness. Although not mentioned by the mental health professionals in this case, some of the visions Kristen reports experiencing ("seeing" her dead father, for example) are common among persons suffering from post-traumatic stress. These mental health concerns do not diminish her quest for spiritual understanding or her need for advocacy in this area.

5. What do we know about Betty Hunter's spirituality? Might a social worker with a different religious or ethnic background (e.g., Catholic, fundamentalist Protestant, Native American, atheist) approach this situation differently?

   We know very little about Betty's own spiritual development. She appears to be somewhat susceptible to superstition and admits to not knowing much about Catholicism. Perhaps she is in a period of her life where she is getting in touch with her spiritual needs. Clearly she is sensitive to, and respects, her client's spirituality and her need for spiritual expression. She feels no need to proselytize, and, in fact, seems to emphasize the practical benefits of a spiritual regimen for Kristen. A Catholic worker might be in a better position to help Kristen reestablish her tenuous connections with the Church, while a worker from an evangelical tradition might be inclined to share her or his own spiritual beliefs.

6. What losses has Kristen suffered in her life? What has been done to help her deal with them

so far? What else could have been done? Is there any way to satisfactorily answer the client's question, "Why did this happen to me?" Is religion or spirituality a legitimate resource in this situation?

Kristen's father committed suicide and she has lost meaningful contact with her siblings, her mother, other relatives, several caretakers, and many friends and acquaintances. She has lost her innocence, her childhood, and any expectations for a "normal life." It is unclear whether Kristen has had psychotherapy to deal with these losses. From the information given, it appears that Betty is sensitive to this and has made efforts to keep Kristen in contact with her mother as much as possible. Because her family has never provided consistent emotional support for Kristen, perhaps Betty should focus on helping her establish new and dependable sources of connection and support, whether spiritual or social.

The visit to Kristen's father's grave is a good example of one way of helping a child deal with her past. Other visits could be planned to her childhood home, her day-care center, her school, her first foster home, etc. Lifebooks are another intervention often used with children who have been through multiple placements.

Of course there is no objective, rational, or satisfactory explanation for why some children suffer neglect, abuse, and abandonment while others have relatively happy childhoods. For all of human history philosophers and religious leaders have struggled to provide explanations for the suffering of innocents. It would be inappropriate for the worker or clinician to impose his or her own beliefs on the client, but there may be something in clients' spiritual traditions that addresses such issues in a way that allows them to accept or overcome hardships and to move on.

7. Many child welfare clients, especially girls, are more than willing to trade sex for affection and to view having a baby as a way to have someone to love and to be loved by. What can be done to help them develop feelings of worth and belonging when they have been abandoned or have lost their connections to their family of origin? Is this issue social and psychological or spiritual?

    There is a parallel between the concerns of youngsters "adrift" in the child welfare system and broader questions addressed by religion. Children and adolescents who have lost their parents and families are left asking not only, "Who am I?" but also, "Whose am I?" For all human beings, healthy self-esteem is based not only on accomplishments, competencies, and skills, but also on reliable connections to others. "To whom do I belong?" "Who cares about me?" "Who will be there for me?" are all common human concerns. For example, a review of popular Biblical passages demonstrates the need for reassurance by continually asserting that humans are the children of a loving God and that they will never be abandoned.

Action

8. When is it appropriate to raise issues about a client's spirituality? Should these issues take a back seat to discussion of the client's other needs? Is it necessary for Betty to justify meeting spiritual needs in terms of practical outcomes? As a professional social worker (and employee of a public agency), what is appropriate for Betty to say or do regarding her client's religion and spirituality? Can Betty be confident that she is advocating for what her client needs and wants, or should Kristen be invited to join the meeting to speak for herself?

    While ensuring that children's basic needs for safety, shelter, nutrition, health care, and education are met, the child welfare system may inadvertently sever ties with parents and other family members and, after multiple moves, may leave children without cultural or spiritual roots. Kristen has repeatedly demonstrated her interest in rituals and her search for spiritual meaning. Her need to address her losses suggests that a spiritual component could be added to her treatment plan. Interventions based on consumers' belief systems have been empirically validated (see Hodge, 2001, in Suggested Readings).

9. If the rest of the team chooses to deny Kristen's request to attend the funeral and ignores Betty's suggestion for an alternative spiritual experience, should Betty pursue this spiritual dimension on her own? Why or why not? What do you think her supervisor would say about it?

    Attending to a client's spiritual needs is a concept that may be new for many human service providers. It is a topic seldom addressed in social work texts and one that instructors may not feel comfortable in addressing. Betty has tried to solicit the support of other team members without much apparent success. She may want to meet alone with Kristen to discuss options. It may be that Betty can work individually to address Kristen's spiritual needs, perhaps enlisting the assistance of a certified clinical-pastoral counselor or a Native American shaman. She should advise the team of her intentions, and also seek consultation from her supervisor. In addition, support, or at least permission, from Kristen's mother should be sought.

Teaching Suggestions

The instructor could begin with a question about how this case is similar to or different from typical child welfare cases. What standard social work interventions (the use of lifebooks, for example) can be used to help children deal with issues of grief and loss?

Another possibility might be to explore the use of rituals in American life in general and in nontraditional situations specifically. Students could be encouraged to describe innovative rituals they helped create or witnessed (e.g., a commitment ceremony for a same-sex couple, a celebration of a step-parent adoption). Talk about what elements and symbols are common to rituals across various cultures (e.g., a celebrant or leader, light or

candles, music, flowers, offerings, readings or speeches, special clothing, shared food and drink, unique setting, etc.) Which of these are particularly meaningful to the students? What would they suggest be included in designing a ritual for Kristen?

Suggested Readings

Fowler, J. W. (1981). *The stages of faith: The psychology of human development and the quest for meaning.* San Francisco: Harper & Row.

Hodge, D. R. (2001). Spiritual assessment: A review of major qualitative methods and a new framework for assessing spirituality. *Social Work, 46,* 203-241.

Medina, L. R. (March, 1990). Adoption rituals needed to enhance sense of 'family.' *Adopted Child, 9*(3), 1-4.

(*Adopted Child* is published by Lois Ruskai Medina, P.O. Box 9362, Moscow, Idaho, 83843)

Robbins, S. P., Chatterjee, P., & Canda, E. R. (1998). Chapter 12: Transpersonal theory. In S. P. Robbins, P. Chatterjee, & E. R. Canda (Eds.), *Contemporary human behavior theory: A critical perspective for social work* (pp. 359-393). Boston: Allyn and Bacon.

Additional Notes

22.part a
Developing Community in Truman Village
Wendy Sellers Campbell and Terry A. Wolfer

Michelle Rawls, the coordinator of Village of Hope Family Support Center, opened the door and entered the after-school program. As she greeted the program assistants, Doris Thompson and Martha White, Michelle noticed that Doris's breath reeked of beer. It was not the first time.

"Doris, I think you're drinking and—"

Before she could finish, Doris stormed out of the building, leaving Michelle alone in the room with 35 children and a confused program assistant.

"Miss Michelle," one of the children began, "why did our teacher leave?"

Michelle Rawls

With more than 20 years experience as a social worker, Michelle Rawls worked as the director of the Human Services concentration at Hinds Technical College in Jackson, Mississippi. But her commitment to social work extended beyond her job: she volunteered over 20 hours per week as a community developer. A short, feisty woman, she was inspired by the teachings of Jane Addams and believed that grassroots, community-based programs were essential to successful social work. She enjoyed the challenge of working in low-income, underdeveloped neighborhoods and felt those experiences were the heart of social work. Michelle had confided to a colleague that she often felt more at home with people of color than with those of her own White culture: "I prefer sitting on old five-gallon buckets and swapping tales in the moonlight to afternoon tea parties and bridge games with the local Junior League."

In 1997, Michelle received an invitation from Melvin Singleton, the local chief of police and a well-respected African American leader in Jackson, to pursue volunteer work with him in Truman Village, an apartment complex on the edge of Jackson in Hinds County. Michelle had come to know Singleton while working with residents of a public housing development in Jackson. They had become friends after she joined Asbury United Methodist Church, an historic African American congregation where Singleton also served as the associate pastor. The Asbury congregation wanted to develop more community outreach programs and solicited Singleton's help as both pastor and police chief.

Truman Village

At Singleton's request, Michelle agreed to take part in the outreach program for Truman Village. Although it was only blocks from the middle-class River View Terrace neighborhood, Truman Village seemed to Michelle like a third-world community. Rows of faded yellow, one-story, two-bedroom concrete block units sprawled across a hillside. Except for occasional clumps of grass, the treeless area around the buildings was barren. In all, there were 100 unfurnished units, each providing 650 square feet. About 500 people lived in Truman Village, an average of five people per household. Families paid $250 per month in rent, and most received public assistance.

"I have seen some destitute things" Michelle remembered, describing her first visit to the village, "but this shocked me because of the conditions. It was really nasty."

Constructed in 1951, the entire village belonged to one man, McQueen Jones. A tall, 72-year-old White man, Jones lived about 20 minutes away in an affluent suburb west of Jackson. As landlord, he worked daily at the complex's rental office and could often be seen riding about the neighborhood in his old pickup truck. He looked out for his tenants, providing clothing and toys for families at Christmas, and employing occupants as maintenance workers on-site. Although Jones was not interested in making major improvements to the village, he managed to win the confidence of many tenants, and they kept him abreast of the local gossip and rumors.

Despite the severe poverty, and perhaps because of it, Michelle expressed a passion for working with this community: "I felt a connection to the community because I saw little ones, little kids."

At the request of Asbury Church, Michelle and Chief Singleton agreed to meet with community members to determine the needs and issues. Michelle knew that the first step in effective community development involved seeking out leaders. She quickly found Ma Freeman at Freeman's Deli.

Ma Freeman, who was a 6-feet-1-inch-tall African American woman with snowy white hair and a large frame, had lived in or near Truman Village for more than 60 years. She raised her children in the neighborhood, where they played outside near raw sewage and without recreational equipment. Having risen through the ranks at Truman Village, Ma Freeman now owned her own liquor and convenience store, Freeman's Deli. She opened her store promptly each day, selling wine and beer to the local community from morning to night. On Sundays, she ignored state laws, opening her store at 6:00 A.M. and selling alcohol for 5 hours until the 11:00 A.M. church service began. Then, Ma Freeman closed shop, prepared herself for church, and sang loudly and proudly in the church choir. Together with Chief Singleton, Ma Freeman, and her daughter, Willa Hawkins, Michelle organized a strengths-based assessment within Truman Village.

"What do you mean, *strengths*-based," several residents asked Michelle. "What's good about this community? Nothing!" But with patience and persistence, Michelle discovered some strengths. She recalled, "Everyone saw the community as a viable, close-knit community where people looked out for each other. If a person needed something, someone was always there to help out." Many residents seemed proud of the neighborhood children and wanted to build a safer environment to protect them from increasing violence and drug abuse.

At the first formal neighborhood meeting that Michelle organized, several residents said, "We want Sheriff Daley to come speak to our community." Seizing the opportunity to meet a need and to build credibility, Michelle quickly complied with the request. Within a week, she arranged for Sheriff Daley to speak to residents in a dilapidated building behind Freeman's Deli. Sixty-five people showed up and demanded that the sheriff place a police substation in Truman Village.

A few days later, Sheriff Daley assigned a deputy sheriff to patrol Truman Village and, with the assistance of McQueen Jones, established a police substation in a vacant apartment. Mr. Jones remodeled the apartment and provided it for the sheriff's use at no charge.

Founding the Village of Hope Family Support Center

Next, Michelle focused on the provision of activities for the children of Truman Village. She decided to create an after-school program in the community and staff it with community residents.

With the help of Asbury Church, private community donations, and a grant from the state Department of Social Services, Michelle developed a center for the children in Truman Village. She based the new Village of Hope Family Support Center on the Hull House model and felt excited about following in Addams' footsteps.

As Michelle explained later, "I was to be the consultant. At the last minute we had to cut back on spending, and so the chief asked me to take on the position of coordinator of the after-school program. The chief would assume the dual role of consultant and director. As coordinator, I was in charge of all day-to-day operations of the program." Singleton worked without pay, but for her more extensive efforts, Michelle drew a part-time salary.

As program coordinator, Michelle worked up to 25 hours per week, including Saturdays. But to adequately staff the center, she needed to hire two program assistants. Michelle knew from her social work experience that one way to empower and engage community leaders was to give them ownership in community development decisions. So she asked Ma Freeman for advice. Ma Freeman wholeheartedly recommended Martha, a young woman pursuing an associate's degree in computer technology, and Doris, an older mother and neighborhood babysitter. Michelle hired them both on the spot. Doris and Martha ran the after-school center daily from 2 to 6 P.M. and they worked well together as they were already good friends. The two provided care and services for some 25 to 30 children each day. As program coordinator, Michelle supervised Doris and Martha and monitored the growing success of the program.

While establishing the center, Michelle also worked with Chief Singleton to develop Village of Hope Fellowship, a new church in the neighborhood. Singleton served as the pastor of the new church, and nearly a 100 Truman Village residents attended the weekly services.

Doris Thompson

As Michelle learned, Doris had dropped out of high school but had survived off her sharp wit and natural intelligence for 42 years. Her neighbors, including Ma Freeman, admired Doris for her discipline and her ability to keep the neighborhood children in line. A member of Village of Hope Fellowship, Doris cleaned Chief Singleton's ministerial robes for free at the dry cleaners where she worked part-time.

Rumors, however, began to circulate about Doris's drinking problem. At first, Michelle tried to ignore the talk and give Doris the benefit of the doubt, but eventually she was forced to have several conversations with Doris about the matter. One day, however, Michelle dropped in on the after-school program and personally smelled the alcohol on Doris's breath. "It was obvious," Michelle said. "Doris reeked of alcohol."

"Doris, I think you're drinking, and—"

Before Michelle could continue, Doris stormed out of the building, leaving Michelle alone in the room with Martha and 35 children. Michelle stayed to help Martha finish the day, but was not sure what to do next.

22.part b
Developing Community in Truman Village
Wendy Sellers Campbell and Terry A. Wolfer

Taking Action

Michelle took direct action to prevent the situation from getting out of hand: "I wrote her up. We could not tolerate the drinking and leaving the job." But within a week, Michelle smelled alcohol on Doris's breath again. This time, she fired Doris immediately.

Michelle was not surprised, however, when Doris went to Singleton for help. As she explained, "Chief Singleton is the epitome of a soft-hearted minister. All you have to do is look like a wet puppy dog."

Later that day, Michelle received a call from Singleton. "Michelle," he said, "I have talked with Doris. She won't drink on the job again. I have reinstated her as program assistant." Michelle felt powerless to argue with the chief. As program director, he had the ultimate authority in program decisions.

The next day, Doris came back to work at the Family Support Program. But her drinking continued, and Michelle grew increasingly frustrated with the situation. Finally, she decided it was time to confront Chief Singleton and to convince him to give up his control over the program, to avoid the triangulation that Doris had used before.

"Chief," Michelle began, "hand it over to me. You can't say 'no' to anybody. You let me deal with it. I have to deal with the day-to-day crap anyhow."

Somewhat to Michelle's surprise, Singleton quickly agreed. "Michelle, you're right. My role here is being a minister. You take over as program consultant and find someone to hire as program coordinator.

"Thanks, Chief. The community needs you most as pastor of Village of Hope Fellowship."

As program consultant, Michelle decided to rethink her vision for the Family Support Program. She concluded that it was best to look outside of Truman Village and hire people with college and professional experience.

Quanna Robinson-Hayward, a recent MSW graduate, seemed perfect for the job. She was a short, squat African American woman in her mid-forties. She had served in the Navy for 18 years and carried the stereotypical military persona, including a gruff voice and stern personality. Quanna had grown up in a neighborhood similar to Truman Village, and therefore she identified with the community and was confident that she would be readily accepted. Furthermore, as a recovering alcoholic, she understood the influence of alcohol abuse on community breakdown.

Quanna began her work as program coordinator, supervising Doris and Michelle, and running the day-to-day operations of the after-school program. Unlike Michelle, however, Quanna never attended the Village of Hope Fellowship and did not participate in community meetings and activities outside of work. As a result, Michelle thought, Quanna had trouble gaining the trust of Truman Village. In fact, Quanna's overall managerial style was far less involved than Michelle's. "Doris? I just don't deal with her," Quanna had said one day.

In casual conversation, Michelle eventually learned that village residents saw Quanna as an outsider, despite her personal characteristics and history, and some began to ask, "Is Quanna gay?" Michelle did not know or care.

Michelle continued to drop in on the Family Support Program periodically, and once again smelled alcohol on Doris' breath.

"This is it, Chief," Michelle warned Singleton. "Give me your position as program director and I will handle the situation with Doris." Just as Singleton had relinquished his role as program consultant, he now gave up his role as program director.

The next day, in her new role as program director, Michelle confronted Doris privately and fired her: "Doris, you have been given plenty of opportunities to quit drinking alcohol on the job. I am going to let you go."

Because Martha had already left the program to pursue a new computer job, Michelle replaced both Martha and Doris with college students who were interested in issues related to child development.

"Not long before, Chief and I, with the approval of Martha and Doris, had agreed to not provide the after-school program for free," recalled Michelle. "We were going to charge $5 per week But after her firing, Doris turned the tables on us, spreading rumors in the community about us taking the money and spending it on ourselves."

A Community Meeting

A few days after she fired Doris, Michelle received a call from Maurice Freeman, Ma Freeman's son and leader of the monthly community meetings. "Michelle," he said, "we would like you to attend our next community meeting. We need for you to address some questions."

"Oh hell," thought Michelle, "something's up."

The next evening, she entered the packed community hall, the same building used by the church that she and Chief Singleton helped to form four years before. Only this time, Michelle stood alone without the backing of her good friend, the minister and chief of police. "On a good month we may see 30 people at the community meeting," Michelle had later explained. "I walked in there and it was packed. There were over 100 people in the sanctuary!"

Michelle saw the faces of the community peering back at her: Martha, Doris, and of course, Ma Freeman. But it was Miss Pearl, a small, frail woman who had lived in the community for years and who received family services from Michelle's program who shouted the first questions: "Why was Doris fired? And why did you bring in outsiders and a queer?"

Taken aback by the challenge, Michelle feared that the past four years of community building now depended on her response at this one evening meeting. Michelle muttered to herself, "Where in the hell are you, Chief Singleton? You should be listening to this."

22.teaching note
Developing Community in Truman Village
Wendy Sellers Campbell and Terry A. Wolfer

Case Synopsis

Michelle Rawls, a White social worker, co-led a church-based community development program in a low-income, African American neighborhood. She collaborated with pastor and police chief Melvin Singleton and other community members to develop a grassroots Family Support Center, and she initially hired two women from the community to work in this center's after-school program for children. However, one of the women, Doris, was drinking alcohol on the job and reacted strongly when confronted by Michelle. When Part A ended, Michelle had to decide how to deal with this staff member. In Part B, Michelle eventually decided to fire Doris and hired professional staff from outside the community. Subsequently, the residents reacted against Michelle's decision and confronted her one evening at their monthly community meeting in the church. At that point Michelle needed to decide more broadly about how to respond to the concerns of these community members.

Learning Outcomes Related to Religion and Spirituality

The case discussion will facilitate the work of students as they

1. Identify how organized religion potentially relates to the community development process, as both a resource and complicating factor.

2. Understand, more specifically, how religious congregations may provide a base for community development efforts, both within the community and as an outside sponsor.

3. Identify multiple roles individuals assume within a community, and understand the importance of setting professional boundaries. Recognize the potential benefits and difficulties of multiple dual relationships in church-based community development (e.g., community member and organizer, church member and pastor, supervisee and supervisor).

Other Learning Outcomes for Which This Case Can Be Used

The case discussion will facilitate the work of students as they

4. Recognize the complexity of carrying out community development work on a grassroots level, and the importance of interpersonal relationships in this process.

5. Gain awareness of how their own race, gender, sexual orientation, and socioeconomic status may affect community development efforts.

6. Identify essential principles of community development and how these contribute to its success.

7. Synthesize their knowledge of interpersonal and community development skills with broader concepts of race, culture, class, and religion.

Course and Levels for Which the Case Is Intended

This case was written for a master's level capstone course in social work, but may also be used for specialized instruction in community development, social organizing, program development, and social policy.

The case is written in two parts. Part A should be used as usual (i.e., given to students in advance of class for reading and analysis). The entire class discussion may focus on formulating and resolving the problems posed in Part A, and end at that point. Alternately, **after concluding discussion of Part A, instructors may wish to provide students with Part B.** Allowing students a few minutes to read Part B in class presents the opportunity for further discussion of problems overlooked, maintained, or created by the social worker's initial responses. By comparing their initial formulations and recommendations with what Michelle actually did, further discussion can help students to consider the implications of various decisions and gain deeper understanding of the case. To preserve the integrity of the initial discussion, Part B should be not be provided to students until after the class has concluded its discussion of Part A. For more information about how to use this two-part case, see the Teaching Suggestions at the end of this teaching note.

Discussion Questions Related to Religion and Spirituality

Establishing the Facts

1. What is known about Truman Village as a place?

    Truman Village (or, the village) is a privately-owned, low-income housing development in Hinds County, on the outskirts of Jackson. Each cement block unit is 650 square feet, and there are 100 units in the village. McQueen Jones is the landlord of the village, and although he works at the village daily, he is not interested in making any major upgrades to the impoverished property.

2. What is known about Michelle's relationship with Truman Village?

    Michelle became connected with the village through outreach efforts with Asbury United Methodist Church. Over the years, her relationship with the village has grown from a volunteer situation to her becoming a paid employee. She continues to spend time with members of the community and to participate in local activities, such as monthly meetings and church services.

3. What is Chief Singleton's relationship with Truman Village?

    Singleton also began participating in the village as an outreach worker with Asbury United Methodist Church. He then became an employee within the village through the Village of Hope Foundation, and he also serves a dual role as pastor of the Village of Hope Fellowship. Members of the community look to him for support during periods of conflict with Michelle.

4. What steps has Michelle taken to develop the community?

    Michelle identified and worked with local community leaders and conducted a community-wide needs assessment. She then partnered with agencies such as the state Department of Social Services and the Hinds County Sheriff's Department to establish programs within the village. She initiated the Family Support Center and employed people from the community to work there. Throughout, she engaged with community members informally and in grassroots meetings.

Analysis (Part A)

5. How does the community respond to outsiders? How do their responses differ towards various people? Why?

    The community responds to outsiders in different ways. In regards to Michelle, the community members allow her to participate in church gatherings and monthly meetings and to socialize with them in the evening. During periods of conflict, however, the community gangs up on Michelle and turns to Chief Singleton for support.

    In regards to the chief, the community allows him to serve as their pastor. Members of the community approach him in times of conflict and use him against

Michelle. The community also provides favors for the chief, including Doris who dry cleans his ministerial robes for free.

The community responds less well to other outsiders, including Quanna and the graduate students. The community spreads rumors about Quanna and is not happy with her new position at the Family Support Center.

The different responses to outsiders probably involve various issues, including race, class, and educational level. But they also stem from interpersonal relationships and whether or not community members have learned to trust particular individuals. Such relationships develop over time, as community developers and residents have opportunities to work and play together.

To some extent, these differing perspectives simply reflect what community members perceive to be their own best interests and can be viewed as a response to the question, "What have you done for me lately?"

6. What do various people have at stake in the Family Support Center? For example, what are Michelle's interests?

The Family Support Center means many things to many people. For example, Michelle has been with the program since its conception. She developed the center and wants to ensure that it succeeds. She also has her professional reputation on the line with this program, both inside and outside the immediate community. She has a longstanding personal relationship with Chief Singleton. The chief has a stake in the center primarily through his connection with the church because many of the people in his congregation have children participating in the center. Doris and Martha have their livelihood at stake in the center, as they both depend on it for income. These two women also have personal reputations within the local community. Truman Village has an investment in the program as well. The center provides a way to ensure the growth and development of neighborhood children. Perhaps more importantly, it also provides an arena for building community power, a largely new experience in their social context.

7. How has leadership evolved at the center? How has this affected the center and the community?

Michelle originally worked as a volunteer in community outreach and then she helped develop the center. Once she and the chief established the center, Michelle was hired as program coordinator. She wanted to be the program consultant, an unpaid and less intensive position, but because of funding considerations, she assumed the role of coordinator. The chief assumed the dual role of program consultant and program director.

This leadership changed once Michelle began having problems with Doris. She eventually persuaded the chief to give up his role as program consultant, and then she took over that position, with the coordinator position going to Quanna. This change in leadership has affected the center as leaders have moved from volunteer to paid positions. Michelle's leadership was also compromised on two accounts when the chief rehired Doris. This role confusion led to problems in supervision. Community members also began to regard the chief as the top leader and by-passed Michelle. This situation only undermined Michelle's authority and leadership.

8. How do the Family Support Center and the Village of Hope Fellowship relate? How does the church contribute to the community development process? To what extent is it effective?

The Family Support Center and the Village of Hope Fellowship both grew out of the outreach efforts sponsored by Asbury United Methodist Church. Members of the congregation are employed by and participate in services offered through the center. The church provides an area for community members to be unified. Additionally, community members use the church facilities once a month at the community meetings. This reciprocal relationship works to the benefit of both the center and the Village of Hope Fellowship. The center recruits members from the congregation and provides needed services. The fellowship creates a unified community and validates the existence of the center. Problems arise when outsiders to the community move into either the center or the fellowship, because these outsiders have less connection to the community and are more susceptible to fear, mistrust, and suspicion from the residents.

9. How is organized religion a resource and a liability in this case?

Organized religion works to provide unification and community solidarity, and the church functions as both a sanctuary and a facility for monthly meetings. Problems arise when outsiders move into the community, because the church serves as a bulwark to newcomers, and as a result, there is a division in the community. The way in which the congregation rallies behind Doris potentially undermines the success of the center and Michelle's efforts.

10. What is the nature of the landlord's relationship with Truman Village?

   As its owner, McQueen Jones operates a full-time rental office within the village, and he is on-site everyday. Although Jones has low standards for the village, he employs some of the residents as maintenance workers and he cooperated with the community's desire for a sheriff's substation by providing an apartment at no charge. Jones has close relationships with community members, as evidenced by his access to the rumor mill. Though superficially benign, these relationships appear paternalistic.

11. How has Michelle gained partial acceptance from the community? Why is she not fully accepted?

   Over a lengthy four-year period, Michelle has participated in the life of the community in a number of different ways including weekly church services, monthly community meetings, daily work at the center, and frequent informal socializing. But she is not fully accepted because she is still an outsider, and differences of race, class, culture, educational level, and professional position remain relevant in varying degrees. To some extent, the ongoing level of acceptance by community members will fluctuate with her actions.

12. Has Michelle succeeded in empowering the community? Why or why not?

   On one level, Michelle has succeeded in empowering the community. A one-time collection of residents has begun to act as a group, conducting their own monthly community meetings, and inviting Michelle to attend. This group expresses their new power when they confront Michelle at a community meeting. The community is now gaining its own voice. This is small but significant progress for people who previously were ignored by outside community leaders.

On another level, Michelle has only partially succeeded in empowering the community. She has helped create a number of programs and services, but issues of authority and trust interfere with the overall operations of the programs. These tensions emerge in the final community meeting. Michelle is left with a fragmented program and the residents' mistrust of her as community developer.

Furthermore, this is limited success for a four-year process of community development. At this point, Michelle has not significantly helped to develop indigenous leaders from this community, and the center is not ready to operate without her leadership.

Action (Part A)

13. How should Michelle handle Doris in her role as a professional social worker? As a church member?

   There are various ways in which Michelle can handle Doris as a professional. She can confront her and stand firm in her decision to fire her. She can call a collaborative meeting of stakeholders within the center to work out an acceptable compromise to all participants. She can also re-hire Doris with a plan for preventing further problems.

As a church member, Michelle can ask for assistance from the chief as pastor of the church. She can address the congregation about the issue on Sunday. She can develop a way for the congregation to be more a part of the center. She can have Doris continue to have a stake in the center through partnerships with the fellowship. Somehow, she may need to continue relating to Doris at the fellowship, even if she persists in firing her.

14. How may Michelle's response impact the overall community development effort? What are the possible consequences of various alternatives?

   If Michelle decides to confront Doris and stand her ground, she risks losing the respect and the trust of the community. She also stands to add to the divisiveness between community insiders and outsiders. If Michelle opts to re-hire Doris, she risks facing more problems related to alcoholism in the workplace, and she may potentially face liability issues if a child is hurt by Doris's neglect. Michelle may rely on the chief's support and assistance, but this decision may only reinforce the community's perception that Michelle does not command the same respect and authority as Chief Singleton.

Analysis (Part B)

15. At the community meeting, what does Michelle stand to gain? To lose?

Michelle stands to gain the respect and trust of the community and to renew the life and interest of the center. She also stands to gain a better relationship with Doris and reinforce, within the community, that she is a friend and not a foe.

She stands to lose the respect of the community, her professional integrity, and her leadership over the center. She may also lose community support for the center and thus four years of community development efforts. She may potentially lose the support of the chief. Her reputation is on the line both within the community and on a broader level.

16. What are the advantages and disadvantages of hiring professional staff over community members?

Professional staff bring experience and expertise to the program. The social workers have received training in social work values and ethics and in community development. The after-school teachers that Michelle hires bring knowledge related to educational development in children. Professional staff may also have a more neutral perspective on the community development process. They are less enmeshed in the community culture and politics. They are in a better position to maintain boundaries around professional development.

The disadvantage of professional staff is mainly that these individuals must gain the trust and respect of the community. They do not have a long history of relationship building with community members, nor the same orientation for building these organic relationships over time. Often they represent a different culture, class, race, or ethnicity. Professional staff may have different values and ethics than community members, and residents may perceive these differences as an attempt by professionals to "take over" their community. There is often a great deal of mistrust surrounding the motives of professionals in community development. There may also be resentment and jealousy on the part of the residents.

Community members enter into programs with the

established trust and confidence of fellow residents. They understand the history and culture of a community and are able to move seamlessly within this context. Residents may have considerable insight into how to develop a community based on unspoken politics and alliances. These persons need little training on the strengths of the community.

Community members exhibit some disadvantages in that they may be too enmeshed in the community. It may be difficult for members to discern personal versus staff roles, and they may have difficulties in maintaining boundaries with fellow residents during work hours. They may also form alliances with neighbors and friends to the detriment of the overall development and progress of the programs.

17. What is the nature of Quanna's relationship with the community? How does it differ from Michelle's?

Quanna enters the community as a professional outsider. She makes no effort to integrate with the residents by participating in meetings and activities, and she perceives her job as strictly a professional role. Quanna arrives with a shared African American culture and a history of poverty and alcoholism in her own life, and she perceives these personal qualities as a reason for assured success in the community development process, even surpassing Michelle in building connections with the village. Conversely, the community perceives Quanna as a threat and shuns her. They spread rumors about her sexual orientation, alienating her from fellow residents.

Quanna's role in the community differs from that of Michelle, who has a history of relationship building with residents of the village. Michelle, although White and of a higher socioeconomic class, extends beyond Quanna in her efforts to engage with residents through community meetings, church, and social activities. Michelle has earned the respect of many members of the community through active participation in the development process. Her efforts give her more connection with the village and the center.

Action (Part B)

18. How can Michelle respond to Ms. Pearl and the other participants at the meeting? How will her response affect the community development process?

Michelle can decide to respond to Ms. Pearl and defend her own actions and the actions of Quanna, but this response will most likely further alienate Michelle from the community. She may decide to handle the conflict with Doris on a private level and not in front of the entire group at the meeting. This decision will strengthen communication between Michelle and Doris but it does little to satisfy the immediate concerns of the residents. Michelle can offer to bring Quanna into the next community meeting so that residents can get to know her better. This decision may enhance the connection between Quanna and the community but does little to satisfy Doris. Michelle must take into account how her response will affect the residents, Doris, Quanna, and the broader community development process.

19. How should Michelle direct the future of the center? What should be Michelle's ongoing role with the center?

    There are several different actions that Michelle may take. She may continue as planned with the center and ignore the reactions at the meeting. She can work to reintegrate the community with the center so that they feel more ownership and connection. She can work on hiring more residents of the village so that the center becomes a mix of outsiders and insiders.

    Michelle can also have the Village of Hope take over the center, and she can pull out as program consultant. She can continue to have a minimal role in the program but hire someone else as consultant. Or, Michelle can continue as the program director and assume more responsibility and leadership over the center. Her role can also involve working with the community on a plan that would progressively give more ownership of the center to the village and lessen her own authority and responsibilities.

Teaching Suggestions

This case comes in two parts, the first of which can be distributed to students ahead of class to allow for their usual preparation. The second part can be distributed midway through the class following a discussion of the first section.

The instructor may wish to begin with the usual questions of fact and analysis. Midway through the analysis of Part A, have students brainstorm, in small groups, what various people in the case have at stake. Encourage students to look at the ways in which the key players' roles are intertwined and how boundaries become difficult to discern. Also encourage students to probe into the question of insiders versus outsiders in community development. Ask students questions about the nature of the relationship between the church and the center. Does this enmeshed relationship work? Why or why not? Encourage students to think about what Asbury United Methodist Church had to gain from outreach to Truman Village. Ask students about the multiple relationship of Singleton as pastor, police chief, and program director. How does this strengthen or undermine the church, the community, and the center? After a discussion of how Michelle can respond to Doris and the consequences of various alternatives, the instructor can provide students with Part B.

Allow students time to read Part B, and then resume the discussion. During this analysis, encourage students to look beyond Michelle's immediate reaction to the larger picture of what her response and actions will mean to the community development process. Engage students in a discussion of race and class within this scenario and probe students as to what race and class mean within the context of community development in the village. The instructor may ask students to draw an eco-map of the community, demonstrating the enmeshed roles and depicting the complicated process of community development.

Additional Notes

———

About the Editors and Contributors

Editors

T. Laine Scales, PhD, is assistant professor of social work and associate director of the Center for Family and Community Ministries at Baylor University, Waco, Texas. Her research interests include social welfare history, spirituality and religion in social work, and rural social work. She has published one book, 11 articles and chapters, and delivered over 20 presentations in these research areas. *All That Fits a Woman: Training Southern Baptist Women for Charity and Mission, 1907-1926* was published by Mercer University Press (2000). Currently, Dr. Scales is co-editing the second edition of *Christianity and Social Work: Readings on the Integration of Christianity and Social Work Practice* and writing a history of the Carver School of Church Social Work, Louisville, Kentucky. She is also co-leading an interdisciplinary research team studying the role of Latina women in congregational leadership in the United States and Mexico. Dr. Scales has held state-level leadership positions in the National Association of Social Workers, Texas Chapter.

Terry A. Wolfer, PhD, is associate professor at the University of South Carolina College of Social Work, where he teaches primarily micro and macro social work practice, research/evaluation, and a case-based capstone course. Dr. Wolfer has provided leadership for use of case method in social work education. He co-led development of the innovative, case-based capstone course at the University of South Carolina. For that course, he has authored or co-authored deci-

sion cases on child welfare, mental health, death and dying, and religion and spirituality. He also co-authored an article on the collaborative faculty process for developing and teaching the course. Currently, he is completing research on learning outcomes for case-based instruction. In addition, he is currently developing a collection of decision cases on social work micro practice. For three years, he and Michael Welsh have led a Faculty Development Institute at the Council on Social Work Education, Annual Program Meeting on case method teaching.

David A. Sherwood, PhD, is professor of social work and coordinator of the Physical and Mental Health MSW Concentration, Baylor University School of Social Work. He is editor of the journal *Social Work & Christianity*, serves as an accreditation site visit chair for the Council on Social Work Education, and has led two BSW programs to accreditation. He has contributed to and edited several books, including *Charitable Choice* (2001). Dr. Sherwood is past president of the North American Association of Christians in Social Work and received the association's Award for Distinguished Service in 1998. He has written extensively regarding social work ethics, ethical integration of personal beliefs and professional social work practice, and spirituality and religion in social work practice. He is currently involved in a three-year research project funded by the Lilly Endowment investigating the effects of involvement in community social service on the religious faith of the volunteers.

Diana R. Garland, PhD, is professor and chair of the Baylor University School of Social Work. She also serves as director of the Baylor Center for Family and Community Ministries. She is editor of the journal *Family Ministry: Empowering Through Faith* and senior editor of the publication *AudioMagazine in Family Ministry.* She is author of 14 books, including *Family Ministry: A Comprehensive Guide* (InterVarsity Press), *Church Social Work* (North American Association of Christian Social Workers, NACSW), and *Church Agencies: Serving Children and Families in Crisis* (Child Welfare League of America, CWLA). Before moving to Baylor University, she served as professor of social work for 17 years and was dean of the Carver School of Church Social Work at the Southern Baptist Theological Seminary in Kentucky. Currently, she is the primary investigator for two projects funded by the Lilly Endowment, one examining the relationship between community ministries and the faith of Christian volunteers, and the other exploring the role of faith in family life.

Beryl Hugen, PhD, is professor of social work and practicum coordinator in the Department of Social Work and Sociology at Calvin College, Grand Rapids, Michigan. He has 12 years of practice experience in a variety of mental health and child welfare settings. Dr. Hugen has published in the area of mental health (family and severe mental illness), the integration of spirituality and religion and social work practice, and social work history. He is editor of *Christianity and Social Work: Readings on the Integration of Christian Faith and Social Work Practice*, and co-editor of *Spiritual and Religious Traditions in Social Work Practice.* Currently, he is a research partner on a project entitled Service and Faith: The Impact on Christian Faith and Congregational Life of Organized Community Caring, funded by the Lilly Endowment.

Sharon Weaver Pittman, Ph.D, is professor and chair of the Social Work Department at Andrews University, Berrien Springs, Michigan. Her research interests include international women's issues with special emphasis on displaced peoples. She also is active in faith-based research and educational evaluation projects. She has served as senior editor of *Dialog*, the journal of the Adventist Association of International Development Professionals. She has served on the Council of Social Work Education

Annual Program Meeting presentation review board and has published articles in *Afflia: Journal of Women and Social Work, Journal of International Social Work, Journal of Social Work Research and Evaluation,* and *Reflections: Narratives of Professional Helping.* She has written numerous book reviews and is currently developing training materials for disaster response and working with displaced peoples.

Contributors

Roger Aker, MSW, is the director of Love in the Name of Christ of Nacogdoches, Texas, a community clearinghouse that assists people by referring those in need to church volunteers. Previous experience includes 20 years of direct and indirect service to children and families.

Nancy K. Brown, PhD, is an assistant professor at the University of South Carolina College of Social Work. She completed her MSW and PhD at the University at Albany in New York. Dr. Brown practiced for many years in the areas of addiction, teen pregnancy, and family therapy. Her research interests have focused primarily on women and addiction; she is currently involved in research on recovering parents' views on substance abuse prevention.

Wendy Sellers Campbell, MSW, MA, is director of Hispanic/Latino Initiatives at the Center for Child and Family Studies, University of South Carolina. She was previously a Peace Corps volunteer in Nicaragua and has worked on a number of projects related to community development with Hispanic/Latinos in South Carolina. She is also currently pursuing a PhD in social work with an emphasis on empowerment theory and female migrant workers.

David Davis, MSW, serves as a counselor and program director for the Advocacy Center for Crime Victims and Children in Waco, Texas. His additional work history includes two years of foreign service, two years of Child Protective Services in Texas, and five years of program development and executive leadership with Hill Country Community Ministries and Austin Metropolitan Ministries. Mr. Davis also serves as a field faculty member of Baylor University's Graduate School of Social Work.

Pam Doty-Nation, MDiv, has been the executive director of Habitat for Humanity of Kent County in Grand Rapids, Michigan, since January

1999. For eight years prior to her work at Habitat, she was the director of Transitional Housing for Homeless Families at Dwelling Place of Grand Rapids. She is an ordained minister in the United Church of Christ.

Karen Grubb Gilbert, MRE (Social Work Concentration), is the minister of missions at Wilshire Baptist Church in Dallas, Texas. She works as an integral member of the church staff, responsible for planning, leading, and evaluating a comprehensive program of mission strategy, action, and education. Training, motivating, and pastoral care of volunteers is a large part of her work. She builds relationships and partnerships with the community, both local and global.

Leola Furman, PhD, is associate professor emeritus of social work, University of North Dakota. She has conducted a national survey on the way social workers integrate religion and spirituality in direct practice. Findings from this survey are included in the book *Spiritual Diversity and Social Work Practice: The Heart of Helping,* which she co-authored with Edward Canda. She has replicated this research in England and is in the process of replicating the same research among social workers in Norway. Additionally, she has conducted research on collaboration among social workers and clergy.

Erlene Grise-Owens, EdD, is assistant professor in the Spalding University School of Social Work. She has taught social work and held administrative roles, including director of field education, for almost 10 years. Her practice experience includes child welfare, clinical social work, and faith-based contexts. She serves on the editorial board of the journal *Family Ministry: Empowering Through Faith.* Her publication topics include gender equity, leadership, and religion and spirituality.

Helen Wilson Harris, MSW, is the director of field education for the Baylor University School of Social Work. She has previously served in administration and clinical services in hospice, medical social work, residential child care, and foster care and adoptions. Her research interests include grief and loss, ethics and social work practice, and congregational social work.

Ann Fleck-Henderson, PhD, is professor at Simmons College School of Social Work and chair of the Human Behavior in the Social Environment Sequence. She has worked in a college counseling office, psychiatric units, and domestic violence organizations. Her academic interests include intellectual and ethical development, domestic violence, and social work education.

Evelyn Hoffman, author and award-winning television host and producer, is the founder of Chaverah, a senior adult enrichment program for the Jewish community in Waco, Texas. Ms. Hoffman serves on the board of contributors for the Waco Tribune-Herald and is a recipient of the National Media OWL Award for excellence in television, video, and film in the field of aging. Ms. Hoffman was honored by the Waco Conference of Christians and Jews as the 1984 Humanitarian of the Year. She was a contributor to *Chicken Soup for the Golden Soul* and to *War Letters.*

Doreen L. Holding Eagle, BSW, is director and case manager of an urban Native American program in North Dakota. She also serves as a commissioner with the first Human Relations Commission ever established in North Dakota. She is currently working on her first research project for the North Dakota Department of Health.

Miriam McNown Johnson, PhD, is associate professor at the University of South Carolina College of Social Work. She has had 20 years of practice experience working with children in out-of-home placements and their families. She has published articles on topics related to residential group care and social work education.

Elisabeth Kenny, MSW, is the field instruction specialist with the Child Welfare Professional Development Project of the Stephen F. Austin State University School of Social Work, Nacogdoches Texas. Ms. Kenny teaches field students preparing to work for Child Protective Services. For 10 years she served as a caseworker for Child Protective Services in Texas and worked for other child development and protective agencies in Texas and Arkansas.

Claudette Lee, MSW, is assistant professor and practicum coordinator for the University of Nebraska at Omaha School of Social Work. She teaches both graduate and undergraduate students. She formerly taught at Iowa State University. She is a certified and licensed mental health practitioner for the state of Nebraska and practiced as a family therapist for many years in Nebraska, Iowa, and Ohio.

Raymond Lisauckis, MSSW, is a program coordinator and direct service provider with the Department of Veterans' Affairs Central Texas Health Care System. He is a lecturer in the Baylor University School of Social Work and has worked primarily in the medical and rehabilitation areas. His interests include current issues of human diversity and cultural awareness.

Michael P. Melendez, MSW, is associate professor at Simmons College Graduate School of Social Work, teaching primarily in the clinical practice sequence. Since 1985, he has maintained a private practice and has provided consultation for culturally competent practice. He is past president of the board of directors of the Latino Health Institute, past board president of AIDS Action Committee, and is a doctoral candidate at Case Western Reserve University.

Linda B. Morales, PhD, is assistant professor in the Stephen F. Austin State University School of Social Work. Prior to teaching at SFASU, she was a social worker in the mental health field for over 20 years. Her research interests include multicultural social work issues and rural social work.

Dennis R. Myers, PhD, is professor of social work and gerontology and director of graduate studies for the Baylor University School of Social Work. Dr. Myers presents and publishes in the area of gerontology with a focus on the family in later life and aging and mental health. He is associate director of a research initiative, Service and Faith: The Impact on Christian Faith and Congregational Life of Organized Community Caring, funded by the Lilly Endowment, and is actively involved with the Alzheimer's Association.

Luis A. Perez, MSW, serves as city district pastor, pastoral administrator, and director of social ministries at Bethel Christian Fellowship in Rochester, New York. In addition, he teaches part time in the Department of Social Work, Nazareth College, and serves as a chaplain to the Monroe County Children's Detention Center. Mr. Perez is a community activist advocating for children and families, with particular focus on the Latino population. These interests led him to run for mayor of Rochester in November of 2001.

Michael E. Sherr, MSW, is a doctoral student in the University of South Carolina College of Social Work. He has practice experience with children, adolescents, and their families as a hospice social worker and a mental health clinician. He currently provides consultation to a few religious congregations and a faith-based ministry for single women with children in North Carolina.

Carol A. Sherwood, MSN, is a psychiatric mental health nurse practitioner and member of the nursing faculty at McLennan Community College, Waco, Texas. She has served on the nursing faculties of Simmons College and Roberts Wesleyan College. She has directed an intensive family preservation program and developed a community mental health program for the Visiting Nurses Association. Her clinical practice and interests focus on women's issues. She has developed a Congregational Health Ministry in her church.

Harvey Stalwick, PhD, is professor and director of the Social Work Program, Concordia College, Moorhead, Minnesota. For over 20 years, he was professor and dean of the Faculty of Social Work at the University of Regina, Saskatchewan, Canada. There he specialized in increasing access to education for persons in the human services, community development, and indigenous child welfare services. Recent interests include the honoring of human rights and social answers that come directly from people acting on their own experiences.

Elizabeth H. Timmons, MSW, has been a practicing social worker for 20 years. She has worked with crime victims and their families through protective services, private practice, and in a rape crisis agency. Ms. Timmons is currently working with persons who have mental retardation and developmental disabilities. She has worked as a field supervisor, instructor and agency liaison in all of these settings and was named the Texas Field Educator's Consortium Field Instructor of the Year in 2000.